Her Excellency
Jeanne Sauvé

Her Excellency Jeanne Sauvé

Shirley E. Woods

Macmillan of Canada
A Division of Canada Publishing Corporation
Toronto, Ontario, Canada

Canadian Cataloguing in Publication Data

Woods, Shirley E., date.
    Her Excellency Jeanne Sauvé

Includes index.
ISBN 0-7715-9899-8

1. Sauvé, Jeanne, 1922-   . 2. Governors general —
Canada — Biography. 3. Canada — Politics and
government — 1963-   *. I. Title.

FC626.S38W66 1986   971.064'092'4   C86-093820-4
F1034.3.S38W66 1986

Edited by Maggie MacDonald
Designed by Margot Boland Graphic Design

Macmillan of Canada
A Division of Canada Publishing Corporation

Printed in Canada

for Sandrea

CONTENTS

PREFACE

My first meeting with a governor general took place in February of 1938, when I was four. In those days we lived in a sparsely populated suburb of Ottawa a mile or two from Rideau Hall. For amusement that winter, I used to hide behind one of the stone pillars at the end of our driveway and ambush passersby. Aside from the milkman in his sleigh there was very little traffic and hence there were few targets. The only pedestrians I could depend upon were two men in greatcoats who walked by our house almost every afternoon. They provided excellent sport until one day my mother caught me in the act of trying to plaster them with snowballs. Mother rushed down the driveway, grabbed me by the ear, and unceremoniously dragged me from the scene. Later, I learned that one of the men was Shuldham (later Sir Shuldham) Redfern, Secretary to the Governor General, and the other was the Great Man himself, Lord Tweedsmuir.

Tweedsmuir was succeeded by the Earl of Athlone, whose wife was Princess Alice. Because of the Blitz, their grandson, Richard Abel-Smith, was sent to Canada with them, and Richard was a classmate of mine at Ashbury. Being a school friend, I was asked to a number of children's parties given for him at Rideau Hall. Prior to these affairs I was polished and scrubbed to a high gloss, and repeatedly admonished to be on my best behaviour. The parties always started on a restrained note, which lasted until it was time to play musical chairs in the ballroom. Then all hell would break loose. March music for the game was provided by a military band, which really got the adrenalin flowing. I vividly remember an arthritic footman being knocked ass-over-teakettle by two little boys who converged on him while he was trying to remove a chair. Princess Alice, who was tiny and birdlike, presided over the parties. Despite her diminutive size she was a force to be reckoned with, and we were in awe of her.

Athlone was succeeded in 1946 by Field Marshal Viscount Alexander, a distinguished soldier. He was the last, and possibly the most popular, British peer to hold the office. I knew his daughter Rose, who was a teenager and later a debutante during her stay in Ottawa. Being a contemporary of Rose's, I was invited to dances given for her each year. These invitations had a certain cachet because Government House ranked at the top of the social pecking order. By this time I considered myself quite adult, and wore white tie and tails, but my mother still continued to admonish me to be on my best behaviour, with the added warning not to drink too much. I didn't always follow her advice, but the parties were great fun and the highlight of the Christmas season.

Vincent Massey had the difficult task of being the first Canadian governor general. Not only was Alexander a tough act to follow, but some hard-line monarchists said that the office would lose its prestige with a commoner as governor general. How wrong they were. Massey was a patrician of the first order, and an exceptionally cultured man. Lord Cranborne (Lord Privy Seal in Churchill's government) said of him, "Fine chap, Vincent, but he does make one feel a bit of a savage."

At the age of nineteen I joined the Governor General's Foot Guards. One of the ceremonial duties of this militia regiment is to provide a guard of honour when the Governor General opens a new session of Parliament. I was a junior officer on the guard for the opening of Parliament in the winter of 1954. Wearing Athol Grey coats and bearskins, we formed up in front of the Peace Tower and waited for the arrival of the Governor General. Despite his age and the bitter cold, Massey came in an open horse-drawn landau escorted by Mounties with pennons flying from their lances. It was a stirring sight. When the state carriage stopped in front of us, the order was given for a royal salute, the band broke into "God Save the Queen", the clock in the Peace Tower struck the hour, and a nearby battery of field guns fired the first salvo of a twenty-one-gun salute. The noise was deafening. Each time the clock struck, or a gun would fire, I could feel the sound reverberate through my stomach. Massey, in full court dress (including the white plumed hat), inspected the guard and went through the ceremony with aplomb. You couldn't have asked for a more regal performance.

Major-General Georges Vanier was a marvellous choice as the first French-Canadian governor general. He had served with gallantry during the First World War, in which he lost a leg, and had also been an outstanding diplomat. Both he and his stately wife, Pauline, were fluently bilingual, and deeply concerned with the need for harmony between Canada's two founding races. They brought an elegance and a warmth to Rideau Hall that is remembered to this day. As a couple, they set a standard that has yet to be surpassed.

Roland Michener followed Georges Vanier. A Rhodes Scholar, he had been a Conservative cabinet minister and later Speaker of the House of Commons. When Prime Minister Pearson asked him to be governor general, he was serving as Canada's High Commissioner to India. Michener brought an element of enthusiasm and vigour to his role that revitalized the viceregal image. I was often invited to curl with him on the outdoor rink at Rideau Hall. These were casual pick-up games, and the players were a mixed bag with widely varying levels of proficiency. Although Michener was a keen competitor who liked to win, he was a good sport on the ice and a gracious host after the match.

Jules Léger, the younger brother of Paul-Émile Cardinal Léger, had been a career diplomat. He was a scholarly man with a fine intellect and a great interest in the arts. However, six months after being sworn into office, he suffered a severe stroke, from which he never fully recovered. He tried valiantly to fulfil his role, and his charming wife, Gabrielle, took over many of his engagements, but during his tenure his health proved to be a serious handicap.

The choice of Ed Schreyer as his successor surprised many people. Schreyer, a lifelong politician and former provincial premier, went straight from the Manitoba legislature, where he was Leader of the Opposition, to the viceregal post. This was unusual, because the role of governor general is non-political, and the holder of the office should have no political ties. (Both Roland Michener and Jeanne Sauvé were disinfected from party politics by a stint as Speaker of the House of Commons.) Having been appointed at the age of forty-four, Schreyer was also the youngest Canadian governor general. I curled with him a number of times at Government House, and found him to be a sincere but rather uncommunicative man.

No one was particularly surprised when Jeanne Sauvé was appointed to succeed Schreyer. Tradition required a French governor general, and it was also high time that a woman should occupy the post.

I didn't know much about Madame Sauvé, except that she had been a controversial figure on Parliament Hill. Curious to know more, I did some research and asked well-informed friends about her. What I learned intrigued me, and whetted my appetite to write her biography. I knew, however, that it would be futile to do so unless I obtained her co-operation.

Madame Sauvé considered my request for more than two months before she finally consented to the project. Although Her Excellency was generous in her co-operation, this is not an ''official'' biography. She did not read or approve any part of the manuscript, nor is she responsible for its contents. By the same token, I have been free to write what I wished, and the opinions expressed are entirely my own.

S.E.W.
Ottawa
March 1986

Chapter 1

PRUD'HOMME

Ottawa enjoyed a golden October in 1984. On the twenty-ninth of the month the capital still basked in the warmth of Indian summer. At Government House the trees were bare, but the grass was bright and the grounds had the clean-swept look of a deer park.

On the stroke of noon that day a cavalcade of four cars left the side entrance of Rideau Hall. The lead car in the procession was a black limousine with a small blue flag on its fender and licence plates that bore no lettering, just a raised gold crown on a scarlet background. Sitting beside the uniformed chauffeur was a young naval officer, an aide-de-camp, with braided gold cords looped around his right shoulder.

The passenger in the limousine was a petite woman with stylishly coifed white hair, flawless skin, and unforgettable blue-green eyes. She was elegantly dressed in a burgundy tweed suit with a matching silk blouse and gold jewellery. Despite the balmy temperature, she wore a mink hat, and a full-length mink coat lay on the seat beside her.

The woman was Her Excellency The Right Honourable Jeanne Sauvé, P.C., C.C., C.M.M., C.D., D.H.L., D.S., D.L., Governor General of Canada. The office of governor general, the representative of the Crown, dates back to Samuel de Champlain, Governor of New France in 1627. Madame Sauvé, the first woman in Canadian history to hold this post, was the sixtieth viceroy since Champlain and

1

the twenty-third since Confederation. Appointed by the sovereign, the Governor General is above politics, and represents all Canadians.

To better understand the problems and aspirations of the people, the Governor General travels extensively throughout the country. On this sunny October afternoon, Madame Sauvé was setting out on a state visit to Saskatchewan. A few hours earlier she had been briefed to expect winter conditions in the West, which was the reason she was taking a fur coat.

As soon as the cavalcade passed through the gates of Government House and turned onto Sussex Drive, the second car in the procession, a grey sedan, began to tail-gate the viceregal car. The sedan almost touched bumpers all the way to the Ottawa airport, and it continually strayed across the white line.

Inside the grey sedan were two men and a woman. The man at the wheel drove with intense concentration, while the other two stared out of the windows like tourists. But they weren't tourists. They were plainclothes RCMP officers, and all three were armed.

In security parlance the grey sedan was a "crash car", whose role was to prevent an assassin from pulling in behind the limousine. By straddling the white line, the sedan was also able to keep other vehicles from pulling abreast of the viceregal car. Had a motorist attempted to do so, the sedan would have blocked the passing lane and, if necessary, caused a collision — hence the term crash car.

Twenty minutes after leaving Rideau Hall, the cavalcade pulled up on the tarmac at Canadian Forces Base Uplands. Almost before the limousine had slid to a stop, the aide-de-camp was standing at the rear door. He opened the door and saluted. Her Excellency stepped out, and was greeted by the Base Commander. Near by, the occupants of the security car kept a watchful eye on their charge. While Madame Sauvé exchanged a few words with the commanding officer, the Secretary to the Governor General hustled the members of her entourage aboard the waiting aircraft. He did this to ensure that protocol would be observed: the Governor General is always the last to board a plane or a ship, and the first to disembark. When the viceregal party was aboard, the Base Commander escorted

Madame Sauvé to the foot of the ramp and gave her a farewell salute. Moments later the aircraft taxied down the runway and took off for Saskatchewan.

The flight in the Convair Cosmopolitan, one of the few propeller-driven VIP aircraft operated by #412 Transport Squadron, took five hours. Madame Sauvé could easily have taken a Canadair Challenger 600 jet, and had been encouraged to do so, but she's a white-knuckle flier. Having heard horror stories from cabinet colleagues about the Challenger 600, until June of 1985 she refused to fly in that plane. Although the Cosmopolitan is slow, it's both reliable and comfortable. The rear section, which Madame Sauvé occupied, is furnished like a living-room, with a sofa and upholstered chairs. The forward section, where the rest of the viceregal party sat, has tables covered in white linen and is similar to a railway dining-car.

One of the highlights of the Saskatchewan tour was to be a visit to the village of Prud'homme, Jeanne Sauvé's birthplace. She was looking forward to this with great anticipation because it would be the first time she had been back to Prud'homme since leaving at the age of three. As her husband, His Excellency The Honourable Maurice Sauvé, was unable to accompany her, she had invited her brother, Jean Benoit, and her widowed eldest sister, Berthe Belisle, along to share the homecoming. In all there were ten in the party, including Esmond Butler, Secretary to the Governor General; her Press Secretary, Marie Bender; her Attaché and English-speech writer, Liane Benoit; and her dresser, Thelma Francoeur.

An hour after they left Ottawa, lunch was served by a uniformed steward. After the meal, most of the party settled back for a nap. When they awoke, the landscape beneath the plane had changed from brown to white, confirming that the West was indeed in the grip of winter.

Late in the afternoon Madame Sauvé came forward to discuss arrangements for a press conference. On the table beside Marie Bender was a popular women's magazine that Liane Benoit had been reading. The cover of the magazine showed a sultry beauty and the titles of the feature articles. Picking up the magazine, Madame Sauvé read one of the titles aloud, "How Women on Their Way to the Top Find Time to Make Love". The embarrassed silence that followed turned into laughter when she added, "I must read that!"

Just before dusk the plane touched down at Regina Airport. On hand to welcome the Governor General were the Lieutenant-Governor, Frederick Johnson, Premier Grant Devine, and Mayor Larry Schneider, with their wives. A clutch of photographers shivered beside the dignitaries, while an equally chilled television crew stood by to film the arrival. The door opened and Madame Sauvé stepped onto the ramp. As she did so a blast of icy wind blew her hair across her face. Realizing she had made a tactical error, she quickly ducked back into the cabin to rearrange her coiffure, and then, with one hand holding her hair in place, walked serenely down the steps.

After shaking hands with her hosts she was whisked away in a long grey limousine to the press conference. The car was the Premier's personal limousine, which he had placed at her disposal for the duration of the tour. Following the press conference she was driven to the Hotel Saskatchewan, where they literally rolled out the red carpet for her. At the entrance of the hotel she was greeted by the manager, flanked by the senior members of his staff, including the head chef in his tall white hat. Madame Sauvé was presented with a bouquet of flowers by the manager's eight-year-old daughter and then escorted to the royal suite on the eighth floor.

The other members of the viceregal party were also given rooms on the eighth floor. The rooms on either side of the royal suite, however, were occupied by plainclothes Mounties with electronic detection equipment.

Because there were no official functions for the rest of the day, Madame Sauvé's aide-de-camp asked if he might be excused, explaining that his grandparents who lived on a farm outside Regina had hoped to visit him. She not only agreed to his request, but said she'd be pleased to meet his grandparents. That evening before dinner the viceregal party and the staff of the Saskatchewan protocol office were invited to the royal suite for a drink. It was meant to be a relaxed get-together — the purpose was for the two groups to meet each other — but for the first twenty minutes the conversation was stilted and formal.

Then the aide came in with his grandparents. The old couple looked out of place, as they hadn't expected to meet the Governor General, and weren't dressed for the occasion. The aide started to introduce his grandparents to Her Excellency, but before he could finish, his grandmother embraced Madame Sauvé and gave her a kiss on the cheek. This stopped all conversation because it's customary to greet the Governor General with a handshake, and women often bob a curtsey. Unperturbed by this breach of protocol, Madame Sauvé returned the embrace warmly and asked the aide and his grandparents to join her. For the next ten minutes she ignored her other guests while the four of them had a good chat. When the old couple left, they almost floated out of the room.

The official part of the tour began the next morning. Plans had been made for the Governor General to ride in an open landau to the Legislative Building for a ceremonial welcome by the province, but this was cancelled because of the weather. It was so cold that Wascana Lake was frozen over and the migrating Canada geese were forced to huddle forlornly on the ice. The wind chill also forced the band and the one-hundred-man guard of honour to move indoors. Fortunately the Saskatchewan legislature is such a large building that everyone, including several hundred flag-waving schoolchildren and at least as many adults, was able to fit into the marble-columned rotunda. During the walkabout after the ceremony, Madame Sauvé spoke to many of the youngsters. One little boy, when asked if he was a Scout, was momentarily tongue-tied, but then replied quite firmly that he was a Wolf Cub.

Later, Madame Sauvé was shown the Legislative Chamber by the Speaker of the Assembly. As a former House of Commons Speaker, she was particularly interested in the seating arrangement and the provincial rules of procedure. And, as a former broadcaster, she was also intrigued by the sophisticated video equipment used to film the sittings. Her visit ended with a coffee reception hosted by

Premier Devine, where she met the members of his cabinet and the Leader of the Opposition.

The next item on her agenda was a tour of the Chip and Dale Group Home. The Chip and Dale home is a special facility for the care of severely handicapped children. It is the only one of its kind in Regina, and one of the few in Canada. Being a mother, Madame Sauvé felt great sympathy for the young patients and spent some time with each one of them. At the conclusion of the tour she cut a birthday cake to mark the first anniversary of the home. In her address to the staff she congratulated them on their skill and devotion to the children.

From the Chip and Dale home she went on to a private lunch with the Lieutenant-Governor. They dined at Government House, a solid Victorian mansion with high ceilings, winding staircases, a ballroom, and a conservatory. This building has recently been restored to its former grandeur after many years of neglect. The restoration process was done with such care that even the wallpaper was duplicated from faded scraps of the original paper, so that the rooms appear as they did at the turn of the century. Today, Government House is both a museum and the official residence of the Lieutenant-Governor. After lunch Madame Sauvé was given a guided tour of the mansion.

In the afternoon she visited the Mounted Police headquarters in Regina. This large establishment, known as "F" Division, includes the Training Depot for recruits. Her Excellency was greeted by the Commissioner of the Force and by the Commanding Officer of the Depot, who gave her a tour of the new headquarters building. She was then taken to meet Assistant Commissioner Bill Neill, the Commanding Officer of "F" Division.

Bill Neill is a burly man with short fair hair and an open, friendly face. He would have been downstairs to welcome the Governor General but a few days earlier had broken his leg and was in a hip-length cast. The fact that Madame Sauvé had to come to his office to meet him caused him some embarrassment. When she entered the room he managed to rise to his feet to shake hands but then collapsed awkwardly into his chair. After inquiring about his health, she proceeded to question him closely on the role of women in the Force. Although she is not a radical feminist, Madame Sauvé believes firmly in equal rights for women. Having zeroed in on the subject, she pursued it relentlessly. Neill became increasingly uncomfortable under her interrogation until Bob Simmonds, the Commissioner, smoothly intervened. Simmonds, who combines the military bearing of a soldier with the quiet authority of a university president, fielded her questions to everyone's satisfaction.

At the Training Depot Her Excellency addressed the recruits; then the viceregal party drove to the Mounted Police chapel, which is the oldest building in Regina. This little stucco church is filled with history. Flags that flew at Fort Walsh in 1875 hang on either side of the altar, and the wooden walls have memorial tablets dating back to the North West Rebellion. The rear wall is literally covered with small plaques commemorating the deaths of members of the Force killed on duty. Madame Sauvé was particularly touched by the memorial to Margaret Clay, the thirty-two-year-old wife of Staff Sergeant Clay who headed a detachment at Chesterfield Inlet. Margaret Clay died on 19 September 1924 while her husband was away on patrol. When she had gone out to feed the sled dogs, she had slipped, and the dogs had mauled her to death.

After visiting the chapel Madame Sauvé had tea at the Officers' Mess. About fifty officers and their wives were presented to her at this reception, and she chatted with many of them. At four o'clock she returned to the Hotel Saskatchewan.

Having made five off-the-cuff speeches since breakfast, she still had a major speech to deliver that night at a state dinner given by Premier Grant Devine. As soon as she got to her suite she called in Liane Benoit, her niece and English-speech writer, and together they made some last-minute changes to her address. This process is not without hazard, because Her Excellency is fond of making pencilled corrections, which later she sometimes has difficulty reading.

For the dinner Madame Sauvé wore an emerald-green silk ball gown with long sleeves and a fitted bodice. The colour complemented her eyes and provided a stunning contrast with her white hair. On her shoulder was a red-and-white bow with the insignia of a Companion of the Order of Canada, and at her waist she wore a row of miniature decorations. At twenty minutes past seven Commander K. C. McCaw, an honorary aide-de-camp, and Michael Jackson, the provincial Director of Protocol, escorted her downstairs to a pre-dinner reception in the Victoria Room.

The purpose of the dinner was to honour Jeanne Sauvé and other prominent people from Saskatchewan who had made their mark in the world. The guests, some of whom hadn't been back to Saskatchewan for years, came from all walks of life. When everyone was seated, it was impressive to see how many leading Canadians had been born in the sparsely populated province. Among the four hundred present were the Governor of the Bank of Canada and the Deputy Governor, the presidents of Imperial Oil and Gulf Canada, the Anglican Archbishop of Winnipeg, three university presidents, the Clerk of the House of Commons, the Commissioner of the Royal Canadian Mounted Police, columnist Allan Fotheringham, journalist Pamela Wallin, and folk singer Joni Mitchell. Aside from these luminaries, there were more than fifty men and women who were members of the Order of Canada.

In his welcoming address Premier Devine repeatedly mispronounced the Governor General's first name, calling her Jean, rhyming with "bean", instead of Jeanne, which rhymes with "man". Madame Sauvé's speech captured the mood of the evening. She began with some amusing anecdotes about Prud'homme, her birthplace. She also observed that if all the people in the room suddenly quit their jobs, large segments of the country would cease to function. On a more serious note, she paid tribute to the pioneers who worked so hard to establish the province, and who received no recognition during their lifetimes. At the conclusion of her address she was given a standing ovation.

After dinner the special guests and their spouses were invited to a private reception in an upstairs suite. Although it was a small gathering, and a select one, there was a plain-clothes Mountie in attendance. She was difficult to spot, however, because she blended in with the crowd. Young, slim, and attractive, she wore a demure dress and little make-up, and carried a small evening purse. The purse contained a Smith and Wesson snub-nosed .38-calibre revolver. When Her Excellency left the party, this young lady was one of those who escorted her back to the royal suite.

During the night another blizzard swept the province. The next morning blowing snow reduced visibility to zero, which forced the Regina Airport to cancel all flights. Many of the out-of-town guests who had attended the dinner were stranded for the day. Madame Sauvé's schedule was also disrupted. She had planned to fly to Saskatoon immediately after breakfast, but her Travel Officer advised her that this was now impossible. The question then was whether to wait, in hope that the storm would subside, or to simply cancel the day's events. Knowing how much effort had gone into the program — especially her visit to Prud'homme — she was determined to keep her engagements. It took some frantic phone calls, but within minutes her schedule was rearranged.

When she left the hotel shortly after ten o'clock that morning all the formalities were observed, including the red carpet, but instead of stepping into the back seat of a limousine, Her Excellency mounted the steps of a chartered city bus. Under the circumstances it was the fastest way to cover the 250 kilometres from Regina to Saskatoon, where she was to be the guest of honour at a huge civic luncheon. Madame Sauvé and her sister, Madame Belisle, sat in the front seat opposite the driver while the rest of the viceregal party occupied the rear of the bus. Inspector Larry Callens, who was in charge of security, was also aboard and kept in constant radio contact with his headquarters. It was a tedious journey, relieved only by brief glimpses of snow-covered prairie. An hour out of Regina the bus stopped at a tiny roadside restaurant. The owner of the establishment was mystified to see a city bus outside his door, and even more perplexed when a naval officer, in full uniform with gold aiguillette, came in and ordered a dozen coffees "to go". The rest of the trip was un-eventful, and at a quarter to two the bus pulled up at the Centennial Auditorium in Saskatoon.

Because it had been impossible to notify everyone of the change in schedule, some of the guests had been waiting at their tables for more than two hours. Only a handful had left, which was a tribute both to Jeanne Sauvé and to Saskatchewan hospitality. His Worship Cliff Wright, Saskatoon's popular mayor, noted in his speech that it was Halloween, and while it wasn't dark yet he had already had his trick and his treat; the trick was the weather, the treat was the presence of the Governor General.

When Madame Sauvé emerged from the Centennial Auditorium the weather had cleared sufficiently for her to travel to her next engagement in her limousine. The rest of the viceregal party piled into the bus for the trip to Canadian Forces Base Dana, a radar base on a hill sixty kilometres northeast of Saskatoon. The cavalcade was met on the highway by a military police car and escorted into the base. As the limousine entered the main gate the Quarter Guard smartly presented arms, but as soon as the viceregal car turned the corner the soldiers of the guard broke ranks and ran for the warmth of their barracks.

Madame Sauvé was welcomed by the Base Commander, who took her to the dining hall where the students of Radar Hill School were awaiting her arrival. After being presented with a bouquet of flowers by two five-year-olds, Her Excellency chatted with chil-dren in each of the classes. Then she addressed the whole room. With a twinkle in her eye she observed that everyone had told her how much they enjoyed school. For this reason, she knew that they would not want a holiday (which she had planned to give them). There was a moment of disbelief, and then a chorus of anguished protests from the children. Madame Sauvé feigned surprise at their reaction, but after pretending to think about it she relented and agreed that they should have a holiday the next day. This brought shrieks of delight and three loud cheers.

Leaving the children on this high note, she was escorted to the mess, where she met the military and civilian personnel of the base and their spouses. As Commander-in-Chief of the Armed Forces she congratulated the personnel on their high standard of conduct and stressed the importance of the radar station to the security of the nation. The Base Commander thanked her for coming and presented her with a station plaque. The Quarter Guard was magically in place to salute as Her Excellency's limousine left the base.

On the way to Prud'homme the viceregal flag fell off the fender of the limousine twice, because the sub-zero temperature kept breaking the seal of the suction cups. Each time this happened the ADC had to jump out of the car and, scrambling on the icy road, reattach the flag. His antics caused a certain amount of unseemly laughter from his friends who were riding behind in the bus. Just as the light was fading the cavalcade turned off onto a side road. A few minutes later a sign proclaimed the village of Prud'homme and the proud fact that it was the birthplace of Governor General Jeanne Sauvé. In the distance were the silhouettes of three grain elevators, one of which had been built by Jeanne Sauvé's father.

Her Excellency was received at the Roman Catholic church of Saints Donatien and Rogatien. She had both a spiritual and a family connection with this church, for she had been baptized there, and her father had built its wooden belfry. Waiting at the foot of the steps was the mayor of Prud'homme, Steve Sopotyk, and Father Gaston Massé, the parish priest. On either side of them stood scarlet-coated Mounties in fur hats, who saluted when Her Excellency stepped from the car. She mounted the steps under a gleaming arch of swords provided by a guard of honour of the Knights of Columbus wearing long capes and white plumed hats. When she entered the church there was a momentary hush, and then everyone stood up. She proceeded up the aisle to the front of the church as the choir sang "Les Voix de chez nous". The other members of the viceregal party followed behind her and were seated in the first two pews.

While Madame Sauvé was signing the guest book, Esmond Butler looked around the packed church and asked one of the residents in a whisper, "What is the population of Prud'homme?" The man gave the matter considerable thought before whispering in reply, "I can't tell you exactly, but it's around two hundred and twenty-three."

After the signing three people connected with Madame Sauvé's past were presented to her: the daughter of her godparents, Madame Lucille Courchène, who had come from Surrey, B.C., for the occasion; Madame Delima Denis, the daughter of the midwife who has assisted at her birth; and Madame Annette Loiselle, who was baptized on the same day, and had the same godparents. Madame Sauvé, who was visibly moved by her homecoming, and the warmth of her welcome, began her speech in French. Seeing the blank looks from her audience she suddenly realized that they didn't understand a word. This was a shock, because when she was a child Prud'homme had been a French settlement. Now most of the population is of Ukrainian or Hungarian descent, and English is the predominant language. Without hesitation she switched to English and repeated her remarks. The choir then sang a number of songs, among them the haunting "Un Canadien errant", while she was presented with a bouquet of flowers and given a number of presents, including a copy of her baptismal certificate — which she said she would hang at Rideau Hall to remind her of where she came from. The ceremony at the church ended with a viewing of historical items on display near the altar. As she left the church the whole crowd sang "O Canada".

From the church she was taken to see the house in which she was born. After a quick tour of the one-storey frame dwelling she went on to the Silver Age Hall. Once again the Knights of Columbus provided a guard of honour. The Silver Age Hall is a long wooden building used for a variety of senior-citizen and community activities. The entire village of Prud'homme as well as the mayors of surrounding municipalities was waiting in the hall for her. Mayor Sopotyk presented a number of leading citizens and their spouses to Madame Sauvé before she settled down to watch a performance of Ukrainian dancing. The dancers, who ranged in age from eight to eighteen, were dressed in folk costumes made by their mothers.

There were four sets, all of whom were good, but the ones who stole the show were the young ones, especially two little boys who performed a rousing Cossack number. Because they had been at the hall when the Governor General was at the church, the dancers didn't know that she had given the schoolchildren a holiday the following day. When she went over to thank the dancers she made a special point of telling them the good news. Tea, with sandwiches and fancy cakes made by local volunteers, was served to the viceregal party. Her Excellency then made a short speech and was given two more gifts: a ceramic grain elevator, and the first copy of the history of Prud'homme.

Madame Sauvé's departure from the hall took about twenty minutes because she was besieged by a crowd of well-wishers, all of whom wanted to shake hands with her. Some people, when they finally found themselves face to face with the Governor General, were so nervous that they were speechless, while others reacted with a flood of words and were reluctant to let go of her hand. Many of the villagers accompanied her outside and stood coatless in the blowing snow to wave goodbye. As she drove away there were tears in her eyes. For the residents of Prud'homme — and for Jeanne Sauvé — it had been an unforgettable day.

Jeanne was born in Prud'homme on 26 April 1922, the fifth child of Charles and Anna Benoit. Charles, who came from Ottawa, was tall and slim with black hair and blue eyes. He was a quiet man with a wry sense of humour, whose favourite pleasure was to settle down with an interesting book. His wife Anna (née Vaillant) came from Ste. Cécile de Masham, a village in the province of Quebec a few miles outside of Ottawa. She was a small woman with fair hair and good features. Anna's main interest was her children, and she was perfectly content to play the traditional role of homemaker.

In 1911 Charles Benoit had gone west to seek his fortune. This meant leaving all that was familiar to him — including the French-speaking milieu in which he had been brought up — for the uncertain prospects of a life in pioneer country. Charles was not alone, however, but was one of many eastern Canadians who went west at that time. Also, more than a thousand immigrants were entering Canada each day, and these newcomers added to the flood of immigration to the prairie provinces. Both the Canadian government and the railways encouraged immigration by touting the Western Dream, the former to increase settlement in the area, the latter to increase rail revenues. However, instead of homesteading on a quarter section of raw land, as many did, Charles chose to go to Saskatoon. Since he was a family man with a wife and a nine-month-old daughter, Berthe, his decision may have been influenced by an advertisement in the Ottawa papers (paid for by the Saskatoon Board of Trade) which had as its headline: "Saskatoon for Sociability and for Cultured, Kind-Hearted People". This ad read in part:

Any deep-seated fallacy is hard to eradicate; although many of such are wildly absurd; but, none is more so than that our Western City life is crude and uncouth. Strangers labouring under such an impression will be pleasantly disillusioned from the moment of their arrival in Saskatoon. Life here is by no means crude and uncouth: on the contrary, it is cultured and refined. The general prosperity has not outcropped in vulgarity; but, rather in an unostentatious indulgence in such things simple, comfortable and beautiful as are dear to the soul of a tasteful and well-bred people.

Nor is life here by any means stale, flat and unprofitable, save to those who so will it: there is ever an endless chain of bright happenings, there is always an atmosphere of colour and sparkle and go, and the very fragrance of the joy of life. . . .

Charles Benoit made some lifelong friends, but he didn't make his fortune in Saskatoon. Nor did he experience an "endless chain of bright happenings". Indeed, prosperity proved so elusive that he ended up as a tram conductor. After six years, he left Saskatoon and returned to Ottawa.

For the next two years he worked as a carpenter and learned the construction business. During this period he built a substantial wooden house for his in-laws at their farm near Masham. (This house is still occupied by descendants of the Vaillant family.) Work in the Ottawa area, however, became increasingly scarce owing to the large number of veterans returning from the First World War who entered the construction trade.

A few months after the Armistice, Charles received a letter from a Saskatoon friend, a man by the name of Turcotte. Mr. Turcotte had just been appointed station-master at Howell, a village on the transcontinental rail line some thirty miles northeast of Saskatoon. In his letter Turcotte urged Charles to come to Howell, because the village was growing at a great rate and there were all sorts of building opportunities. Another attractive feature was that the population of Howell was largely of French stock. The chance to make a fresh start appealed to Charles, and he accepted Turcotte's invitation. In the spring of 1919 he and Anna with their three children, Berthe, Lina, and Armand, made the long journey by train back to Saskatchewan.

When Charles Benoit and his family arrived at Howell it was still a frontier community. Twenty-five years earlier the site had been a hunting area used by Cree Indians and Métis. The first settler was Joseph Marcotte, who in 1897 immigrated from Quebec and established a ranch there that encompassed four townships. Three years later Joseph Marcotte married an Austrian immigrant, Anielka Belenski. The couple called their homestead the Blue Bell Ranch, because of the profusion of little blue flowers that grew on the surrounding prairie. When the Grand Trunk line came through, Marcotte was the sole supplier of fresh meat to the construction crews. The railway workers in turn renamed the locality Marcotte's Crossing. The name was changed again in 1903, after the Marcottes had a daughter who was christened Lally, the first white child to be born in the district. In her honour, and in recognition of the railway, the site became known as Lally's Siding. Settlers followed in the wake of the railway, and by 1906 there were enough people in the area to justify a post office. The post office was officially named Howell, after a Winnipeg lawyer and surveyor who had been of service to Joseph Marcotte. Thus in a period of less than ten years the settlement was known by four different names.

Virtually all the residents of Howell were French, and the village had a French convent run by the Order of the Daughters of Providence. Many of the farms surrounding Howell were owned by Hungarians or Ukrainians. (Berthe, Jeanne's eldest sister, remembers visits to the Benoit house by Ukrainian women in long skirts and babushkas who sold vegetables door to door.) The village had no industry but served as a depot for the railway and depended upon trade from the farms in the area. By the time Charles Benoit arrived, Howell consisted of a few dozen houses, the church of Saints Donatien and Rogatien, a small convent, a bank, a hotel, a general store, a barber-shop and poolroom, two livery stables, and two grain elevators. Initially, Charles found plenty of work. He built several houses, which he lived in briefly and then sold for a profit, a number of huge barns, and a grain elevator. He was also a foreman on the construction of Howell's largest building, a new four-storey convent, and he erected the bell tower on the church.

In August of 1919, his wife Anna had a third daughter, Annette. Two years later, during her next pregnancy, Anna became dangerously ill with pneumonia. She was nursed back to health by the local midwife, Madame Mathilde Lafrenière. When a healthy girl was delivered on 26 April 1922 by Dr. Martial Lavoie, assisted by Madame Lafrenière, Anna christened the child Marie Jeanne Mathilde — the name Mathilde being in recognition of Madame Lafrenière's nursing skill. Although the baby's first name was Marie, from the time she was an infant she was called Jeanne.

Shortly after Jeanne's birth a controversy developed among the residents of Howell over the name of the village. Because most of the population was francophone it was felt that the community should have a French name. But they couldn't agree on the new name. Some people wanted it to be Marcotteville, some thought Lallytown was more appropriate, and there were even a few who wanted to retain the old name. Father Bourdel, who had come as a missionary from France and founded the parish, lobbied to have the village named Hélène or Ste. Hélène. He chose these names to honour the memory of Mademoiselle Hélène DeJoie, who had died in the Spanish flu epidemic in 1918, and who had been a generous benefactress to the parish. While the various names were being debated at heated meetings, Dr. Lavoie quietly wrote to The Honourable J. M. Ulrich in Ottawa stating that it was the wish of the village to change its name to Prud'homme. Dr. Lavoie selected this name to honour Monseigneur J. Henri Prud'homme, the newly appointed Roman Catholic bishop of Prince Albert. Lavoie's request was accepted, and on 15 November 1922 the name was officially changed to Prud'homme. This is why Jeanne, who was baptized six months earlier, has Howell on her baptismal certificate. Shortly after settling the question to his personal satisfaction, the good doctor left town.

The two-storey white clapboard house in which Jeanne was born was later sold by Charles Benoit. It changed hands several times and was eventually bought by a couple with serious marital problems. This couple had a violent quarrel which ended with the wife going home to her mother. While she was away, her husband had the house put on a flatcar and trucked to another town. On her return, his wife was confronted with a vacant lot. Many years later, when Jeanne was appointed governor general, the village elders tried to put a plaque on her birthplace, but they couldn't find it, so they compromised by putting a plaque on another house in which she had lived.

After the building boom subsided in Prud'homme, Charles Benoit established a farm implement business. It wasn't a success and once again he turned to construction. In 1923 he moved his family to Dana, a small community a few miles from Prud'homme, where there was still a demand for housing. Later, he built houses for workers at nearby Muskiki Lake, which had a salt extraction plant. The Benoits' second son and sixth child, Jean, was born at Muskiki Springs in June of 1924.

Because Charles and Anna Benoit considered the education of their children to be of prime importance, they sent their two eldest girls east in October of 1924. Fourteen-year-old Berthe, who had completed her schooling at the Prud'homme convent (and led her class each year), was going to finish her education in Ottawa and attend teachers' college. Lina, who was a bright twelve-year-old, but who had been deaf since birth, was going to be educated at a French institute for the deaf in Montreal.

The rest of the family returned to Ottawa in December of the following year. A major reason for the move was Charles Benoit's desire for all his children to get a sound French education. Besides being his home, Ottawa had a number of good French schools and a French university.

It was night when the family boarded the eastbound transcontinental at Prud'homme, and Anna immediately put the children to bed. Three-year-old Jeanne, who was a chatterbox, shared an upper berth with her six-year-old sister, Annette. The two little girls woke very early the next morning and were soon giggling and laughing in their new surroundings. Suddenly the curtains of the berth were ripped open and the porter told them in a stern voice to be quiet. Jeanne and Annette, who had never seen a black man before, were terrified by the sight of the porter's dark face. After he closed the curtains they didn't make another sound until their mother got them down from their berth for breakfast.

The train journey from Prud'homme to Ottawa took three days and four nights. This gave Charles and Anna time to reflect upon the past and to plan for the future. For Jeanne and the other young ones, the trip seemed to take forever. On the third day, as the train rattled across Ontario, the Benoit children began to realize that the move to Ottawa was a turning-point in their lives, and boredom gave way to a mounting sense of anticipation.

Chapter 2

FORMATIVE YEARS
Ottawa, 1925–42

Jeanne, helped by the porter, was the first of the Benoit family to get off the train in Ottawa. She was wearing her proudest possession, a red wool coat trimmed with white rabbit fur. Hand in hand, she and Annette led the family procession down the platform. Close behind them came her mother, carrying baby Jean, while her father and her ten-year-old brother Armand, laden with luggage, brought up the rear.

Unlike the quiet little station in Prud'homme, Union Station was crowded and noisy, and the air smelt of soot. Everyone seemed to be in a hurry, and the snatches of conversation Jeanne heard were in English. As they trudged along the platform they passed a gigantic locomotive that made ominous sounds as though about to explode, and hissed steam from its boiler. Eventually the family emerged from the grimy corridor between the trains into the station's brightly lit concourse. To everyone's relief, the Benoit and Vaillant grandparents were waiting there to greet them.

Grandfather Benoit scooped Jeanne into his arms and asked her where she got her stylish red coat. She replied in French, but used an English sentence structure. Although she was only three, this minor faux pas — which later became a family joke — dismayed her grandfather. It also caused Charles Benoit some embarrassment, because he was proud of the family's French heritage and determined that his children should speak good French. To this end, one of the few rules Jeanne's father insisted upon was that only French be spoken in their home.

After staying with Anna's parents at Ste. Cécile de Masham for the first few weeks, Charles Benoit rented a house in Ottawa. The house was on Carling Avenue in the parish of St. Jean Baptiste, on the west side of the city. As well as having a close-knit French community, this working-class district contained a number of other ethnic groups, including Italians, Chinese, Poles, and Germans. What made it attractive to Charles was the quality of the French Roman Catholic separate schools in the area, and the range of parish activities for young people.

The core of the parish was on Empress Street, a side street running north from Somerset Street, the main commercial thoroughfare. At the corner of Somerset and Empress was l'École St. Jean Baptiste, a boys' school run by the Christian Brothers, which Armand and Jean attended. Opposite the boys' school was the parish recreation hall, la Salle St. Jean Baptiste, which had a bowling alley in the basement, and an auditorium on the top floor where plays and other forms of entertainment were staged. On the same side of the street as l'École St. Jean Baptiste was the Dominican monastery, an impressive stone building with ample grounds surrounded by a high stone wall. Beside the monastery, at the intersection of Primrose Avenue, was St. Jean Baptiste church, which was also run by the Dominican Fathers. Opposite the church, set on a promontory facing the Gatineau Hills and overlooking the Lebreton Flats, was another stone building, the Notre Dame du Rosaire convent. This school, which Jeanne and her sisters attended, was run by the Sisters of Charity, or, as they are more familiarly known, the Grey Nuns.

During the first three years in Ottawa, while Charles Benoit was establishing himself in the contracting business, the family moved three times. Following the birth of Lucille, in July of 1926, the family left Carling Avenue for a larger rented house on Larch Street. A year later they moved a block away to Poplar Street, which was a ten-minute walk from Empress Avenue. That September, Jeanne entered the first grade of the Notre Dame du Rosaire convent.

Being a cheerful little girl with an inquiring mind, she loved school from the outset. She was also proud of her school uniform, which was a black serge dress with a pleated bodice and skirt, long sleeves, and white collar and cuffs. (The stiff white celluloid collar and cuffs had to be cleaned each night with a toothbrush, using soap and water.) Summer and winter the girls wore long black lisle stockings with black shoes.

When she was in the elementary grades, Jeanne often came home from the convent wearing a rosette for achievement in class. On these occasions her father would greet her by saying, "Here's my little Indian chief," and she would be required to recite her lesson for him. She was accustomed to this sort of attention, because when she was very small her father would sometimes stand her on the kitchen table so she could amuse the family with her wit and eloquence. Fortunately, Charles and Anna were able to make each one of their children feel special, and for this reason there was no jealousy in the family. Indeed, performing was a favourite family pastime. At the Poplar Street house, Charles built a stage for the children in a large shed adjoining the kitchen. This theatre became a neighbourhood attraction, where patrons were charged an admission fee of one button to watch plays written, directed, and acted by the Benoit clan.

Jeanne's grandmother Vaillant also had a strong influence upon her. Théodosie Vaillant was a tiny woman with tremendous energy and a puckish sense of humour. She and Jeanne had an unspoken bond because, besides being similar in looks, they were similar in temperament. One of the things the Benoit children enjoyed most each summer was staying with their grandmother at the family farm outside of Ste. Cécile de Masham. Normally two or three of the children would go together for these visits. Jeanne usually went with her older sister Annette and her younger brother Jean. Charles Benoit would put them on the bus in Ottawa and give them a bag of candies to sustain them on the twenty-mile journey.

The farm was situated in gently rolling country in the valley of the Gatineau River. At that time it had neither plumbing nor electricity. Light was provided by oil lamps, cooking was done on a wood stove, and the toilet was a two-hole outdoor privy. The farm had a magical quality for the Benoit children, as there were endless things to do. Jeanne loved to romp in the fields among the wildflowers, breathing the scent of clover and new-mown hay. Her brother Jean spent many happy hours fishing in the brook that ran through a corner of the property. His fishing outfit consisted of an alder switch with a few feet of line, a small hook, and a plentiful supply of worms. The trick to catching fish was to approach each pool quietly, and with great stealth to drop the worm at the head of the current. Often he would feel a rubbery pluck on his line and with a quick flip out would come a pan-sized speckled trout. Jeanne and Annette were permitted to accompany Jean on these expeditions, but because they were girls they weren't allowed to fish. (The only woman who defied this convention was an English aunt who lived in Arnprior — and she was regarded as an eccentric.) Once or twice each visit the family would have a picnic at the sugar bush which was two fields away from the house. Even though the weather was fine they would always eat their sandwiches in the little sugaring hut.

Playing in the barn was another favourite pastime. Although they were not allowed to do it, they would climb high up into the rafters and plunge into the hay. After a few jumps their clothes and their hair would be covered with straw and everyone would be sneezing from the dust, but it was great sport. The attic in the barn also held a special fascination for Annette because it contained all sorts of relics such as a spinning wheel, a pair of old bedsteads, a cutter, and hair-curling irons and other antique implements.

Because it was a working farm, the Benoit children were not permitted to ride the horses or even to sit on the hay wagon while haying was in progress. But they did help with a number of chores. As a special treat their grandmother would let them feed the chickens, and they were given the additional responsibility of collecting the eggs. Another chore was cranking the handle of the cream separator. Jeanne would often become mesmerized watching the twin streams of milk and cream pour steadily from the machine. To keep the cream fresh until it was picked up by the dairy, it was put in a tall can and set in a box in the brook downstream from an icy spring. This simple method of refrigeration kept the cream in perfect condition.

The farm was owned by grandmother Vaillant, but because she was a widow it was operated by one of her sons. This son had a large family and there was usually a new baby in the house each year. After lunch Jeanne used to get great pleasure from holding her newest baby cousin and rocking it to sleep. After supper, when the fields had taken on the texture of velvet in the fading light, she would go with her cousins and the dog to the pasture to fetch the cattle. The act of bringing home the cattle was for Jeanne a symbolic and satisfying way to end the day.

The highlight of every visit was going to church with grandmother Vaillant in the buggy. The glossy black buggy was drawn by a privileged horse named Marlin, who was not worked at any other time of the week. Marlin's harness was adorned with brass bells that Jeanne's grandfather had painstakingly collected over a period of years. Of varying sizes, they each had a different tone. The buggy's high seat was just wide enough to accommodate grandmother Vaillant and her son, with one Benoit child wedged in between them. The ride from the farm to the church in Ste. Cécile de Masham took about an hour. When Jeanne entered the church with her grandmother, people would stare at them, which made her feel like a celebrity. After Mass the members of the congregation, most of whom lived on the surrounding farms, would gossip on the steps of the church. One Sunday, following church, Jeanne accompanied her grandmother to a lively political meeting in the village hall across the street. It was the first one she had ever been to, and she thoroughly enjoyed it.

When Jeanne was twelve, her aunt who lived on the farm died in childbirth. This family tragedy meant that grandmother Vaillant had to take a full-time role in raising her son's eight children. As a result of the increased workload on the farm, it was no longer feasible for the Benoit children to come as guests. For Jeanne, the visits to the farm had taught her to appreciate nature and had brought her into solid contact with reality. As a child she was inclined to theorize about life, but on the farm there was no room for the abstract, one had to be practical. Looking back on her holidays with her grandmother, she was moved to exclaim, "Thank God I had them, because if I hadn't, I would have been impossible!"

Although life in the city was not the same as a holiday in the country, there were plenty of recreational activities in Ottawa. Booth Park, a ten-minute walk from the Benoit house, was a large playground complete with swings, horseshoe pitches, and two baseball diamonds. The Plante Baths, a city-owned indoor swimming-pool, was a few minutes' walk in the opposite direction. Jeanne, who loved tennis, used to play almost every day of the summer on the asphalt court at the convent. Because of the noise, the nuns only allowed the girls to use the court after three o'clock in the afternoon. This rule was strictly observed, but the girls were so keen that they would play until dark. In the winter there was good skiing on the hill behind the Arboretum at the Experimental Farm. To get there, Jeanne would ski from her house down Somerset Street until she came to the railroad tracks, and then pole along the tracks to the hill. By today's standards the hill would be considered a beginners' slope, but it was a fair climb (there was no tow) and you picked up nice speed on the run down to Dow's Lake. The parish also organized sleigh rides for the young people, and there was skating on the rink at the Dominican monastery.

With seven children in the family it was Jeanne's responsibility to keep a motherly eye on the two youngest, Jean and Lucille. When her brother Jean was ten he caught influenza just before Christmas, and couldn't go out until mid-January. To cheer him up, and to ensure that his first skating party would be a success, Jeanne coerced the most popular girl of his age into skating with him. Unfortunately, her plan didn't work out as she had hoped. After Jeanne made the introductions, her brother took the young lady's arm and without saying a word skated once around the rink. At the end of the circuit, he made an abrupt farewell and bolted back to his chums at the other end of the ice. This was the first and the last time that Jeanne tried to fix her brother up with a date. Jean, for his part, found it such a traumatic experience that he had nothing to do with girls for another five years.

When she was thirteen, Jeanne was recruited into the Guides catholiques (Girl Guides) by one of the Dominican fathers. That summer, as the head of a troop of six Guides, she supervised activities for younger children at the parish recreation centre. She was terribly earnest about Guiding and wholeheartedly embraced its high ideals, but one of the principles — truthfulness — caused her a great deal of soul-searching. Looking back at this moral thorn of her teens, she recently remarked, "I worried so much about truthfulness that I must have had a problem in that area!"

Although Charles and Anna Benoit always used the formal "vous" rather than the more familiar "tu" when addressing their children, Jeanne grew up in a warm and loving household. She had a particularly close relationship with her father, who taught her to solve problems by means of logic and to deal with difficult situations in a rational manner. Charles used this approach to discipline his children; if one of them got out of line, he never used force but would reason with the offender. This made the children feel that they were responsible for their own behaviour, and they considered themselves much luckier than most of their friends. At meals he would include them in discussions on politics or current events as though they were adults, which reinforced their sense of personal responsibility. The family also shared a common goal, which was to ensure that everyone got a good education.

On weekdays Anna would do the dishes after supper so the children would be free to devote all their time to their homework. On Saturdays, Charles would take the children to the Ottawa Public Library or to the National Museum. The library trips were also for his benefit, because he would return the books he had read during the previous week and come home with a fresh armload of reading material. At the museum, he and the children would see documentary films or listen to lectures. He also took them several times to visit the Parliament Buildings. On one occasion, Charles pointed out the statue of Agnes Macphail, who had made history by being the first woman to be elected to the House, and told Jeanne that one day she too might be elected to Parliament. Jeanne thought the idea was totally absurd.

Jeanne led her class at the convent year after year. The nuns liked her, and so did her fellow students. One reason for her popularity was that she was a team player. If a classmate was having difficulty with her homework, Jeanne would help her, and in class she only answered questions when specifically asked to do so — she didn't show off by trying to answer every question. Outside of class she was also a leader. An excellent public speaker, when the bishop or some other VIP visited the convent Jeanne was usually chosen to give the welcoming address. In her graduation year she won a speaking contest among students from a number of Ottawa schools where each contestant had to make a speech in French and then in English. Many years later, a CBC interviewer asked one of her teachers, Sister Marguerite Myre, if Jeanne had had *any* faults. Sister Marguerite replied, "No, but then I only saw her at school; maybe she had some at home."

Religion was an integral part of Jeanne's childhood. As a devout Roman Catholic she attended church each Sunday as well as on feast days. At the convent the nuns taught her catechism in class, and she later took lectures on philosophy and theology at the Dominican monastery. She also participated in a round of religious activities such as festivals, plays, and chorales at St. Jean Baptiste church. Her religious zeal prompted one of the nuns at the convent, Sister Marie Varnelle — who may have hoped that Jeanne was considering a religious vocation — to ask her what she would like to be when she grew up. Jeanne thought about it for a moment and then replied, "I would like to be well dressed." Sister Marie was not amused.

Jeanne's success didn't go to her head because she had the nagging fear that she didn't deserve it. Throughout her school years she worried that favouritism was the reason she got high marks and was chosen for leading roles. She felt especially badly when she passed her older sister Annette in grade seven. Annette, however, bore no resentment and told a friend, "Why should I be angry that Jeanne passed me when she's passed everyone else too?" It was only when Jeanne wrote her matriculation exams, which were set and marked by the province, that her fears of being the teachers' pet were laid to rest. These exams were particularly difficult for French-speaking students because all the answers, except for Latin translations, had to be written in English. Jeanne won First Class Honours, and was awarded a scholarship by the Rideau Convent in Ottawa to study for a Bachelor of Arts degree.

It was at this point that Jeanne suffered the first serious reverse in her life. When she told her father that she had won the scholarship, he said that she couldn't accept it, because he couldn't afford the cost of her room and board as he was still paying separate-school fees for Jean and Lucille. In fact, Charles could have afforded the expense, but he had just come through the Depression and he was being overly cautious. Jeanne pleaded with her father for days, but he wouldn't change his mind. As a result, she had to give up her dream of university and go to work. She was bitterly disappointed, and cried herself to sleep for weeks.

When Jeanne graduated from the convent in June of 1940 she had just turned eighteen. She had a slim, athletic figure and her hair, which had been ash blonde when she was a child, had turned a deep honey colour. Her features were attractive, especially her blue-green eyes, but she was definitely not a glamour girl. One of her schoolmates recollected that Jeanne was always well groomed and smelt of good soap (adding that this was not the case with all her contemporaries). To her father's displeasure, she looked and dressed like a typical American bobby-soxer. As far as boys were concerned, she had had a number of crushes but very few dates and no steady boyfriends. This was not surprising, because social activities in the parish were group-oriented, which discouraged boys and girls from pairing off with each other.

Later that summer Jeanne found what she thought was the perfect solution to her university problem. An advertisement in the paper offered high wages to students who were willing to pick fruit in the Niagara Peninsula. In a few months she could make enough money to pay for her first year's room and board. Charles and Anna, however, did not agree with her. At that time it was all right for boys to take summer jobs, but it was not thought appropriate for girls from respectable families to do so. Once again Jeanne was reduced to tears of frustration.

Eventually Jeanne came to a compromise — she would work during the day and attend night classes at the university. She qualified as a translator and got a job in the government working for the Department of National Defence. Most of her work consisted of translating letters written in French to the Minister, James Ralston. It was not a stimulating occupation. She also enrolled in night courses for a B.A. at the University of Ottawa. By coincidence, Sister Marguerite Myre, one of her teachers at the convent, was in the same class. After class she often walked home with Sister Marguerite, who, because of her vows of poverty, would not allow herself the luxury of taking a streetcar.

She and Sister Marguerite had a lot to talk about, as Jeanne was still involved in parish activities and the Jeunesse étudiante catholique. The Jeunesse étudiante catholique, or Young Catholic Students, was a lay religious movement that had started in Europe and had come to Canada in the early thirties. Although it was an apostolic movement, it had practical social overtones. The primary aim of the movement was to help young people cope with the stresses of the post-First World War era and the Depression by introducing an element of religious faith into their daily lives. Jeanne had been asked, as a gesture of piety and public service, to join the JEC by one of the nuns at the convent. As the representative for her school on the diocesan council she had done such a good job that she was later appointed president of the JEC for the Ottawa diocese.

In the spring of 1942, the government advertised for girls to work at the Canadian Information Office in Washington. Jeanne thought this was an exciting opportunity, but her parents were appalled at the idea of their daughter, who had just turned twenty, living in a foreign country. Charles flatly refused to let her apply for the posting. This was a setback for Jeanne, but it paved the way for another option she had been considering — that of working in Montreal.

During the previous two years she had attended several national meetings of the JEC in Montreal and Quebec City. Her performance at these gatherings attracted the attention of a number of influential people in the organization who earmarked her as a potential staff member for the Centrale (headquarters) in Montreal. Aside from her leadership qualities, Jeanne was fluently bilingual, a rare qualification in the predominantly francophone movement. Alexandrine Leduc, a pretty, dark-haired, dynamic young woman who was in charge of Ontario and the western provinces for the JEC, made the initial approach to recruit her. Alex remembers her first impression of Jeanne: "She was highly intelligent, she was nice, and she had good judgement — just what we needed. She was also fun." After talking with Jeanne in Ottawa, Alex told Father Lalande, the chaplain at the Centrale, "That one has to come to Montreal."

Jeanne, however, was not at all sure that she wanted to make the commitment that working for the JEC would entail. It meant leaving her family and turning her back on all that was familiar in her life. She agonized over the decision for some time but was eventually persuaded to go by the Dominican parish priest, who then spoke with her parents. Although the priest had managed to sell Jeanne on the idea, he was unable to persuade Charles Benoit to let his daughter work at the Centrale. However, when Jeanne broached the subject of working in Washington, her parents were so alarmed by that prospect that they relented and agreed to let her go to

Montreal — reasoning that it was the lesser of two evils, and had the advantage of being only a few hours away.

It was a wrench for Jeanne to leave the family, made even more painful by the belief that she was abandoning her youngest sister, Lucille. Her mother was also upset, and constantly fretted over how long she would be gone. Jeanne's father, who felt she was throwing her life away, was deeply saddened by her departure, but hid his emotion by gruffly telling Anna:

"You might as well get used to it. She's never coming back."

Chapter 3

A TASTE OF LEADERSHIP
Montreal, 1942–48

Jeanne considered her decision to work at the Centrale, the head-quarters of the Jeunesse étudiante catholique, as serious as entering a convent. However, once she made the commitment, she never looked back. On 31 August 1942 she sent a telegram to Jacqueline Ratté, her future room-mate in Montreal. Jacqueline, who was from Quebec City and was the same age as Jeanne, still has the wire, which reads: "ARRIVING WINDSOR STATION SEVEN TEN PM STOP PUMP THE ORGAN RAISE THE FLUTES."

Knowing that the Jeunesse étudiante catholique could provide little for its volunteers, Jeanne brought her own bedding, towels, and kitchen utensils. The JEC was so strapped for funds that the out-of-town workers were paid nothing except a subsistence allowance of seven dollars a week. They were, however, given rent-free accommodation by the Fathers of the Holy Cross, who sponsored the movement. For the first six months Jeanne and Jacqueline shared a room on the third floor of the Fides Publishing building on St. Denis Street. This location was only a few minutes' walk from the Centrale, and, more important, the building was owned by the Fathers of the Holy Cross. Apart from these obvious advantages, it was less than ideal for the girls. Their room, which was formerly an office, had no cooking facilities, and the bathroom was two corridors away. When they returned home after dark, it gave the girls an eerie feeling to hear their steps echo in the deserted building as they clumped up the three flights of stairs to their quarters.

Even so, Jeanne loved Montreal and she loved the freedom of being on her own. Living in a cosmopolitan city steeped in French culture, where French was the dominant language, was a heady experience for her. By 1942 the Depression was nothing more than a bad memory and, despite war rationing, Montreal hummed with activity. Being a major rail junction and port, the city was rife with war rumours as thousands of servicemen passed through on their way overseas, and refugees trickled in from Europe. The refugees, some of whom were renowned artists and intellectuals, enriched Montreal's cultural community, while the soldiers, many of whom were enjoying a final fling before embarkation, enriched the coffers of Montreal's brothels and "blind pigs". (Venereal disease was so prevalent among Montreal's prostitutes that at one stage the Department of National Defence considered placing the city out of bounds to all transient servicemen.)

During the war there was also a more serious and disturbing aspect to the social structure in Montreal — the deep split between the English and the French communities over conscription.

In the province of Quebec, the prevailing attitude was that the war was an English problem which didn't concern French Canadians. This view was encouraged by both the Church and the provincial authorities. In 1940 the ebullient mayor of Montreal, Camillien Houde, urged the populace to defy the federal government by not registering their names for military service. Houde was arrested for civil disobedience and interned until August 1944. (His stand was so popular that when he was released, more than fifty thousand people turned out to welcome him home.) When a plebiscite was held on the question of compulsory military service in the spring of 1942, nearly seventy-three per cent of Quebecers voted against conscription, while more than eighty per cent of the rest of country voted for it. The results of the plebiscite caused bitter resentment, and polarized the French and the English of Canada. Because of Quebec's opposition, conscription was delayed until November 1944.

Although thousands of French Canadians volunteered for overseas service, and a good number of Quebec units served with distinction, many young francophones in Quebec, including such notables as Pierre Trudeau, refused to take part in the war. Their justification — that it was an English conflict — was received with hostility in English Canada. English Canadians believed that anyone who failed to support the war effort was shirking his duty. Some of the brightest young French Canadians who turned their backs on the war channelled their energy into trying to improve the social situation within the province of Quebec. Having been exposed to harsh anglophone criticism, including charges of cowardice, most of the young men at the JEC made no secret of the fact that they loathed the English. Their attitude shocked Jeanne, who once told a fellow volunteer, Marie Tessier-Lavigne, "You know, I haven't been brought up like that. I don't consider the English my enemies, they are part of us." Both of Jeanne's brothers had enlisted, Armand in the army and Jean in the air force.

By scrimping on her expenses, Jeanne was able to buy a few books and to see French movies and plays on a fairly regular basis. At that time it was possible to get a three-course meal for sixty-five cents, and at the Palestre nationale, a community sports complex at the corner of Cherrier and St. Hubert, you could buy a bowl of good soup, an indifferent main course, and an excellent piece of pie for just twenty-five cents. Later, in their quest for cheap eating-places, Jeanne and Jacqueline discovered an inexpensive Italian restaurant on the second floor of a building on Ste. Catherine Street. Despite its bargain prices, the restaurant had very few patrons. Soon a dozen or so of the staff of the Centrale were eating there each week at a table reserved for them by the kindly proprietor. They stopped going to the restaurant abruptly after being warned by a city detective that the place was a notorious Mafia hangout.

Jeanne usually had breakfast and sometimes lunch at the Centrale, which was just around the corner at 430 Sherbrooke Street East. This large house, which resembled a rabbit warren, contained numerous offices, a printing press in the basement, a dormitory for the male out-of-town volunteers, and a cafeteria. When she worked late, as she frequently did, she would also have her supper there.

Her first job at the Centrale was as a *propagandiste*, whose task was to spread the doctrine of the movement. The word "propaganda" (which fell into disrepute during the Second World War because it was synonymous with false information) actually originated with the College of the Congregation, the committee of cardinals in Rome in charge of foreign missions. As a bilingual *propagandiste*, Jeanne travelled extensively, visiting colleges and religious institutions outside of Quebec. She also wrote articles for the two newspapers published by the JEC, and she carried on a prodigious correspondence. To better understand Jeanne's role in the JEC, we should glance at the history of the movement.

The Jeunesse étudiante catholique was a specialized branch of the Catholic Action Movement. The purpose of the Catholic Action Movement, started by Pope Pius XI after the First World War, was to promote a spiritual revival and to instil Christian values in the daily lives of young people. The founder of the branch known as the Jeunesse étudiante catholique was l'Abbé Joseph Cardijn, a Belgian priest and a mystic. Cardijn was far ahead of his time in that he had an ecumenical outlook, which caused him to be branded as a maverick by some of the Catholic hierarchy. Also, when he was formulating his doctrine he consulted a variety of world youth leaders, including communists and fascists. One of his most influential advisers was Sir Robert (later Lord) Baden-Powell, the founder of the Boy Scouts, whom he visited in England. Convinced that the dogmatic approach of the Church was out of date, Cardijn developed a system based on three steps: Voir, Juger, Agir (Look, Judge, Act) that had tremendous appeal to the young. Further, Cardijn believed that, to be effective, his movement must have specialized branches, and these branches should be run by lay people with the spiritual assistance of chaplains. To this end, he founded the Jeunesse ouvrière catholique (JOC) for young workers, the Jeunesse agricole catholique (JAC) for farmers, and the Jeunesse étudiante catholique (JEC) for students. During the Depression, when many young people were disillusioned and out of work, his movement spread like wildfire. In 1931 the movement came to Canada. Father Henri Roy, a Canadian Oblate, started a branch of the Jeunesse ouvrière catholique in the province of Quebec. In the same year another Quebec priest, Father Brault, founded a branch of the Jeunesse agricole catholique, and the Canadian Fathers of the Holy Cross established a branch of the Jeunesse étudiante catholique.

Meanwhile, a distinguished cleric, teacher, and writer, Canon Lionel Groulx, had already founded a youth movement in Quebec called l'Association catholique de la jeunesse canadienne-française (ACJC). Groulx, a fiery Quebec nationalist, modelled the ACJC after l'Action française, a right-wing youth movement in France with racist and anti-Semitic overtones that was later condemned by Pius XI. Mixing politics with religion, Groulx aimed his message at students of classical colleges and young professionals — the intellectual elite. In consequence, the ACJC had a severely limited appeal, and the movement never really got off the ground. In the late 1920s, the powerful Jesuit Order took over the ACJC, giving it an even more radical nationalistic twist. The Jesuits, with five classical colleges and the sponsorship of a number of large organizations, including the Sacred Heart Society, were confident that they could broaden the membership base and revitalize the ACJC.

The arrival of Cardijn's movement on the Canadian scene put the cat among the pigeons. At first the Jesuits tried to ignore Cardijn's movement, but this proved impossible when the total membership of the JOC, JAC, and JEC surpassed that of the ACJC. In the mid-thirties, the Jesuits made an unsuccessful attempt to merge the Canadian branches of Cardijn's movement with their movement. After being rebuffed, the ideological battle lines were drawn — the Jesuits and most of the Quebec religious hierarchy, including a number of the bishops, against the Fathers of the Holy Cross, the Dominicans, the Oblates, a few bishops, and most of the younger clergy.

The struggle between the two factions was over the need for changes within the Church and questions of doctrine. The Jesuits and other Roman Catholic conservatives were opposed to any form of change and determined to maintain the status quo. Cardijn's doctrine of "Look, Judge, and Act" not only brought into question the dogma of the Church, but implied that young people were responsible enough to make their own religious judgements. This was heresy to the Jesuits, who expected — and got — blind obedience from their charges. Cardijn's belief that lay people should play an active role in Church affairs also infuriated conservative clerics, who considered it a form of Protestantism. Another area of bitter disagreement was nationalism. Cardijn had a global outlook, and while he was all for improving social conditions, he didn't believe nationalism was the answer, because it would restrict religious thought to geographic boundaries. The Jesuits, in contrast, were zealous Quebec nationalists. As an example of the rivalry within the top ranks of the Church, Bishop Charbonneau of Montreal was an ally of the JEC, while Monseigneur Georges Courchesne, Bishop of Rimouski, was so hostile to the movement that at the Centrale he was nicknamed Bishop Cours*chisme*.

When Jeanne joined the Centrale in 1942 the province of Quebec was in many respects a ghetto. For years the provincial government and the Roman Catholic hierarchy, working hand in glove, had conditioned Quebecers to a siege mentality, preaching that the only way to protect the French language and their culture was to look inward rather than outward. Quebecers were told that their principal enemy was the federal government, and that all the province's social and economic ills were caused by external influences. The JEC refused to accept this self-serving doctrine and chose to address the realities of the day. These included the problem of a powerful and repressive Church, the lack of modern educational facilities, and the critical need for better social services. In its newspapers, in correspondence with diocesan representatives, and in meetings, the JEC exposed these problems, exhorting its members to "Look, Judge, and Act" for change. By the early forties, when the JEC had representatives in more than seventeen hundred educational institutions, it was a force to be reckoned with. Pierre Juneau, who worked closely with Jeanne, summed up the attitude of the JEC volunteers in these words: "We considered ourselves religious but anti-clerical; it was a liberation movement, we wanted to liberate people's minds from dried-up traditions."

The JEC attracted the idealistic and ambitious young, many of whom were destined to play leading roles on the provincial and national stages. Gérard Pelletier, a deceptively soft-spoken intellectual with an iron will who headed the Boys' section went on to become editor of *La Presse*, a senior cabinet minister in the Trudeau government, Canada's ambassador to the United Nations, and ambassador to France. After Pelletier left to study in Europe, he was succeeded by Pierre Juneau, a forceful administrator who also rose to cabinet level in the Trudeau government, and was Secretary of State, the first chairman of the Canadian Radio-television and Telecommunications Commission, and subsequently president of the Canadian Broadcasting Corporation. Marc Lalonde is another former president of the Boys' section of the JEC. Before being elected to Parliament, Lalonde was a Special Assistant to Prime Minister Pearson and Principal Secretary to Prime Minister Trudeau. He went on to hold a number of important cabinet portfolios, including Justice and Finance, and worked effectively on behalf of Canadian unity. Claude Ryan, the distinguished journalist and former leader of the Quebec Liberal party, is one of many provincial politicians (including some prominent separatists) who were associated with the JEC.

The Centrale of the JEC consisted of a Boys' section and a Girls' section, each with its own president. The two sections operated independently, but joined forces on a number of common projects such as the summer camps for schoolchildren, editorial seminars for school newspaper editors, and the two newspapers. One of these newspapers, *François*, started by Alexandrine Leduc, was aimed at primary and young secondary school students, while the other, *La Vie étudiante*, was written for senior high school and college students. Published twice monthly, the two papers had a circulation of more than fifty thousand. When Jeanne arrived at the Centrale, Gérard Pelletier was editor of the senior paper and president of the

Boys' section. Alex Leduc had just left the Centrale, having married Gérard Pelletier, but was still editing the junior newspaper. Jeanne, who succeeded Alex as liaison with the JEC groups outside of Quebec, worked on both papers.

The fact that the young men and women at the Centrale worked together and often had out-of-town editorial meetings was another source of displeasure to reactionaries in the Church. These conservatives suspected all manner of immoral behaviour and railed against it from their pulpits. Their suspicions were totally unfounded: the gatherings were usually held at a religious institution, such as the Holy Cross Fathers' monastery at Ste. Scholastique, and not only did the young men and women occupy separate quarters, but the boys were billeted with the priests. Furthermore, they were always accompanied by a chaplain from the Centrale.

One of the best-loved chaplains was Father Germain-Marie Lalande, who later became Superior General of the Holy Cross Order in Rome. A wiry little man with strong features, Lalande radiated goodwill and had a marvellous rapport with the young people. When asked for advice he had the ability to put himself in the other person's shoes, and he invariably came up with the right answer — even though it might not be the one you wanted to hear. Another favourite chaplain was Father Maurice Lafond, who was subsequently Superior of the Provincial Order. Father Lafond was a tall, dignified priest with an extraordinary intellect, who exerted a great influence upon the staff of the Centrale. Jeanne and many of her contemporaries have kept in touch with these two spiritual advisers ever since their days at the JEC.

Although Jeanne and Jacqueline Ratté didn't mind their quarters in the Fides building (they were working so hard, they considered their room merely a place to collapse at the end of the day), their parents complained to the Fathers of the Holy Cross. As a result, after six months on St. Denis Street Jeanne and Jacqueline moved to a rambling house in Outremont which was the home of les Compagnons de St-Laurent, a theatre group sponsored by the Fathers of the Holy Cross. It was much less lonely there, as Alex and Gérard Pelletier (who acted as their chaperones) had an apartment in the house, as did the singer Félix Leclerc and his wife. Also, the theatre troupe practised at all hours in the basement of the house, and it was not unusual for the girls to be woken in the middle of the night to give their opinion on a rehearsal. On Sundays Father Legault, the resident priest and guiding light, would celebrate Mass in the theatre.

Jeanne threw herself into her work at the Centrale with gusto. She was well organized and she loved the challenge of her job. Her schoolgirl aggressiveness was now channelled into an intellectual force, and at the age of twenty she had a confidence and maturity far beyond her years. Her style then, as it is today, was to carefully analyse a situation before dealing with it. This logical approach prompted one of her contemporaries to say that she was "very much a daughter of the Dominicans and Saint Thomas Aquinas". Once, during an editorial conference, Father Lalande innocently paid her the compliment of saying that she thought like a man. Jeanne (who used to be flattered when told this by the nuns at her convent) was furious, because she considered it both patronizing and an insult to her femininity.

She was also a superb communicator, able to speak and to write with exceptional clarity. It was nothing for her to address a large audience without notes, and unlike most writers she didn't bother with rough drafts, but composed directly on her typewriter. Jeanne's reserved manner gave some people the impression that she was cold and aloof. However, her friends knew that this was a façade; she was in fact a warm and sympathetic person, easily moved to tears and laughter. Everyone at the Centrale agreed that she was a leader.

In 1943, a year after she joined the Centrale, Jeanne was appointed president of the Girls' section. A few months later, Father Lalande took her on a speaking tour to the west coast. The purpose of the tour was to expand the movement by enlisting more English-speaking schools and religious institutions. To save money, they brought a huge hamper of sandwiches with them on the train and travelled coach class, which meant that they sat up most of the way across Canada. En route they stopped at several cities to meet with diocesan leaders and to fulfil speaking engagements; sometimes Jeanne made five or six speeches in as many hours. On the night train from Winnipeg to Calgary a burly drunk tried to molest Jeanne on her way to the washroom. It was a frightening situation because the ill-lit vestibule was sealed from the coach by a door and the other passengers, including Father Lalande, were asleep. Jeanne cooled the man's ardour by grabbing the emergency cord and threatening to stop the train. Afterwards she made light of the incident, but for many months it haunted her dreams.

The two missionaries stayed more than a week in Vancouver and were warmly received everywhere, even though Jeanne deliberately mispronounced some English words in her speeches to emphasize the fact that she was a francophone from Quebec. Both a memorable and an exhausting trip, it was excellent training for a future governor general.

During the previous year Jeanne had become, as her father had feared, a budding Quebec nationalist. However, the western tour so impressed her and broadened her vision of the country that when she returned to Montreal she was once again a federalist. Unfortunately, owing to the long-standing rivalry between English and French Roman Catholics, the tour failed to garner many recruits for the JEC.

While it was difficult to sell English Canadians on the JEC, the opposite was true of colleges in the United States. Father Lalande and Jeanne were welcomed by institutions throughout New England and as far west as Chicago. Often Jeanne addressed the entire congregation or student body, which might number three hundred priests or a thousand students. Their favourite university was Notre Dame in Indiana (famous for its theological college as well as for its football team), run by the Fathers of the Holy Cross. The only unpleasant incident to occur in the United States happened at a diocesan meeting in Cleveland. Jeanne was introduced to the large audience by Father Lalande as a typical young staff worker of the JEC. After she had spoken, a crusty member of the Church hierarchy got up and denounced her speech, noting that the Devil operated in various guises — including that of female lay workers. Jeanne was flabbergasted by this attack but could do absolutely nothing about it.

Occasionally Jeanne encountered a hostile reception in the province of Quebec, but there was also a curious reverse phenomenon. Quite often when she addressed congregations of nuns she was listened to with respect bordering on reverence. This was puzzling, because Jeanne was a lay worker barely out of her teens. Eventually she learned the reason for the nuns' reaction — it was so bizarre for a young woman without religious training to lecture them that they assumed she must be inspired by the Holy Spirit.

At the Centrale there was no such delusion; although Jeanne was obviously a devout Roman Catholic, she was respected rather for her organizational and administrative talents. Even her title was of little consequence, because everyone was a volunteer, and what counted was the ability of the individual. When she took over as president she tried to structure her section like a business office, with a clearly defined pecking order, but later resigned herself to the fuzzy volunteer arrangement. One reason for her acceptance of the status quo was that by sheer force of personality she usually got her way. Reminiscing recently, one of her former staff recalled, "She could really make us work!" Jeanne was also able to hold her own with the successive leaders of the Boys' Section, Gérard Pelletier and Pierre Juneau. As well as being a partner, she was a good friend of both men, although Juneau sometimes exasperated her because he was not as quick to grasp situations or to express himself as she was. One of her talents, which served her well in later years when she was a cabinet minister, was the speed with which she could understand a complex problem, and come to grips with it. At group discussions Jeanne and the other girls would often tease Juneau by chanting "À course, Pierre, à course!", which roughly translated means "Hurry up, Pierre, get the lead out!" Since then Jeanne's path has crossed those of her former team-mates Gérard Pelletier and Pierre Juneau many times.

Shortly after becoming president Jeanne expanded her section by enlisting three more out-of-town volunteers: Fernande Martin, Berthe Deschênes, and Françoise Chamard, all of whom had been JEC leaders in their home diocese. The manner in which Fernande Martin was recruited was typical of Jeanne's approach. Fernande, a shy and sweet-natured girl with a bubbly sense of humour, lived in St. Hyacinthe, near Montreal. Although she was eager to work at the Centrale, she was the youngest of eight children and her mother was reluctant to let her leave home. Jeanne made a special trip to St. Hyacinthe, sat down with Madame Martin, and persuaded her to allow Fernande to work for the JEC. Jeanne's sales pitch was based on logic, but expressed with sympathy and emotion. At the end of the meeting Madame Martin, Fernande, and Jeanne were all in tears. Following this traumatic episode Jeanne felt justified in claiming that she was Fernande's surrogate mother.

Billeting the new girls proved a problem, because there wasn't enough room for them at the Compagnons de St-Laurent house in Outremont. As a result, Jeanne and the three out-of-town volunteers moved into an apartment on Laval Street near St. Denis. This flat, which consisted of a double room with a single window, had neither hot water nor kitchen facilities. Fernande Martin's father was incensed at the primitive arrangement and complained to Father Lafond. Father Lafond explained that the Order couldn't afford better accommodation because it was already in debt to the bank. Monsieur Martin, a businessman, told the priest, "If you are going to drown, it doesn't really matter whether you drown in ten feet or in thirty feet of water." Accepting this pragmatic advice, the Order increased its loan and used the proceeds to finance an apartment for the girls on St. Hubert Street, near Laurier. Although the neighbourhood left something to be desired, the new apartment was comparatively luxurious, as it had two double bedrooms, a living-room, and a kitchen. The only thing it lacked was furniture.

Jeanne was given two hundred dollars (which she spent at Dupuis Frères) to furnish the place.

The girls got along surprisingly well together. One reason they were able to avoid quarrelling was that all of them had a sense of humour, especially Berthe Deschênes, who had an infectious belly-laugh. Another reason was that everyone was fully occupied, and frequently on the road. In this connection a friend estimated that Jeanne visited every French-speaking diocese in Canada at least twice each year. Looking back on the St. Hubert Street days, Berthe re-called, "Jeanne was our mother, she took care of us and was very attentive if we got homesick or ill." Forty years later, despite long separations and diverse careers, the four are still friends.

While they were working at the Centrale the girls had very little social life. Aside from the odd movie, performances of le Théâtre du Nouveau Monde (which was affiliated with les Compagnons de St-Laurent), and Sunday dinners at the homes of local members of the Centrale, there were few outings. Occasionally the staff of the JEC would put on a show of their own in which everyone took part. Jeanne was particularly fond of folk-dancing. Outdoor enter-tainment consisted of two weeks at one of the JEC student camps in the summer, and a few skiing parties in the winter. The girls didn't feel socially deprived, however, because they met a lot of interesting people, including foreign visitors, at the Centrale.

Nor was there much in the way of romance, as it was an unwrit-ten rule that if a girl got seriously involved with a boy on the staff, the girl was obliged to leave. Those romances that did occur were carried on very discreetly, and usually led to marriage; for instance, Gérard Pelletier married Alexandrine Leduc and Pierre Juneau mar-ried Fernande Martin. By today's standards, the code of behaviour among these properly brought-up young Roman Catholics was decorous in the extreme. Hard liquor wasn't part of the social scene, drugs were unknown, and religious pressures posed a formidable barrier to premarital sex. This rigid code didn't prevent boys and girls from being attracted to each other, but it did ensure that the ensuing relationship would be a relatively platonic one.

Jeanne had her share of admirers. One of the first was Ambroise Lafortune, a popular and enthusiastic young Scout leader who was often around the Centrale. He was much fonder of Jeanne than she was of him. In November 1943, at a meeting of student journalists hosted by the Oblates in Ville La Salle, Ambroise played a prank on Jeanne that he hoped would attract her attention and earn her gratitude. He hid her purse, with the intention of producing it after everyone else failed to find it. He couldn't have chosen a worse time to do this. After the purse was hidden, the meeting was interrupted by the chairman, Gérard Pelletier, who announced that Jeanne's father had just died and her purse containing her train ticket to Ottawa was lost. Ambroise sheepishly "found" the purse. On their last date together Ambroise told Jeanne that he was entering the priesthood. He is now known as "Père Ambroise" and not only has served the Church for many years but is also an influential author and television personality.

Another person who worshipped Jeanne from afar was Guy Cormier, an articulate *propagandiste* with a flair for journalism. After leaving the JEC, Cormier rose to a senior position with the newspaper *La Presse*. For her part, Jeanne was briefly infatuated with three different young men. However, from the outset she knew that there was no future to any of these relationships because all three were destined for the priesthood.

The most important man in Jeanne's life before she met Maurice Sauvé had been her father. His death in 1943 was a severe blow from which she took a long time to recover. Being a private person, even though she was swept by homesickness and depression, she kept her grief to herself. Several months after her father died she confided to one of her room-mates, "You can't understand how deep my sorrow is — it's still terrible."

Until the late forties, Jeanne hardly gave a thought to marriage. Her main interest was the JEC movement. Being so deeply committed to the cause, she tended to ignore the personal side of her life. These were fervent years, not only in the religious sense but also in the social sense. Students were living in an authoritarian world, especially in the province of Quebec, which by the end of 1944 was once again in the grip of Maurice Duplessis, after five years of repressive government by the Liberals under Adélard Godbout. The message of the JEC was political reform, religious enlightenment, and better social services. Jeanne devoted all her energy to achieving these goals.

The influence of the JEC reached its peak in June 1946, the year the Canadian movement celebrated its fifteenth anniversary. More than twenty-five thousand people, including students from across North America and from Europe, attended the celebration. The main events included a gigantic pageant and a Mass celebrated by hundreds of priests and bishops at Delorimier Stadium in Montreal. Jeanne addressed the gathering at the stadium and also spoke at a luncheon of VIP's at the Cercle Universitaire. (Surprisingly enough, she found the speech to the select group much more intimidating than her address to the huge crowd.) By all accounts, the Fifteenth Anniversary Congress was a great success.

Jeanne and the rest of the staff of the JEC worked for months to ensure that it would be. One of the logistical problems was how to provide lunch for twenty-five thousand people at the stadium. This was solved by a team of volunteers who worked all night making sandwiches for box lunches. The sandwich operation was headed by Jean Cadieux, who went on to become rector of the University of Moncton. Another ticklish problem was how to control the giant parade through the streets of Montreal. To get the right person for this job it was necessary to reach outside the membership of the JEC. The man selected was a twenty-two-year-old University of Montreal law student who in 1943 had gained notoriety (and his picture in *Time* magazine) for organizing and leading the largest anti-conscription parade in Canada's history. His name was Maurice Sauvé.

Maurice Sauvé was a tall, lanky fellow with a shock of black hair, high colouring, and dark good looks. He carried himself with the authoritative air of a successful politician. Highly competent and superbly organized, he spoke with a conviction that brooked no argument. Although he could be overbearing at times, he could also be extremely charming — a fact that was not lost on the young women.

For Maurice, the job of organizing the JEC parade was a piece of cake. Drawing upon his past experience and using a map of the city of Montreal, he traced the parade route and then deftly pinpointed the various spots that would require cordoning, signs, loudspeakers, or JEC personnel for crowd control. Maurice planned it so meticulously that even though he was not there on the big day (he was working as a bellhop on a Canada Steamships cruise boat), the parade went off like clockwork.

Jeanne and Maurice first met at a party for the organizers of the Congress. Maurice noticed Jeanne immediately, and after working his way through the crowd engaged her in conversation. Jeanne wasn't particularly impressed, although she found him attractive — strong men have always appealed to her — and he was quite different from the serious boys on the staff of the JEC. For these reasons she remembered him.

That October, Maurice went to Ottawa to visit Lucille Robillard, whom he had met on a cruise boat during the summer. When he arrived, however, he learned that Lucille was ill with flu and couldn't see him. So that his trip wouldn't be a total loss, Lucille suggested that he might like to take out her cousin, Jeanne Benoit, who was also in Ottawa that weekend. Maurice agreed with alacrity. Jeanne and Maurice spent a pleasant but uneventful evening talking in the living-room of the Benoit house. From Jeanne's point of view, there was nothing to the date — "and anyway he was my cousin's boyfriend, not mine." Following that weekend, Maurice made it a practice to drop into the Centrale to chat with Jeanne and her friends. An amusing raconteur, he regaled them with tales of his escapades on the cruise boats and other worldly exploits. The young women liked him, and enjoyed his stories, but privately they considered him something of a playboy.

In December 1946, a university friend asked Maurice if he would substitute for him at his holiday job at the Quebec Liquor Commission. Maurice, who earned enough each summer that he didn't need to work during the school year, agreed to help out his friend. One day a customer, filled with Christmas cheer, gave him two tickets to a hockey game at the Forum. Maurice, having never seen les Canadiens play, was delighted. After giving the matter much thought, he invited Jeanne to share his good fortune. Neither Jeanne nor Maurice remember the score of the game, but both agree it was their first "real" date.

Between Christmas and New Year's, Maurice attended the annual meeting of the National Federation of Canadian University Students in Toronto. With the backing of the McGill delegates, he was elected president, the first French Canadian to hold this office in the sixteen-year history of the federation. One reason for electing him was the need for a bilingual leader who could bring all the Canadian universities, including Quebec degree-granting institutions, into the federation. Maurice, who had been taught English by an Irish Jesuit (which is why he speaks English with a slight brogue), was a persuasive speaker in both languages. Also, when he chaired meetings he had the knack of getting people to reach a consensus with the minimum of fuss. As expected, he was a highly effective president. During 1947 he visited every university in Canada, and by the end of the year he had managed to enlist all of them in the federation.

Prior to becoming president of NFCUS, Maurice was a staunch Quebec nationalist, having learned his history from the Jesuits at Collège Ste-Marie. History can be deceptive, because each historian has a slightly different perception of past events. The Jesuit version of Canada's history was that ever since the Conquest the English had systematically abused the French. A keen history student, Maurice once made a list of twelve major encounters where French Canadians had ended up with the short end of the stick. Because he had never been outside of Quebec, travelling from coast to coast was an eye-opener. As an anti-conscriptionist, and as one who had been taught that the English were his enemy, he was astounded by the friendly reception he received at universities across the country. He was also profoundly impressed by the variety of cultures and the sheer size of Canada. Although he wasn't conscious of it at the time, while he was president of the National Federation of Canadian University Students his political views gradually changed, and when he stepped down at the end of the year, he was well on his way to becoming a federalist.

During 1947 Jeanne and Maurice saw an increasing amount of each other, but both continued to date other people. It wasn't until January 1948, when Maurice won a scholarship to study at the London School of Economics, that their relationship became more serious. Maurice's plans for the next four years included acquiring a wife who would accompany him to England that autumn. His reasoning was that if he didn't get married before he left, by the time he returned to Canada all the girls he knew — at least the pick of the crop — would be married. (There was also the hazard that if he went to Europe as a bachelor he might marry someone overseas, which could pose a cultural problem for his bride when he brought her back to Canada.) His criteria for the ideal wife were, by the standards of the day, somewhat unusual.

Maurice was looking for a woman who was intellectually his equal, with a strong streak of independence, who would be willing to forgo having children until his career was established, and who would also pursue her own career. In Quebec at that time, such a woman was exceedingly difficult to find. All the girls in his circle had been educated at the same convents, with the same social values. Upon graduation, most of these girls either married or became nuns. If they married, their sole focus was their husband and their children — nothing more.

Jeanne answered his criteria. Aside from finding her immensely attractive, in Maurice's words "Jeanne was bright, she was autonomous, she didn't want to be a servant to her husband, and she wanted to pursue a career." Having selected Jeanne, all he had to do was to persuade her to marry him. Maurice, who was described by a former girlfriend as a *force nature*, embarked on a whirlwind courtship. Although she was in love with Maurice, Jeanne took her time making up her mind whether to marry him. One reason for her hesitancy was that if she married, it would mean leaving the JEC. Another consideration was Maurice's mother, who was outspokenly opposed to the marriage.

Maurice, who was born in Montreal on 20 September 1923, was the eldest son of Joseph-Honoré and Mélanie Sauvé. Joseph-Honoré had intended to become a doctor, but after receiving his Bachelor of Arts degree he had contracted tuberculosis. Following four years of convalescence he was told that a career in medicine was out of the question — he would have a relapse if he worked indoors — and that he would have to find outdoor employment. An easy-going, affable fellow, he chose to become a travelling salesman. Although a good salesman, he never made much money, and during the Depression the family was forced to move to cheaper quarters several times. Because their father was often on the road, Maurice and his two younger brothers were brought up by their mother. She was the dominant parent; it was from her that the boys inherited their drive and ambition. Refusing to let financial obstacles stand in the way, Mélanie saw to it that her sons received an excellent education. (Her dedication was rewarded: Maurice has done very well in business and politics, Gaston is a renowned heart surgeon and lecturer at the University of Ottawa, and Robert, who lives in Montreal, capped a law career by being appointed judge of the Workmen's Compensation Board.)

Although Maurice was twenty-five when he was courting Jeanne, Mélanie thought that he was too young to get married, and that if he married Jeanne she would lead him around by the nose. Mélanie's ultra-conservative political and religious views undoubtedly coloured her opinion of her future daughter-in-law. Mélanie considered the JEC to be anti-clerical, and she heartily disapproved of Jeanne's role in the activist organization. Thus, while Maurice was using all his charm to woo Jeanne, his mother was doing her utmost (including phone calls to Father Lalande) to torpedo the romance.

For their part, the Benoit family liked Maurice and were in favour of the marriage. Jeanne was now twenty-six, and it was time she settled down. Their only reservation was that Jeanne might be happier with a quieter, more intellectual husband. This view was shared by many of Jeanne's friends at the JEC.

In February 1948 Jeanne finally agreed to marry Maurice. The wedding was set for late September. At the end of May, after graduating with a law degree from the University of Montreal, Maurice once again worked on the cruise boats. To be near him that summer Jeanne took a job as a book-keeper at the Manoir Richelieu hotel in Murray Bay, one of his ports of call.

Jeanne left the Centrale, after heading the Girls' section for six years, with mixed feelings. On one hand she felt a sense of satisfaction with the work she had done, but on the other a sense of regret that the province was still a ghetto.

What she didn't realize was the importance of the role she had played in the fight for social change in Quebec — a struggle that would culminate fifteen years later in the Quiet Revolution.

Nor did she know that over the next three decades she and many of her JEC colleagues would influence the destiny of Canada.

Chapter 4

LONDON AND PARIS
1948–52

Jeanne and Maurice were married in Ottawa at St. Jean Baptiste church, just across the street from Notre Dame du Rosaire convent, on 24 September 1948. The wedding Mass was celebrated by her old friend and spiritual adviser from the JEC, Father Lalande. It was a simple wedding, because Jeanne's mother, who had been a widow for five years, was suffering from a heart ailment. Also, the newlyweds wanted to save their money for Europe. Jeanne, who was given away by her brother Jean, wore a navy-blue dress with matching blue shoes and hat, while Maurice wore a stiff new dark blue suit. About one hundred friends and relatives attended the ceremony.

Maurice's parents arrived in Ottawa the night before the wedding but declined to go to Madame Benoit's that evening for a get-together of the two families. It wasn't until the next day that Jeanne's mother finally met the Sauvés. Maurice's mother made a notable entrance at the church by arriving after the service had begun. Unmoved by the whispered suggestion of an usher that she use a side aisle, she insisted on walking down the centre aisle to her pew. This little incident foreshadowed a relationship with her daughter-in-law that would, at best, be an armed neutrality.

Following the ceremony at the church, Jeanne's sister Berthe gave a wedding breakfast for about twenty-five close relatives at her apartment on Sussex Drive. Madame Benoit had wanted to give the

51

reception, but her heart condition was so serious that her doctor had advised against it. Around noon, the party motored to Montreal, where Jeanne and Maurice spend their wedding night in a honeymoon suite at the Mount Royal hotel.

The next day the newlyweds sailed from Montreal on the *Empress of Canada* for England. Both families and a large contingent of friends from the JEC went down to the dock to see them off. Because the couple planned to be away for four years, it was an emotional farewell. After exchanging hugs and tears with well-wishers on the pier, Jeanne and Maurice stood at the rail for ages waving to them. Finally the ship's horn sounded, the band broke into "Auld Lang Syne", and amid a shower of streamers the liner glided slowly down the St. Lawrence.

The honeymoon voyage proved to be a disappointment, even though, at Mélanie Sauvé's insistence, they travelled first class, a luxury they could ill afford. Not only was their cabin so cramped that they could barely turn around, but they felt uncomfortable with the other first-class passengers, all of whom were much older than they were. To top it off, Jeanne was seasick for most of the way across the Atlantic.

When the ship docked at Liverpool they were met by a representative of the British Council, the organization that had awarded Maurice his scholarship. This helpful man cleared their luggage through customs and arranged for them to stay at a hostel until they could find more permanent lodgings. Within two days they moved to a furnished room in a tiny house in the Denmark Hill district of London.

Their one-room flat lacked privacy, but it was only a short bus ride from the London School of Economics and it was cheap. Cost remained the critical factor; they had come to England with a total of nineteen hundred and fifty dollars, of which fifteen hundred dollars was a bank loan guaranteed by one of Maurice's law professors. Added to this was the scholarship, which had a value of three hundred pounds. After careful calculation, Maurice determined that they must

...ud'homme, September 1922. Left to right: Lina, Annette, baby Jeanne, ...adame Benoit, Berthe, Armand. (Courtesy Berthe Belisle)

...harles Albert Benoit, Jeanne's father. ...Courtesy Jean Benoit)

The Benoit children (Armand absent), Ottawa, 1930.
Left to right: Lucille, Jean, Jeanne, Annette, Lina, Berthe.
(Courtesy Berthe Belisle)

Classroom, Notre Dame du Rosaire convent, Ottawa. Jeanne is in the second row, second from right. (Sauvé family collection)

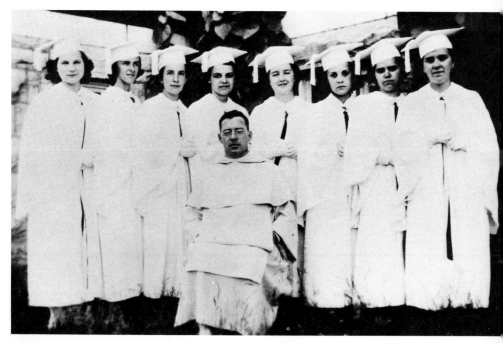

Graduating class of Notre Dame du Rosaire convent with Father Sylvain, Ottawa, 1940. Jeanne is on the extreme left. (Sauvé family collection)

anne, aged thirteen, in her Guide catholique uniform. (Sauvé family
llection)

Jeanne, top right, with her JEC room-mates, Montreal, 1944. Left
foreground, Berthe Deschênes; right foreground, Françoise Chamard; behind
them Fernande Martin. (Courtesy Berthe Bellemare)

The three youngest members of the Benoit family, Ottawa, 1944. Jean in the
centre, Lucille on the left, Jeanne on the right. (Courtesy Jean Benoit)

Sugaring-off party near Montreal, April 1946. Maurice Sauvé on
the left, Jeanne on the right. (Courtesy Berthe Bellemare)

Jeanne and Maurice Sauvé leaving for their wedding reception, 24 September
1948. (Sauvé family collection)

Jeanne, left foreground, conferring with colleagues in a broadcasting studio of Radio-Canada, Montreal. (Courtesy CBC)

Jeanne with Jean-François, 1962.
(Sauvé family collection)

Election night, 30 October 1972. Jeanne being congratulated by fellow Liberal Marcel Roy, while another successful Liberal, Jean-Pierre Goyer, looks on. (Gerry Davidson, *Montreal Star*, Public Archives of Canada, PA-146046)

The Trudeau cabinet, 1972. Jeanne is seated at the far end of the table. (Sauvé family collection)

live on a budget of nine pounds a week. If they spent more than this amount, they would have to scrimp the following week.

Despite their tight financial situation, they loved London. Both were struck by the kindness and politeness they encountered everywhere. Looking back on those days Maurice recalled: "The people of London were very civilized and also civic-minded; if you had to queue, you took your place in the line and no one tried to pass in front of you. There was also a system of trust; if you took a bus, the lady would ask you where you were going, and if you said Elephant and Castle, she would simply take your word for it and tell you the fare — no one cheated." Another pleasant surprise was the attitude of the London bobbies, who were unfailingly courteous to them when they asked for directions.

Critical shortages and strict rationing of food and fuel made life difficult in post-war England. Being young and healthy — and totally wrapped up in each other — Jeanne and Maurice fared better than most people. They had known about the food situation and had brought a hefty supply of tinned goods. After their hoard ran out, they had to pool their ration coupons to buy a quarter-pound of butter and a half-pound of meat each week. They had also known about the scarcity of fuel, but there was nothing they could do about it. As coal was almost unobtainable, the fireplace in their room was useless and the only source of heat was the coin-operated gas oven. To feed the gas meter cost a shilling, which for them was prohibitively expensive. During that first winter it was so cold in their flat that Maurice often wore his overcoat and mitts to study. At bedtime they would pop a shilling in the meter, open the door of the oven, quickly undress, and then race to get under the covers. Even with the oven on full blast, the temperature would still be so low that they could see their breath in the room.

Getting accustomed to the English accent posed another problem, particularly for Maurice, who for the first three months had great difficulty understanding his professors. Regional accents, as well as peculiarities of pronunciation, further confused the issue.

Eventually, they surmounted the language barrier — but they were never able to crack the Cockney dialect.

Once Maurice was settled into his university routine, Jeanne set about looking for a job. Between interviews she would often join him at the LSE and listen to the lectures. Just before Christmas, she was hired by the London City Council as a part-time teacher, teaching French to adults in the evenings. Because she had had no previous experience, she made the mistake of concentrating on grammar rather than teaching conversational French. As a result, this venture didn't last long, nor was it a success.

In the spring of 1949 Jeanne, who was three months pregnant, had a miscarriage. There were no complications, and after being examined by a general practitioner, she was on her feet the next day. She was distressed to lose her baby but accepted the loss philosophically, confident that there was plenty of time in the future to have a family.

Shortly after this incident she was offered another teaching job, which came as a result of having registered at Canada House upon her arrival in London. A secretary at Canada House phoned to ask if she would be interested in tutoring Diana Wilgress, the fourteen-year-old daughter of Dana Wilgress, the newly appointed Canadian High Commissioner. Jeanne was quite definitely interested, and a few days later she had an interview with Mrs. Wilgress at the High Commissioner's temporary residence in Belgravia. At this meeting it was agreed that she would tutor Diana — who needed help in all subjects because she had missed a great deal of school on account of rheumatic fever — to prepare her for entrance into the English school system. Mrs. Wilgress obtained the necessary textbooks, a study in the residence was set aside as a classroom, and for the next year Jeanne taught Diana.

This arrangement worked out beautifully for everyone. At the end of the year Diana had no trouble gaining entrance to one of the best girls' schools in London. (Diana is still convinced that Jeanne, had she wished to, could have had an outstanding career as a teacher.) Jeanne, who enjoyed teaching Diana, was paid the princely sum of five pounds a week. In addition, she was given lunch at the residence each day. These lunches became a source of embarrassment to her after she mentioned to Mrs. Wilgress how much she missed having meat. From then on, whenever she had a meal at the residence, she was always served meat.

Mrs. Wilgress also wangled an invitation for Jeanne to be presented at Court. Going to Buckingham Palace was an exciting prospect, but it raised the problem of what to wear for the occasion. The only suitable dress Jeanne owned was the navy-blue one she had worn at her wedding, but she'd been warned that the King didn't like sombre colours. Her solution — inspired by her uniform at the convent — was to sew pieces of white lace on the collar and cuffs of her wedding dress. The most memorable aspect of the ceremony at the palace for Jeanne was to discover that the King wore make-up. The next day she asked Mrs. Wilgress why this was so, and learned that the King did this to prevent the public from knowing he was gravely ill. This struck Jeanne as a silly subterfuge, but thirty-five years later when she was received at the palace as Canada's governor general, she took extra care with her make-up to disguise the fact that she too had been seriously ill.

In the summer of 1949 Jeanne was interviewed on radio by the London correspondent for the CBC. This interview, which was part of a weekly program beamed to Canada, took place in a grubby studio at the headquarters of the BBC. During the program Jeanne was asked to tell the folks back home about her life in England. She needed no encouragement, and even though she knew her words were going across the airwaves to the entire Canadian network, she spoke easily, without the slightest trace of nervousness, and thoroughly enjoyed herself. This experience, her first time on radio, was the harbinger of her long broadcasting career.

That summer Maurice worked as a waiter for British Railways. When he applied for the job he expected to be questioned closely on his previous experience, but this was not the case. The old man who interviewed him hadn't the slightest interest in his qualifications, just his suit size. Nodding to a rack of uniforms he said, ''If one of those fits you, you're hired.'' Fortunately for Maurice, who was tall and thin, there was one uniform left that fitted him. The next day he was assigned to the train that ran between Euston Station in London and the Border port of Carlisle. Until he got used to the swaying of the dining-car — the road-bed had been bombed during the war — he was terrified that he would dump a loaded tray in the lap of a customer. Because it was an eight-hour run each way, the crew of the train spent the night in a British Railways hotel in Carlisle. Maurice was given four shillings for his accommodation but slept in a cubbyhole that cost only one shilling, and thus was able to pocket three shillings each trip. This windfall, plus his salary and tips, upped his earnings to a respectable ten pounds per week.

At the end of the summer Jeanne and Maurice attended the founding convention of the World Assembly of Youth in Brussels. This gathering of youth leaders, which attracted delegates from about twenty non-communist countries, lasted more than a week. Maurice, who was chosen to head the Canadian delegation because of the outstanding job he had done as president of NFCUS, took a spirited part in the proceedings. As the week progressed it became clear that a majority of the delegates didn't want to elect their founding president from one of the ''superpower'' countries (Britain, the United States, or France). Maurice, a bilingual Canadian living in England, ran as a compromise candidate, and won easily on the first ballot. His term of office was one year, for which he was paid a salary of one thousand American dollars, as well as his travel expenses. As president of the World Assembly of Youth he corresponded and met with youth leaders from all over the world, and also chaired Executive Committee meetings of the Assembly in Brussels every three months.

Maurice enjoyed studying at the London School of Economics, even though the classrooms were run-down and hopelessly over-crowded. Originally designed for one thousand students, the school had an enrolment of more than four thousand. While he was in England, he was the only French Canadian at the LSE (Pierre Trudeau was there before him, and Jacques Parizeau attended later).

In those days the London School of Economics was famous as a hotbed of political thought, with a distinct bias to the left. During Maurice's time, seventeen different communist clubs flourished on campus. He joined one of the staid Roman Catholic clubs, but for entertainment he often attended gatherings where wild-eyed students promoted more radical ideologies.

In the autumn of 1949 the Sauvés moved to a larger flat in the same neighbourhood. Although they didn't have enough furniture (they had to use orange crates for bookshelves), they were much happier there. The flat gave them privacy, it was spacious, and for the first time they were able to entertain their friends. In this connection, rationing was still so severe that dinner guests would either bring their own meat or give Jeanne the equivalent number of coupons. However, with their increased income they could now afford to make brief trips to the continent. Eating was a major attraction on these jaunts. During their first year, travelling had been out of the question, and their indulgences — aside from a subscription to *The Times* — had been limited to cinemas or shilling seats in the back rows of Haymarket theatres.

Their stay in England ended in the summer of 1950. After a brief visit home to Canada, they moved in September to Paris. Jeanne had a job waiting for her as assistant to the director of the Youth Secretariat at the United Nations Educational, Scientific, and Cultural Organization (UNESCO). This job paid an annual salary of five thousand American dollars, which in those days was a fortune. It was at this point that Jeanne became the main bread-winner. Had it not been for her salary, Maurice couldn't have enrolled at the University of Paris to complete his doctorate. Since he had been re-elected president of the World Assembly of Youth for a second term, his total salary was only one thousand dollars that year.

The first thing they noticed on the continent was that life was considerably easier than in England. There was no rationing in France, food was plentiful, and rents were cheap. Paris, the spiritual home of francophones throughout the world, was an enchanting city. The most surprising revelation, which dawned on them gradually, was that moving to France was a greater cultural shock than moving to England. Like many Quebecers, they hadn't realized the extent of the North American influence on the customs of Quebec — an influence that produced a lifestyle in the province that was more English than French.

Initially they rented a furnished flat on the fourth floor of a building in the 16th *arrondissement*. This luxury apartment, which was filled with Empire furniture, overlooked the Bois de Boulogne. It was an ideal place for Jeanne and Maurice to entertain, one of their favourite pleasures. Unlike London, where most of their friends were local residents, in Paris they had an eclectic circle of friends. These included people of all political persuasions and nationalities, as well as many young Quebecers. Marie Tessier-Lavigne, who was working in Paris at the time, and had been with Jeanne at the JEC, remembers a typical dinner party at the Sauvés'. Among the mixed bag of guests that night was an Italian priest, a French trade-union leader, a rabidly anti-Catholic Belgian socialist, a German post-graduate student, and several Canadians, including André Raynauld, who was later president of the Economic Council of Canada, Jérôme Choquette, who became minister of justice in Bourassa's government, and d'Iberville Fortier, one of their closest friends. Fortier had been a classmate of Maurice's at the University of Montreal, and was also studying for his Ph.D. in Economics at the University of Paris. He later joined the Department of External Affairs and, after serving as Canada's ambassador to Italy and to Greece, was appointed Commissioner of Official Languages.

Jeanne worked at the Paris headquarters of UNESCO for the first year while Maurice attended the University of Paris. Although he hadn't completed his degree at the LSE, he was given credit for two years of study towards his doctorate. Jeanne's earnings paid most of their expenses, but as she intended to enrol at the Sorbonne, she was careful to save a substantial amount of her salary each month.

In May of 1951 Jeanne and Maurice took part in a walking pilgrimage from Paris to Chartres, a distance of roughly one hundred kilometres. As they progressed toward Chartres the pilgrims recited prayers, sang hymns, and discussed religious philosophy. At night they slept in the fields or in barns. During the march Jeanne was interviewed for Radio-Canada by d'Iberville Fortier. The tape of this interview, which Fortier still has, reflects Jeanne's intense concern with spiritual matters.

For the thrill of it, and as a learning experience, Maurice also participated in a number of protest marches. France in the early fifties was seething with unrest which manifested itself in strikes, riots, and violent demonstrations. Most of the trouble was inspired by the Communists. Although Maurice didn't have any strong political views — he and Jeanne were primarily concerned with social issues — he often joined his friends in their demonstrations. At that time there was no shortage of things to protest, whether it was NATO, General Eisenhower, the Korean War, Tito's independence, or even Moscow. Both the demonstrators and the Paris riot police, the CRS (Corps Républicain de la Sécurité), were well organized to deal with each other. Maurice once joined a march down the Champs-Elysées, where contingents of protesters, spaced thirty metres apart, stretched from the Place de la Concorde to the Rond-Point. Just as the parade filled the Champs-Elysées, squads of riot police, who had been waiting in ambush, charged from the side streets. Swinging their rolled-up lead-weighted capes like bludgeons, they quickly dispersed the crowd. Maurice and a couple of his friends hid in a public urinal but were rooted out of their refuge, and, as they flew through the door, another pair of police gave them a good crack with their truncheons. Eventually the French government issued a warning that any foreign student who attended a demonstration would be deported. To Jeanne's relief, this threat ended the excitement for Maurice.

In the summer of 1951 Jeanne and Maurice travelled to Ithaca, New York, for the annual meeting of the World Assembly of Youth. For the third consecutive year, Maurice was elected president of the organization. After the meeting, Maurice's parents picked them up and drove them back to Montreal for a short holiday.

To save money, when they returned to Paris that September they moved to a small furnished flat on the Quai de Jemmapes. It was quite a come-down from their elegant apartment overlooking the Bois de Boulogne, and it lacked certain basic amenities such as a refrigerator. For this reason, Jeanne had to do her shopping every day, a task that she grew to enjoy. One of their favourite meals was fresh bread, Camembert cheese, and a bottle of red wine. Except for a few close friends, Jeanne and Maurice did little entertaining in their new apartment.

Although it was in a working-class district, the Quai de Jemmapes had a picturesque Dutch flavour because of the barge traffic on the canal that ran beside it. In the evenings Jeanne and Maurice would often stroll along the canal, pausing from time to time to admire the bridges. Occasionally they would go to a theatre or to a concert, but rarely could they afford to go to a restaurant for dinner. By this time Jeanne was studying at the Sorbonne and Maurice was in the final year of his doctorate. Despite their restricted circumstances, they were supremely happy. D'Iberville Fortier, who saw a lot of them in Paris, said recently, "I have seldom seen such a close couple. They so obviously loved each other — it was a force and a strength for them."

At the Sorbonne, Jeanne took the renowned Cours de l'Alliance pour Étrangers, which deals with the culture and literature of France. Having wanted to go to university since she was a teen-ager, she applied herself and got high marks in all her papers. Each morning she had two classes, with an hour break between them. To pass the time during her break she would have coffee and a croissant at a café across the street. One day a sign in a corridor of the Sorbonne caught her eye: "Don't just be an intellectual — learn to sew!" The cost of the course was just fifty francs, the amount she was spending every morning on her coffee breaks. Jeanne, who loves to sew, and knew that for the next few years she would have to make her own clothes, signed up for the course. She didn't learn much, however, because the students weren't given any fabric to work on but were simply taught the theory of sewing.

In the spring of 1952 Maurice was offered a job by a United Nations agency to manage their headquarters in the Belgian Congo. He declined the offer, even after it was sweetened to include a job for Jeanne. Maurice refused because he and Jeanne felt that if they started working for the UN they would get caught up in it and never return to Canada. In this connection, throughout their stay in Paris they had kept abreast of developments at home by talking to visitors, exchanging letters, and reading Quebec newspapers. Their most stimulating reading was *Cité libre*, the influential and outspoken periodical founded in 1950 by Gérard Pelletier and Pierre Trudeau.

Jeanne graduated from the Sorbonne with a degree in French Civilization in May 1952. On the fourth of July Maurice successfully defended his thesis in front of three professors at the University of Paris and was awarded his Ph.D. in Economics.

In August, after four glorious years abroad, they sailed for Canada. Their reason for returning home was quite simple: in Jeanne's words, "We were committed to Canada."

Chapter 5

MAURICE:
From Union Organizer
to Cabinet Minister

When Jeanne and Maurice stepped off the boat from Europe in the autumn of 1952, both were determined to establish careers. Money was a secondary goal — being idealists and reformers, they wanted to do something that would contribute to society. Because Maurice was the better qualified of the two, by unspoken agreement their first priority was to establish his career.

The situation in Quebec had changed little in the four years they'd been away. If anything, it was worse. For all practical purposes there was now only one political party in the province, the Union Nationale, ruled by Maurice Duplessis with an iron fist. In his memoir, *Years of Impatience* (Methuen, Toronto, 1984), Gérard Pelletier describes Duplessis: "A brilliant manipulator, every kind of conservatism was grist for his mill: social, religious, philosophical, cultural. He was not the only petty dictator to see freedom as a threat and change as a disaster, but he was the most intelligent, the craftiest, the most astute and the least burdened with scruples." In particular, Duplessis considered the unions a threat to his power and he dealt harshly with them. During the Asbestos Strike in 1949, and on several other occasions, he went so far as to use the Provincial Police to crush labour unrest.

While in France, Maurice Sauvé had made up his mind to work for the unions. Before leaving Paris he wrote Gérard Picard, President of the Confédération des Travailleurs catholiques du Canada (CTCC), to ask for a job. This umbrella organization, the predecessor of the Confederation of National Trade Unions (CNTU), appealed to him because it was independent of U.S. affiliates and a strong presence in Quebec. Jean Marchand, who succeeded Picard as president, was at that time Secretary General of the CTCC.

Soon after his ship docked in Montreal, Maurice went to Quebec City for interviews with Picard and Marchand. Both men were impressed with his enthusiasm, but Marchand, despite Maurice's academic credentials — a B.A., a degree in law, and a Ph.D. in economics — wasn't convinced that he would fit into the union movement. However, Maurice pleaded his case so eloquently and with such humility that after several meetings he was offered the position of Technical Adviser to the Labour Council in St. Hyacinthe. He took the job, even though St. Hyacinthe was a backwater, because he wanted to start his career at the grass-roots level.

During his first week in St. Hyacinthe (a town some fifty kilometres east of Montreal), Maurice hustled around and met the leaders of the fifteen unions in the local council. The following week he and Jeanne moved into a large apartment on the second floor of a house on rue Girouard, the street where the town's tycoons lived. Furnishing their eight-room apartment presented a problem because they had no furniture and no money. Indeed, although they had managed to pay their way in Europe, Maurice still owed the original fifteen hundred dollars he had borrowed to go to England. Jeanne's mother came to the rescue by giving them some furniture and lending them a Government of Canada bond for Maurice to use as collateral for a loan from the Caisse Populaire. The proceeds of the loan were spent on a kitchen table, a refrigerator, a good mattress, and other necessities.

Most of the unions in St. Hyacinthe were involved with the textile industry. Maurice worked hard organizing these unions, looking into their grievances, and helping them negotiate their contracts. Often in the evenings he would attend union meetings. In this way he established a warm rapport with the union leaders as well as with many of the rank-and-file members. To his surprise, he discovered that he was far more radical in his outlook than they were. Their innate conservatism, which was partly motivated by fear of losing their jobs if they antagonized their employers, was a constant source of frustration for him. Their conservative attitude also made it very difficult for him to enlist new members for the unions. When he launched a door-to-door campaign he was told time and again by workers that there was no need to join a union. In most instances, the householders wouldn't even discuss the issue, they'd simply shut the door in his face.

A few weeks after they arrived in St. Hyacinthe, Jeanne did a radio show in Montreal, which was the start of her career as a free-lance broadcaster. For the first year she had relatively few bookings and spent her spare time helping Maurice with his work. One of the assignments he gave her was to help organize the employees of Gaylord Products, a local hairpin manufacturer. After speaking with most of the Gaylord workers, she learned that two women in particular could influence the decision to form a union. Jeanne did her best to convince these two that they were being underpaid by the company and needed a union, but they refused to believe her. When she cited statistics and wage scales to back up her argument, they told her that the boss gave everyone a free Coke every day and a turkey at Christmas — which in their opinion was proof that they were being well treated. Eventually, Jeanne gave up in defeat.

Although Maurice's vocation was with the blue-collar workers, his social life was with the business and professional people of the town. This came about because Jeanne had made friends with her neighbours, the wives of the St. Hyacinthe elite. Jeanne got along well in this circle, but Maurice, because of his socialist views, was regarded as a maverick. At dinner parties one of his favourite conversation-stoppers was the flat statement "Anyone who earns more than ten thousand dollars a year is immoral."

For an entirely different reason, he also raised hackles at the headquarters of the CTCC. Before going to St. Hyacinthe, Maurice had been told in confidence by Jean Marchand that the CTCC was secretly considering a general strike. Taking the matter into his own hands, Maurice canvassed the union leaders in St. Hyacinthe for their views on a general strike, and reported back to Marchand that everyone was against it. Marchand was furious with Maurice for letting the cat out of the bag, and gave him a severe tongue-lashing. Maurice, never noted for accepting criticism with grace, bitterly resented Marchand for what he considered his gross over-reaction to the incident. As it turned out, the general strike was postponed.

This clash was significant, because it revealed for the first time the hostility that existed between the two men. The reason they disliked each other is less clear, since both were dedicated union workers, and at that time Marchand, who had earned his spurs in the Asbestos Strike, was so far above Maurice in the union movement that rivalry couldn't have been a factor. While Marchand was a street fighter and Maurice was an untried academic, it is possible that their similarities rather than their differences created the personality conflict: both men came from poor families, both were impulsive activists, both were intensely ambitious, and both had robust egos. Reduced to its simplest terms, they may have sensed from the outset that there wasn't room for both of them on the same stage. Whatever the cause of their enmity, it would simmer for years. In the end, Marchand's ill-will would contribute directly to Maurice's political downfall.

Notwithstanding his quarrel with Marchand, Maurice did a creditable job in St. Hyacinthe. In fact, he was so highly regarded in local circles that l'Abbé Frigaud, the chaplain of the Labour Council, recommended a raise for him. After a year in St. Hyacinthe, Maurice decided that he should broaden his experience and was granted a transfer back to Montreal to work for the Fédération nationale de la métallurgie. This organization had about twenty thousand Quebec members, mostly in the aluminum and shipbuilding industries. For the first six months with the FNM he commuted from St. Hyacinthe, but in May of 1954 he and Jeanne moved back to Montreal. Through Jeanne, who had a growing number of friends in the broadcasting field, they sublet a charming apartment on Sherbrooke Street from an orchestra leader with the CBC.

As a technical adviser to the FNM, Maurice travelled extensively throughout the province visiting various locals. Because he was an economist, it was also his responsibility to prepare briefs for arbitration boards and to compile statistical material for use in negotiating contracts. One of his accomplishments, in partnership with Jean Gérin-Lajoie, was to establish the first system of job evaluation and classification in the Quebec steel industry. While he was with the metal-workers union he spent several weeks in Thetford Mines and Asbestos studying the economic and social consequences of the 1949 strike. He used the results of this research to contribute a chapter to Pierre Trudeau's book on the Asbestos Strike, *La Grève de l'Amiante*, published in 1956 by Éditions Cité libre.

Often he was directly involved in the bargaining process. Although he wasn't afraid to strike, he believed that the best way to wring the maximum from an employer was through negotiation. In Maurice's words, "Employers with whom I dealt were wise enough to know that if they didn't make the concessions we wanted, negotiations would turn sour, and we'd call a strike." This strategy paid off; during his two years with the FNM the only strike he was involved in was a general strike in Shawinigan, and on that occasion he managed to settle with Alcan just before the general strike went into effect.

During the general strike in Shawinigan Falls, Jeanne was asked by Philippe Girard, the chief organizer for the CNTU, to lend a hand. Specifically, Girard wanted Jeanne to stiffen the backs of the women in Shawinigan so that they wouldn't urge their husbands to go back to work. When Jeanne asked him, "What are you negotiating? What are the terms — are they reasonable?" Girard was flabbergasted. He had expected that she would simply do as she was told. However, she insisted on a full explanation of the terms before she would agree to his request.

Jeanne, in fact, didn't tell the women to support the strike. She explained to them over the radio and at meetings the terms of the negotiations, but left the decision up to them. To make it easier for the women to judge the situation objectively, she personally intervened to remove the most serious economic obstacle. Many families had bought household appliances, such as stoves, washing machines, and refrigerators, from local stores on the time-payment plan. When the company pay cheques ceased, so did the instalment payments, which posed the threat of repossession by the merchants. Jeanne visited each of the store owners and said, "Wait for your payments — after this is over you'll still want their business." Most of the merchants agreed to wait for their money.

In the summer of 1955 the federal government announced that a Royal Commission on Canada's Economic Prospects was being convened in Ottawa under the chairmanship of Walter Gordon. When Maurice heard about it he went to Ottawa and asked Maurice Lamontagne, who was a close adviser to Prime Minister St. Laurent, if he could help him get a job on the commission. A few weeks later he was offered a position as assistant secretary, at a salary of ten thousand dollars a year. With this offer in his pocket, he then asked for a leave of absence from the metal-workers union, but was told that if he went to Ottawa there wouldn't be a place for him when he got back. Believing it vital to his career to learn how the federal government operated, Maurice burned his bridges and left the union.

That September Maurice and Jeanne moved to the capital. The move didn't hurt Jeanne's career, as she was able to commute to Montreal each week, and she was also able to pick up some local television work. Accommodation was scarce in Ottawa, but they managed to find a comfortable apartment on Stewart Street, within walking distance of the Commission's office in the Daly Building. Working on the Commission was a stimulating experience for Maurice, because the hand-picked staff represented some of the best professional and academic brains in the country. The chairman, Walter Gordon, was at that time senior partner of the prestigious accounting firm of Clarkson, Gordon, and head of the consulting firm of Woods, Gordon. The Secretary to the Commission and Director of Research, Douglas LePan, was not only an able administrator but a brilliant writer who won the Governor General's Award for both poetry and fiction. Two of the four Assistant Directors of Research (Simon Reisman and Bill Hood) went on to become deputy ministers of finance, the third (Jack Davis) became a cabinet minister, and the fourth (Doug Fullerton) has had an outstanding career in government and finance. One of the hallmarks of the Gordon Commission was that everybody had strong opinions — and wasn't shy about voicing them.

Maurice, who was thirty-two when he joined the Commission, played a relatively minor role. Aside from routine administrative duties, he arranged the hearings in Montreal and Quebec City, and he attended hearings in all the other provinces. One of his responsibilities was to supervise the French translations of the reports. When it came to the final report, he rejected the first draft and, without waiting for authority, plucked four crack translators out of the Department of the Secretary of State. By working round the clock his team was able to rewrite the French report so that it could be published simultaneously with the English version, in November 1957.

The recommendations of the Commission roused a storm of controversy, but no action was taken because in June of that year the Liberals had been defeated in the General Election. This disappointed the members of the Commission, especially Walter Gordon, who had hoped that his Royal Commission would be a launching-pad for his entry into politics. (Gordon had to wait another five years but eventually realized his ambition.) As for Maurice, he was well satisfied with his stint in the capital. He'd been well paid, he'd made a tremendous number of contacts, and he'd learned a lot about the federal government. In January 1958 he got his first taste of federal politics when, at the behest of Walter Gordon, he worked for Mike Pearson at the Liberal Leadership Convention. Maurice stayed on with the Commission until it was dissolved in May 1958. Then, with no plans for the future, he and Jeanne sublet their apartment and left for a holiday in Europe.

Maurice was still undecided whether to go into business or into politics when they returned to Montreal at the end of the summer. His mind was made up by two phone calls. The first was from Maurice Lamontagne, who said that Jean Lesage was looking for an assistant, and that he had suggested Maurice's name to him. (Lesage, a former cabinet minister in Louis St. Laurent's government, had left federal politics after the 1957 defeat, and in May 1958 had been elected leader of the Quebec Liberal party.) The next day Maurice received a call from Claude Ducharme, a Montreal lawyer who'd been a classmate at university. Ducharme also told him that Lesage was looking for an assistant, and that he'd be pleased to arrange a meeting for Maurice with Lesage. Maurice suspected that Lamontagne and Ducharme were working in concert, but he subsequently learned that both were independent referrals.

A few weeks later Lesage invited Maurice to lunch at the Reform Club in Montreal. Over lunch Maurice questioned the Liberal leader closely on his plans for the provincial party. Impressed with Lesage, whom he liked instantly, Maurice said to him at the end of the meal, "I'm not a member of any political party, but I believe the province must have a change of government, and I'd like to work for you." Lesage appeared pleased, but explained that he was considering several other candidates and would let him know later. Maurice waited anxiously by his phone until one morning Lesage called to say, "The job is yours, you can start today." He was given the title of Director of Public Relations and a starting salary of twelve thousand a year.

When Maurice joined the Quebec Liberal party in September 1958 it was a critical time for Lesage. During that summer *Le Devoir* had revealed a natural-gas scandal in which several of Duplessis's ministers were involved. Lesage had pounced on the scandal, but had been publicly rebuked for his attacks by a fellow Liberal, Senator Sarto Fournier, the Mayor of Montreal. The rift between Senator Fournier and the newly elected provincial leader was essentially a clash between the Old Guard and the New Guard of the party. The Old Guard was used to running the show for their own benefit. While they were in control, all decisions were made in the back rooms; the grass-roots membership was ignored. Party bosses selected the candidates; there were no open nomination conventions. Patronage favours, in the form of lucrative contracts, were freely dispensed in exchange for campaign donations. Because of this self-serving arrangement the Old Guard was determined to maintain the status quo, and in certain ridings they had gone so far as to make "sweetheart deals" or non-aggression pacts with their opponents. Senator Fournier's tolerant view of the natural-gas scandal served notice to Lesage that the Old Guard wouldn't tolerate tampering with entrenched party policy.

The split among the provincial Liberals came to a head at the annual meeting in October. The Old Guard put pressure on Lesage to placate Fournier, while the New Guard, which was made up of young reformers, agitated to have Fournier expelled. After much discussion and intense lobbying, the question of whether to expel Fournier was put to a vote. The motion was passed by a majority of about twenty to one. Routing the Old Guard was a momentous victory for Lesage, who emerged as the undisputed leader of the party.

In 1958 the Quebec Liberals were in the political wilderness. Jean Lesage didn't even have a seat in the Assembly; Georges-Émile Lapalme was acting as Leader of the Opposition. The party existed, but it had to be completely rebuilt, and there wasn't much time, as the next election was expected within two years. Lesage set about the rebuilding task with tremendous energy and dedication. Among his priorities was the need to fashion a new platform, to enlist good candidates, and to raise money. A number of standing committees were set up, the most important being the Publicity Committee, of which Maurice was a key member. This committee dealt with election strategy, and was the nerve centre of the party. It met at the party headquarters in Montreal every week from October 1958 until the election in June 1960.

Maurice visited all the ridings in the province to enlist public relations men and to organize election committees. He also supervised a grass-roots survey of the electorate, which had never been done before in Canada. Meticulous organization at every level was the keynote of Lesage's campaign; nothing was left to chance. The party's finances were bolstered by a variety of then novel methods, including door-to-door canvassing and fund-raising dinners. Even the campaign slogan was carefully test-marketed. At the annual meeting in 1959, four boxes with buttons carrying different messages were placed at the entrance door to the hall. The box that emptied first was the one with buttons that read "C'est le temps que ça change" (It's time for a change). This was the slogan used in the election.

The party platform, called the Liberal Manifesto, was formulated after the survey results were analysed. It was written by Maurice and two other members of the executive, René Tremblay and Claude Morin, who closeted themselves for several days at the Maison Montmorency, a Dominican retreat near Quebec City. (Morin went on to become a senior bureaucrat in the Lesage government, but he is best known as a hard-line Parti Québécois minister.) When the election was called, the Liberals were ready. Nothing had to be improvised, everything was in place. Even so, the Liberals knew it would be a tough battle.

Maurice Duplessis had died in office the previous September. He was succeeded by Paul Sauvé, one of his cabinet ministers, who was widely admired in the province. Jeanne interviewed Paul Sauvé for the CBC and, although her husband was working round the clock to unseat his party, she was very impressed with the new leader of the Union Nationale. After the program she exclaimed to a reporter, "He's a wonderful man that all Quebecers can be proud of!" In January 1960, less than four months after he was sworn in, Paul Sauvé died of a heart attack. He was succeeded by Antonio Barrette, another former Duplessis cabinet minister. Barrette lacked the charisma of his predecessor, but under his leadership the Union Nationale was still a formidable political machine.

Eight weeks before the election, which was slated for the twenty-second of June, a closed meeting of Liberal candidates and organizers was held in Montreal. At this meeting it was agreed that the party would campaign on the published Manifesto and not deviate from it. Discipline was fundamental to the campaign strategy. In this connection, the candidates were told precisely how much money would be allocated to each of their ridings, and how it would be spent. This time, unlike the previous election when the Union Nationale had a pipeline into the secret councils of the Liberals, the Liberals had spies in the headquarters of the Union Nationale. Every two weeks the Liberals made a survey of the voting trend. At the outset the UN were ahead, the next survey showed the two parties neck and neck, and then in the stretch the Liberals pulled ahead.

The campaign unfolded exactly as the Liberals had hoped, although there were a few surprises. During the final weeks it was learned that the UN planned to release damaging letters allegedly written by Jean Lesage when he was a federal cabinet minister. Liberal headquarters got copies of the letters and had them analysed by a forensic expert, who stated that they were forgeries. Armed with this written opinion, the Legal Committee of the party sent wires to the media warning that if the letters were published they would be sued. Lesage, at a public meeting, announced that he knew of the forged letters and dared the UN to publish them. This spiked the Union Nationale's guns. The Union Nationale also made innuendoes suggesting that the Liberals were communists, or at best socialists. To combat these charges the Liberals mailed a booklet with the biographies of their candidates to more than a million households in the province. At the end of each biography were two lines mentioning the candidate's relatives in the Roman Catholic clergy; for example, "his elder brother Pierre is a Jesuit priest and his cousin, Annette LeBlanc, is a Sister of Charity." Georges-Émile Lapalme had no relatives in the Church, so they simply wrote, "He has visited the Pope." (René Lévesque, who became a cabinet minister in the Lesage government and later headed the Parti Québécois, was one of the few candidates for whom they could find no religious connection.)

Ten days before the election, Maurice was asked by a commentator from the CBC how the voting would go on election day. His information was so accurate that he was able to tick off the ridings in alphabetical order and correctly predict, with the exception of one riding, the winner of every riding.

On election day Maurice and Jeanne drove from Montreal to Quebec City to be with Jean Lesage when the results came in. It wasn't until eleven o'clock that Lesage was finally declared the winner. The Liberals squeaked in with fifty seats compared to forty-four for the Union Nationale, and there was one Independent member. As soon as the official result was known, Lesage and Maurice jumped into a police cruiser and were driven to a victory celebration at the Quebec Coliseum. The wild ride downtown with tires squealing, lights flashing, and the siren wailing, was something to remember. At the rally Lesage introduced Maurice to the crowd as "one of the main architects of our victory".

The 1960 election was a crucial turning-point in the fortunes of Quebec. Many historians regard it as the beginning of the Quiet Revolution.

The day after the election Maurice returned to Montreal. He had done his job, and his ultimate goal — which he had made clear to Lesage — was federal politics. Paradoxically, this was due in part to his concern for Quebec. Maurice reasoned that the welfare of Quebec was more dependent upon the federal government than upon the provincial government, because federal initiatives were the important ones, and the main motor for the economy. He was also convinced that national unity was vital to the survival of Quebec, and a strong French presence in Ottawa was the best way to preserve the culture and autonomy of the province.

That summer Jeanne and Maurice took a holiday in Europe, a tradition they had started a few years earlier, as soon as they could afford the fare. It was Jeanne's first real holiday since the birth of their son, Jean-François, the previous July. Their only child, Jean-François was a central figure in their lives and a growing source of pleasure for both of them.

When they returned from Europe, Maurice went to work for

the federal Liberal party as a consultant and an organizer in eastern Canada. Although he was working at the federal level, he continued to be involved with the provincial party. In the spring of 1962 he was asked by the Provincial Secretary to see if he could find out what was happening in the Magdalen Islands. The Magdalen Islands, a hook-shaped cluster of windswept dunes in the Gulf of St. Lawrence, had been a Union Nationale stronghold since 1936. In the 1960 election the sitting UN member, Hormidas-Damien Langlais, had been re-elected once again.

On his way back from Moncton, Maurice dropped in to the Magdalen Islands. He was greeted at the airport by the senior Liberal organizer, a man who owned a grocery store, and taken to his home. When they got inside the house the local organizer took the precaution of pulling the blinds for secrecy. Then he proceeded to tell Maurice about the sad political situation in the islands. It was very bleak indeed. Even though the Liberals were in power in Quebec City, the Magdalen Islands were still controlled by the Union Nationale. Langlais continued to visit the islands like a potentate, staying in the bishop's suite at the hospital and using the four provincial policemen as his errand boys to fetch constituents. Virtually all of the government jobs, such as road work, were still being given to supporters of the Union Nationale.

That night five or six Liberals came to the grocer's house for a meeting with Maurice. At the end of a long and depressing discussion everyone agreed that there was no hope for the Liberals in the Magdalens. Maurice flew to the mainland the next day, reported the situation, and then dismissed the matter from his mind.

A month later Prime Minister John Diefenbaker, whose Conservative government was coming apart at the seams, called a federal election. Maurice, encouraged by Jeanne, decided to run for Parliament, but when he tried to get a riding in the Montreal area he was turned down by party headquarters. At that time, the Quebec wing of the federal Liberal party was a closed shop run by the Old Guard. It consisted of well-entrenched MP's, influential party organizers, and some Quebec senators who dominated the executive committee.

Maurice was rebuffed because he had a reputation as a radical, and he made no secret of wanting to reform the party. As there was nothing he could do without the consent of the committee, he busied himself working on behalf of other candidates.

Meanwhile, the former Liberal candidate in the Magdalen Islands declined to run again. In desperation the local Liberal organizer phoned Quebec headquarters and asked if the chap who had visited them (whose name he couldn't remember) would run in the Magdalen Islands. Because it was such a remote outpost, and because the chance of a Liberal's being elected was virtually nil, the party executive told Maurice that, if he wished, he could run there.

It might seem odd that a mainlander would be asked to run, but it was a political tradition in the Magdalen Islands, the smallest constituency in Canada. By custom both the federal and the provincial representatives always came from the mainland. This peculiar arrangement was due to mistrust: the population of twelve thousand was scattered throughout a number of isolated communities, each of which suspected the political motives of the others. Roughly ninety per cent of the population was French and ten per cent was English. The terrain is similar to Prince Edward Island, but the land-holdings are so small that there is little agriculture. Fishing has always been the chief industry. The people of the Magdalens take their politics seriously, and are fiercely partisan. The loyalty of every individual is well known; hence there is practically no swing vote. When a person changes his political allegiance, it is not unusual for him to go on record to that effect by swearing an oath before the parish priest. The islanders love political meetings, and on election days their turnout is phenomenal.

Maurice flew to the Magdalen Islands to discuss his candidature and was interviewed by about twenty-five Liberals. They told him that if he could solve their provincial problems, they would select him as their federal candidate. He protested, saying, "You're putting me in a box," but they pointed out that he was involved with the party at both levels and was therefore in a good position to help them. The upshot was that he took their list of sixty-four grievances (most of which involved petty patronage) back with him to Quebec and settled fifty-eight of them. This feat made him an instant hero. When he returned to the islands for his nomination meeting, twelve hundred people were at the airport to welcome him — which was considerably more than the bishop drew on his yearly pastoral visit.

At the nomination meeting Maurice explained that party responsibilities prevented him from returning to the islands until the last two weeks of the campaign, but that Louis-Philippe Lacroix, his campaign manager, would be his representative during his absence. While he was away, Maurice arranged for a string of political luminaries to visit the Magdalens to speak on his behalf. This was another local tradition — party speakers had to come from the mainland or few people would listen to them.

Jeanne was with Maurice for the final two weeks of the campaign. They rented a house, which they shared with several of Maurice's assistants. Each day Maurice canvassed a different section of the constituency. Jeanne, who by 1962 was a well-known broadcasting personality, also toured the riding, speaking to groups of women voters. At night she would cook dinner, usually lobsters, for everyone. As there were no liquor outlets on the islands, the lobsters would be washed down with white wine brought from the mainland. Owing to the unavailability of liquor, the local people drank a lethal home-brew made from molasses. Maurice refused to try the home-brew, because he knew that if he accepted one drink, he would have to have a drink wherever he went, and he wouldn't last the course.

The election followed the time-honoured pattern. First, there was a giant meeting where the two opponents confronted each other in debate. This was always a lively gathering. Then the candidates went their separate ways, campaigning door-to-door and speaking to groups in the various parishes. The last rally, and the most crucial one for the candidates, was the one that each held on the Saturday night before the Monday election. At these final rallies, which started at eight o'clock and finished precisely at midnight, voters travelled back and forth from one meeting to the other to see which had the largest attendance, and then packed the hall of the candidate with the biggest audience. Thus the outcome of the election was foretold on the Saturday before polling-day.

Maurice's final rally was a barn-burner. Throughout the evening, announcements over the public address system gave the attendance at his opponent's meeting. Excitement mounted as the number kept dropping. Eventually, Maurice's hall was jammed and newcomers had to listen to the speeches outside in their cars. Each time a new total was announced there would be wild applause inside the building, and an answering cacophony of car horns from outside the hall. At half past eleven, when Maurice rose to make the wind-up speech, the hall was suddenly silent. Spellbound on the edge of their seats, the crowd waited for him to speak. Years later, recalling the scene, Maurice said, "At that moment, I could have asked them to kneel." With the audience in the palm of his hand, he spoke until midnight. At the end of his speech he was given a foot-stamping ovation.

After attending Mass the following day, Maurice participated in another quaint local election custom, *la galopade*. This is a contest that takes place on the Sunday before polling-day while the candidates are visiting the homes of uncommitted voters. Played by a variable number of partisans, the object of *la galopade* is to prevent the other party's man from gaining any converts. This is accomplished by harassing the candidate's car at high speeds (forcing it off the road if possible) and by blocking his exit should the candidate reach his destination. As a counter-measure, the candidates travel in three-car convoys. The escort cars contain burly men with bicycle chains whose job is to provide muscle in the event of a brawl, and to remove (by overturning if necessary) cars blocking the laneway. Depending upon the stamina of the players, the contest can go on for hours. *La galopade* is considered good clean fun in the Magdalens, but is frowned upon by the insurance industry.

Maurice survived *la galopade* and, on Monday the eighteenth of June, travelled the length of the islands to visit all twenty-nine polling-stations. At each stop his poll captain would give him an estimate of the vote. As usual, the turnout was heavy; that day ninety-nine per cent of the eligible electors cast their ballots. By the end of his tour he had an indicated majority of 510 votes over his opponent, the Tory incumbent. This proved to be uncannily accurate; when the ballots were counted, his actual majority was 515 (which was subsequently increased to 535 by the Service vote). It was the largest majority in the history of the Magdalens.

Jeanne was delighted with Maurice's victory. She was approaching the peak of her career, and with his election to Parliament they could now both share the public spotlight. Nor was she daunted by the prospect of being a politician's wife. Since her return to Canada she had become fascinated with politics, and she had enjoyed the campaign immensely.

The 1962 election was a triumph for Maurice, but not for the Liberal party, which, with Diefenbaker on the ropes, had counted on picking up fifty seats in Quebec. The Tories obliged by losing thirty-six, but the Grits could only amass thirty-five seats in the province. What scuppered the Liberals was the Social Credit party, under the demagogic leadership of a Rouyn car dealer, Réal Caouette, who came from nowhere to grab twenty-six Quebec ridings. On a national basis, the Progressive Conservatives ended up with 116 seats, the Liberals with 100, the CCF (forerunner of the NDP) with 19, and the Social Credit with 30 seats. Caouette's success cost the Liberals their chance for a majority, and, to add insult to injury, the Social Credit's block of seats gave it the balance of power.

In Quebec, when the Liberals fare badly at the polls, they traditionally find a scapegoat. At a post-mortem meeting in Montreal after the election, Lionel Chevrier, the leader of the Quebec caucus, singled out Maurice to take the blame for the disaster. Maurice, who wasn't prepared to take the rap, pointed out that no one had foreseen the Social Credit avalanche, and even if they had, there was nothing they could have done about it. The only person to speak in Maurice's defence was Bryce Mackasey, a reformer who had been elected against the wishes of the Old Guard.

When Maurice went to Ottawa as an Opposition backbencher in September 1962, he automatically became a member of the

Quebec caucus. The Quebec caucus is an important political entity because the province has historically been the Liberal party's power base, and the Quebec caucus has traditionally spoken for French Canada. (The Tories also have a Quebec caucus, but, aside from the aberrations of the Diefenbaker sweep in 1958 and Mulroney's landslide in 1984, it is normally so small that it could convene in a telephone booth.) Although the members of the Quebec caucus have much in common, and practically all are French, they often engage in Machiavellian struggles with each other. Dissension within the caucus, however, is masked by the complexity of the intrigues, and by the Liberal tradition of party solidarity, which rivals that of the Canadian Medical Association.

In 1962, the entry of some of the newly elected members to the Quebec caucus ruffled the feathers of the Old Guard. The most prominent in this group of reformers, dubbed the "New Guard", was Maurice Sauvé. Maurice was thirty-nine at that time. He still had the high colouring of his youth, but he had filled out and now weighed more than two hundred pounds. Over six feet in height, he towered over most of his colleagues. His size and aggressive manner prompted journalist Ron Collister to write in the Toronto *Telegram* that he resembled "an Irish pug with his back to the bar".

The caucus knew that Maurice wanted an overhaul of the party in Quebec — and that he believed he was the man to do it. Maurice's principal concerns were the selection of candidates and party finances. Specifically, he wanted candidates to be selected by democratic nomination in the ridings, rather than by party hacks, and he wanted to purge the party of its shady funding practices. To achieve these ends, power would have to be wrested from the Old Guard. Not surprisingly, the Old Guard viewed Maurice as a threat, and from the outset he had a host of enemies.

Throughout his political career Maurice had two main preoccupations: the federal party in Quebec, and national unity. One of his fundamental beliefs was that if the country was to remain united, there would have to be a much stronger French presence at the federal level. Also, it was imperative that the federal government become more involved in Quebec's problems. He referred to these tenets in his maiden speech to the House of Commons on 18 December 1962. After raking the Diefenbaker government over the coals for indecision and incompetence, he went on to discuss the position of the French in Canada.

During the winter of 1963 Parliament was embroiled in the nuclear issue, a controversy that was fuelled by the Kennedy administration. Diefenbaker had permitted American Bomarc missiles and Starfighter aircraft to be stationed on Canadian soil, but had refused to allow them to be armed with nuclear warheads. In a surprising about-face, Pearson, who had always been against nuclear weapons, charged Diefenbaker with failing to honour Canada's commitment to NATO. The ensuing want-of-confidence motion toppled Diefenbaker's government, precipitating another election.

Maurice was jubilant because he knew the Liberals would win the election, and he was sure he would be made a cabinet minister. He was partly right: in the April 1963 contest the Liberals won 129 seats, the Tories dropped to 95, the Social Credit slipped to 24, and the NDP came last with 17 seats. The results meant another minority government, but this time it was a Liberal administration. In the Magdalen Islands the turnout was relatively light; only eighty-five per cent of the eligible voters cast their ballots, and Maurice breezed in with a huge majority. The Conservatives hadn't chosen to field a candidate in the Magdalens; Maurice's only opponent had been a twenty-year-old Créditiste.

Five days after the election, Prime Minister Pearson formed his cabinet. To Maurice's dismay, he wasn't given a portfolio. When his name had been suggested for a ministerial post the proposal had been vetoed by Lionel Chevrier and Azellus Denis, the leaders of the Old Guard. Maurice was bitterly disappointed at being passed over, as he considered it a signal to French Canada that he didn't have the backing of the Prime Minister. Wondering what he could do to retrieve the situation, he decided to confront Pearson at his home. Because it was so soon after the election, Pearson was still living at Stornoway, the official residence of the Leader of the

Opposition. Hurrying over to Stornoway, Maurice brushed aside the preliminaries and said to Pearson: "You are ruining my career; if I wasn't representing the Magdalen Islands, I would resign!" Well aware that he was treading a tightrope with his minority, Pearson tried to mollify Maurice by offering him the position of Parliamentary Secretary to Mitchell Sharp, the Minister of Trade and Commerce. Maurice refused it out of hand. They talked a bit more, then Pearson offered him the chairmanship of the Special Committee on National Defence. Maurice accepted this proposal with alacrity. They shook hands on the deal, which ended the crisis.

In one respect it was just as well that Maurice wasn't associated with the cabinet at the outset. During the campaign, the Liberals, in addition to employing gimmicks such as a "Truth Squad" and political colouring books, had made some exceedingly rash promises. Among the most embarrassing was a pledge to introduce, within the first two months of taking office, legislation that would cure the country's social and economic ills. This period of achievement was heralded as the "Sixty Days of Decision". There is no need to dwell on what actually transpired, except to note that on the sixtieth day of decision Walter Gordon, the Minister of Finance, decided to tender his resignation.

The Pearson administration also had to deal with pressing inter-national problems. The most urgent was the nuclear-arms question. During the campaign the Liberals had said that they would honour Canada's nuclear commitment. The decision, however, would not be rammed down the public's throat; it would be debated in Parlia-ment after a thorough examination of Canada's NATO role by an all-party committee.

The appointment of Maurice to head the Special Committee on National Defence raised eyebrows, because his only military experi-ence — if such it might be called — had been to organize an anti-conscription parade, and he knew nothing about national defence. Despite these limitations, he proved to be an effective chairman. One reason for his success was that the members of the committee (who, as Pearson had promised, were drawn from all parties) were well qualified to assess Canada's role in NATO. Maurice didn't contribute a great deal to the committee's discussions, but he was adept at getting the members to reach a consensus. From October to December 1963 the committee met more than forty times, and also travelled to England, Germany, Belgium, France, and the United States for talks with NATO allies. At the end of this period, the Special Committee tabled an 850-page report unanimously recommending acceptance of nuclear arms for Canada. The Committee's recommendation was quickly approved by a free vote in the House of Commons. On New Year's Eve, the first shipment of nuclear warheads was quietly trucked across the border to North Bay, one of the two Canadian Bomarc sites.

In January 1964, Lionel Chevrier was appointed Canada's High Commissioner in London. Three weeks later, as part of a cabinet shuffle, his Old Guard colleague in the cabinet, Azellus Denis, was elevated to the Senate. (The Postmaster General's move to the Upper House may have been hastened to some extent by the revelation that he had used a list of defeated Liberal candidates to dispense patronage.) Denis's and Chevrier's departure cleared the way for Maurice to enter the cabinet. On 3 February, Maurice was appointed minister of forestry and rural development. To placate the Old Guard, Pearson appointed one of their younger adherents, Yvon Dupuis, to the cabinet on the same day. Dupuis, a rabble-rousing orator, had been the Liberals' best weapon against Réal Caouette in the two previous elections.

Maurice's satisfaction at being given a cabinet post was diminished by the fact that Forestry was a minor portfolio. It was also a frustrating one to administer because jurisdiction was largely in the hands of the provinces. The federal Department of Forestry owned a string of research stations, but its main task was to orchestrate federal-provincial agreements. In addition to Forestry, Maurice was put in charge of the Agricultural Rehabilitation and Development Act (ARDA). This presented more of a challenge. Rural development meant dealing with people, rather than trees, which appealed to Maurice.

Shortly after he was appointed to the cabinet, Maurice made an important contribution to Canadian unity by helping to resolve the Canada-Quebec pension deadlock.

This crisis was the result of a 1963 Liberal campaign promise to provide "Better Pensions for All". As soon as it was unveiled, the Pearson government's ill-conceived pay-as-you-go pension plan was rejected by both Quebec and Ontario. Quebec then devised its own funded pension plan, which provided greater benefits but required a share of federal tax revenues. The federal government, however, refused to make any tax concessions. At a federal-provincial conference in Quebec City at the end of March 1964 the federal government presented a compromise solution that failed to satisfy either Ontario or Quebec. This meeting ended on a sour note, with some knowledgeable observers predicting the break-up of Confederation. Lesage, who was determined to go ahead with his own pension plan, scheduled a provincial budget for two weeks later, the seventeenth of April. This budget would levy double taxation on Quebec residents.

Maurice didn't attend the conference, but while it was in progress he received a number of telephone calls from his former colleague, Claude Morin, who had drafted the Quebec Plan. The most alarming call came after the conference ended, when Morin told Maurice that Lesage was going to castigate Ottawa in his budget speech. Maurice contacted Tom Kent, Prime Minister Pearson's chief aide, and the two men decided that they must immediately go to Quebec City to try and salvage the situation. Pearson was surprised at their proposal but agreed to let them go, provided their mission was conducted in secret. With minutes to spare, Maurice and Kent caught the last plane to Quebec. To mask their visit, Kent was registered in the Château Frontenac under the name of Claude Frenette, Maurice's executive assistant. The next morning Claude Morin came to the hotel and the three men hammered out a tentative solution. That afternoon they were spirited through a side door into the Premier's office, where they presented the compromise proposal to Lesage. The Premier not only gave his blessing, but postponed his budget for a week so that the negotiators would have time to sort out the details. Maurice and Tom Kent flew back to Ottawa in a Quebec government aircraft.

From Uplands airport they went straight to the Prime Minister's residence. The solution they proposed appalled Pearson and some of his senior ministers, especially Walter Gordon, but after two hours of discussion everyone agreed to it in principle. The following day, Thursday, Maurice phoned Claude Morin, who arranged that he and Claude Castonguay would come to Ottawa on Saturday to finalize the deal.

This crucial meeting took place in the Privy Council chamber in the East Block of the Parliament Buildings. The negotiating teams talked all afternoon, without reaching any agreement. If anything, the two sides grew further apart in their positions. Finally, just before Morin and Castonguay were about to leave, Tom Kent excused himself and signalled Maurice to join him in the washroom. Standing with his back to the urinals, Maurice quickly outlined Quebec's minimum requirements. Armed with this information, Kent returned to the bargaining-table and by working feverishly was able to stitch together an agreement. It cost the federal government more than two hundred million dollars in the first two years, but it kept the country together. For his part in the drama, the Parliamentary Press Gallery nicknamed Maurice "the James Bond of Confederation".

While the pension crisis was being resolved, another political struggle was in progress behind the scenes. This concerned the leadership of the Quebec caucus, which had come up for grabs following the departure of Lionel Chevrier. The three rivals for the leadership were Maurice Lamontagne, the Secretary of State; Guy Favreau, the Minister of Justice; and Maurice Sauvé. Lamontagne, who had helped Maurice get his job on the Gordon Commission, was the front runner. A cultured intellectual with an impressive record of public service, he had played an important role in the fight against Duplessis. Lamontagne was also an old friend of Pearson, and his closest Quebec adviser. Favreau was a decent and immensely popular man who had been persuaded by Pearson to leave his Montreal law practice to enter politics. On the surface, all three were

Jeanne Sauvé, Minister of the Environment, descending in an elevator at a Northern Quebec mine, 1975. (Sauvé family collection)

Campaigning in Ahuntsic riding, July 1974. (Sauvé family collection)

Election results, July 1974. (Sauvé family collection)

Jeanne Sauvé, Minister of Communications, speaking on Canadian unity, Ritz-Carlton Hotel. Seated is former Senator Thérèse Casgrain. Montreal, March 1976. (Allan R. Leishman, *Montreal Star*, Public Archives of Canada, PA-146048)

Auctioning a Canadian flag at a fund-raising dinner in aid of the mentally retarded, Montreal, May 1977. The flag was bought by industrialist Paul Desmarais for five thousand dollars. (George Bird, *Montreal Star*, Public Archives of Canada, PA-146043)

Presiding over the Commons, 1980.
(Sauvé family collection)

President Reagan's 1981 visit to the House of Commons. In the foreground,
facing the camera, Maurice Sauvé. (Canapress Photo Service)

peaker Jeanne Sauvé hands over constitution resolution to Governor General
:d Schreyer, December 1981. Esmond Butler in background. (*Ottawa*
Citizen)

peaker Jeanne Sauvé with Her Majesty the Queen on her 1982 visit to
'arliament. Jean Marchand, Speaker of the Senate, is on the Queen's right.
Department of the Secretary of State)

Barbecue for the Prince and Princess of Wales at the Speaker's
residence, Kingsmere, June 1983. (Department of the Secretary
of State)

Madame Sauvé passing through the receiving
line at a dinner for the Prince and Princess given
by Governor General Schreyer at Rideau Hall,
June 1983. (Department of the Secretary of State)

The Sauvé residence in the Town of Mount Royal,
Montreal. (M. S. Heney)

Madame Sauvé in the sitting-room off her bedroom,
Montreal. (M. S. Heney)

The Sauvés' country house, St. Charles-sur-Richelieu,
Q. (M. S. Heney)

Madame Sauvé being greeted by her sister Berthe Belisle on her arrival in Ottawa before the investiture. Prime Minister Trudeau and her husband Maurice are on the right, her sister Lucille and brother Jean are among the family members on the left. Union Station, May 1984. (Department of the Secretary of State)

The investiture ceremony in the Senate Chamber, May 1984. (Department of the Secretary of State)

reformers, but Lamontagne and Favreau had received the tacit support of the Old Guard because they were thought to be more mal-
leable than Sauvé. It should also be added that both Lamontagne
and Favreau were politically naive, and much less effective in the
House than Maurice Sauvé.

Pearson, to restore harmony, tried to settle the question by making the leadership a triumvirate. This typically Pearsonian solution
was rejected by the Quebec caucus. The Old Guard then moved
into the vacuum. Guy Rouleau, Pearson's parliamentary secretary,
circulated a letter on the Prime Minister's stationery stating that it
was the wish of the caucus that Favreau be appointed Quebec leader.
This ploy eliminated Lamontagne, whom the Old Guard considered
too weak to stop Sauvé, and made Favreau the favourite. At a meeting in Montreal at the end of April 1964, Favreau was overwhelm-
ingly endorsed as leader of the Quebec caucus. Maurice was so upset at
the turn of events that for the second time he considered resigning
from politics.

Maurice lost the leadership contest because he didn't have a power
base in the caucus. This shortcoming was to haunt him throughout
his career. He had high-level French friends in the civil service,
influential English friends in the cabinet (such as Judy LaMarsh,
Edgar Benson, and Walter Gordon), and solid connections in the
Quebec legislature, but these people couldn't help him in the caucus.
Maurice's basic problem was that he was a loner rather than a team
player. To be successful in politics, particularly in Ottawa, one must
forge alliances, and one must constantly expand them — which Maurice failed to do.

Contemporary journalists wrote many complimentary things
about Maurice, but they also noted that he was intolerant, impatient,
and brutally frank. As a cabinet minister he was admired for his
intelligence and his administrative ability, but his tactlessness alien-
ated many potential allies. In the House of Commons he ignored
the political niceties, and was considered by the Opposition to be as
dangerous as a loose cannon.

For example, when he went to Europe in July 1964 for a Food

and Agriculture Organization meeting, he was told by the Prime
Minister to take his holidays after the meeting and to return to
Canada in late August. Maurice's absence was noted by a Tory
backbencher, Louis-Joseph Pigeon. Day after day Pigeon (who had
earlier cast aspersions on Jeanne's connection with the CBC) rose in
the House to question the government on Maurice's whereabouts.
Pigeon's needling was so successful that the Ottawa *Citizen* joined
in the hue and cry by publishing a critical editorial. When Maurice
returned to the House on 11 August, the first question on the Order Paper was from Mr. Pigeon. Unfortunately for Pigeon, Maurice
had been told that while he was away Pigeon had been arrested and
charged with a homosexual offence involving a young man in Hull.
Here is the Hansard report of their encounter that day:

Mr. L-J Pigeon (Joliette-L'Assomption-Montcalm):
"Mr. Speaker, I have a question for the Minister of Forestry.
*"I should like to ask him whether he enjoyed his stay in Europe and
why he cut his holidays short?"*
Hon. Maurice Sauvé (Minister of Forestry):
*"Mr. Speaker, I spent two weeks in Europe. The first week I was on
official business. The second week, since I thought the House would
adjourn on August 8, I saw fit to take a week's holiday. I felt I needed a
holiday because I was seriously ill last April, as everybody knows.*
*"I feel moreover, that the Hon. member for Joliette-L'Assomption-
Montcalm should have taken a holiday too at the same time."*
Right Hon. J. G. Diefenbaker (Leader of the Opposition):
*"Mr. Speaker, the latter part of that observation has no place in the
records of Parliament, and I am sure the Hon. gentleman will find the
isle of Capri is quite different from the House of Commons."*

Maurice's allusion to Pigeon's brush with the law was greeted
by a stunned silence in the Commons, and so shook the Speaker
that he terminated the Question Period. Pigeon, who was acquitted
when his case came to trial, never again tried to challenge Maurice.

During the autumn of 1964 and the first half of 1965 the Liberal administration was rocked by a series of scandals. Yvon Dupuis became the first cabinet minister in Canadian history to face criminal charges while in office. Dupuis, who was forced to resign, was found guilty on three counts of influence-peddling in connection with an application for a racetrack. He was fined five thousand dollars and sentenced to a year in jail. Later, his conviction was quashed on appeal. René Tremblay, the Minister of Immigration, was involved in furniture purchases from a shady company that subsequently went bankrupt. Maurice Lamontagne also bought furniture from the same company, but, unlike Tremblay, who had paid in full for his goods, Lamontagne still owed a substantial amount for his furniture. The worst scandal, however, was the Rivard Affair.

Lucien Rivard was a gangster who had masterminded an American dope-smuggling ring. In November 1964 he was being held, pending extradition to the United States, in Montreal's Bordeaux Jail. To prevent Rivard's extradition, the Mafia brought pressure to bear on several individuals in the Liberal administration. When this was revealed in the House of Commons by Tory MP Erik Nielsen, it caused an uproar. Guy Rouleau admitted that he had made representations in the case and resigned as Pearson's parliamentary secretary. In response to Nielsen's allegations, a royal commission under Mr. Justice Frédéric Dorion was convened to investigate the whole affair. At the beginning of March 1965, while the Dorion Commission was sifting through the evidence and examining witnesses, Rivard escaped from Bordeaux Jail.

The most disturbing aspect of the scandals was that virtually all those implicated were French Canadians. During that winter there was an outcry from the press demanding reform of the Quebec caucus. Some prominent journalists went so far as to suggest that Pearson should dump Favreau and replace him with Maurice Sauvé. Writing in the *Winnipeg Free Press* on 23 March, Bruce Hutchison had this to say about the Quebec leadership situation:

The vacuum must soon be filled and there is no one to fill it except Mr.

Maurice Sauvé who manages the forestry department with his left hand and, with his right, commands the loyalty of a new generation in Quebec Liberalism.

. . . In Ottawa you will hear two flatly opposite versions of this ebullient creature. One of the capital's most acute observers told me that Mr. Sauvé was the inevitable prime minister in some future day. A major Quebec politician, on the other hand, said that Mr. Sauvé's ruthless climb to power had affronted so many good men that in the end they would combine to destroy him.

When this was written, Maurice was in Europe with Jeanne contemplating his political future. They were on holiday, but Jeanne, as she had from the outset, shared his trials and tribulations. Not only was she his wife, she was also his closest adviser (although he didn't always take her advice). For the past five years, since 1960, they had often performed as a team, speaking to audiences across the country on Quebec and Canadian unity. What concerned Maurice at this juncture was that despite the rash of scandals, Pearson had done nothing to revamp the Quebec wing. Thoroughly frustrated, Maurice was once again thinking of resigning from federal politics.

Instead, he returned to Canada at the end of April and resumed the fight. On the third of June he made a speech to the Montreal Labour Council in which he said that reforms must be carried out before the next election or the impetus for reform would be lost. By inference, this was a criticism of Favreau. The press lauded his speech, but it further isolated him from the Prime Minister.

At the end of June 1965 Judge Dorion tabled his report on the Rivard Affair. Dorion named two assistants to the Minister of Justice who had acted improperly in the extradition case, and criticized Favreau's judgement in his handling of the proceedings. Although he was innocent of any criminal offence, Guy Favreau resigned as minister of justice the following day.

Only cosmetic changes were made when Pearson shuffled his cabinet in the wake of the Dorion Report. Maurice was given no new responsibilities. Guy Favreau retained his position as Quebec lieutenant and was made president of the Privy Council. Maurice Lamontagne and René Tremblay remained in the cabinet.

In mid-July 1965 Lucien Rivard was recaptured and swiftly extradited to Texas, where he received a twenty-year sentence for dope-smuggling.

Despite the horror show that had unfolded during the previous months, Prime Minister Pearson clung to the idea that if he went to the electorate, they would give him a majority. Dazzled by this prospect, on 7 September Pearson called another federal election.

Throughout the summer Maurice had been negotiating with three potential Liberal candidates: Jean Marchand, Gérard Pelletier, and Pierre Trudeau. Maurice was convinced that as a team these three men would do much to reform the Quebec caucus (and he also knew that their presence on the federal stage would put his political career into the shade). Initially only Marchand had planned to run, but Maurice had warned him, "If you come in alone, the Old Guard will do to you what they did to me — they'll screw you." After numerous conversations, including several at Maurice's home, Pelletier and Trudeau agreed to seek election. Marchand was warmly welcomed by the Liberals, but Maurice had difficulty persuading Pearson and Favreau to accept Pelletier and Trudeau, both of whom had been vitriolic critics of the Liberal party. He was, however, able to arrange a meeting between Favreau and the three newcomers at the Windsor Hotel in Montreal on the night of 9 September.

For the first few hours Favreau, Maurice Lamontagne, and Louis "Bob" Giguère, remembering what Trudeau had written about the Liberals, tried to dissuade him from joining the party. While they were doing their best to persuade Trudeau not to join, Maurice Sauvé was insisting with equal vehemence that he should join. Then Pelletier, who had just flown in from Winnipeg, arrived at the viceregal suite. The leaders of the Quebec caucus used the same arguments to try and dissuade Pelletier. Finally, Maurice suggested that Marchand, Pelletier, and Trudeau join him in the bedroom. As soon as the door closed behind them, Maurice said, "Ignore their arguments. Call *La Presse* and *Le Devoir* from the bedside phone and tell them you're holding a press conference tomorrow." When this was done they returned to the living-room and presented Favreau with a *fait accompli*. Favreau was furious, but Maurice told him, "If you don't accept Trudeau and Pelletier, I won't run in the election." The following afternoon the "Three Wise Men", as they became known in English Canada (or "The Three Doves" as they were known in Quebec), announced their intention to run as Liberals in the forthcoming election.

In the 1965 campaign Maurice spent most of his time speaking on behalf of fellow Liberals. He was also instrumental in finding a safe riding for Gérard Pelletier. To do this he persuaded the long-time incumbent of Hochelaga, Raymond Eudes, to give up his seat in exchange for a promise from the Prime Minister that he would be made a senator. Pelletier was elected in Hochelaga, and Eudes was subsequently elevated to the Senate. Although the Conservatives ran a strong candidate in the Magdalens, Maurice was re-elected for the third time with a comfortable majority. Nationally, the Liberal party didn't fare as well. The Liberals got two more seats, but so did the Progressive Conservatives. For the second time Mike Pearson was in the delicate position of heading a minority government.

A few weeks after the November 1965 election Maurice flew to Rome to chair the Annual Conference of the Food and Agriculture Organization. When he left Canada he was unaware that Dr. Marc Arsenault, his Tory opponent in the Magdalens, was about to accuse him of election irregularities. The Tories, who thought they had finally bagged "Mr. Clean", broke the story on 9 December. It was front-page news in both French and English Canada. The headline in the *Globe and Mail* was typical of the coverage. It read: "Election Spells Shenanigans in Sauvé-land". Maurice, who couldn't have left Rome even if he'd wanted to, shrugged off the charges and Diefenbaker's demand for his resignation. Meanwhile, as the furor mounted in Canada, his friends and colleagues became increasingly worried. Doug Fullerton, who had known Maurice since the Gordon Commission, cabled him to say: "STORM REACHING

GALE PROPORTIONS, URGE RETURN SOONEST OR WILL LOSE BY
DEFAULT.''

Jeanne, who had also been in Rome, flew back to Montreal and
was picked up secretly at the airport by Sonny Gordon, one of Maurice's executive assistants. While they were driving to Ottawa,
Gordon briefed her on the extent and seriousness of the charges.
Neither she nor Maurice had appreciated the gravity of the situation. Jeanne immediately phoned Maurice, who agreed to take the
first plane home when the conference ended. In the meantime his
staff in the Magdalens set to work collecting affidavits to refute the
allegations.

Maurice arrived in Ottawa on the evening of 13 December. The
next morning he huddled with his two assistants, Sonny Gordon
and Claude Frenette, and his friend Doug Fullerton. The conference
continued while the foursome travelled to Montreal that afternoon
in the cabinet's private Pullman car. (Maurice was fond of the old-
fashioned comfort of the specially equipped coach, and used it as
often as possible.) That night a brains-trust comprised of friends
and colleagues convened at his house in Outremont. Among those
who dropped in to offer advice were Claude Ducharme, Gérard
Pelletier, Jean-Pierre Goyer, René Lévesque, Jean Marchand, and
Pierre Trudeau. By three o'clock the next morning a detailed press
communiqué, completed with sworn statements, had been drafted.
Just before the sun came up, Maurice boarded the train to return to
Ottawa. While he caught a few hours' sleep, the rebuttal was typed in
French and in English. That afternoon Maurice held a press conference
attended by more than one hundred journalists. It took him forty
minutes to read the text of the thirty-two-page rebuttal.

Only one charge had any real merit. This concerned a telephone
call Maurice had made to his cousin Judge Joseph Dugay on election
day. That morning two Tory supporters had been jailed for threatening Maurice's campaign manager. A Conservative representative
had phoned the judge (who was more than a hundred miles away
by sea in New Carlisle) and tried to have the men released, but
Maurice, fearing a riot, had also phoned to prevent their release. In

the end, the two men were escorted to the polls under guard and allowed to vote. Maurice was clearly wrong to phone the judge, but there were extenuating circumstances, because it was impossible to contact him quickly any other way. Referring to the incident, Judge Dugay told a reporter, "Everybody calls the judge in these parts — I was not angry nor influenced by the call."

The media accepted Maurice's explanations, and the charges were never referred to the Privileges and Elections Committee of the House of Commons. In essence, the whole thing had been a tempest in a teapot. On the other hand the press release, because it was so masterfully crafted, was used by several universities in their political science courses and was also reprinted in full in the first issue of the *Journal of Canadian Studies*.

Pearson's new cabinet, announced two days after Maurice's press conference, included Jean Marchand. Marchand was appointed minister of citizenship (later manpower) and immigration, and heir apparent to Favreau as Pearson's Quebec lieutenant. Although he didn't replace Favreau until January 1967, from this point on Marchand was the unofficial leader of the Quebec caucus. Both Pierre Trudeau and Gérard Pelletier were made parliamentary secretaries. Maurice Lamontagne and Réne Tremblay resigned from the cabinet but continued to represent their constituencies in the Commons.

Maurice, who had wanted to be minister of trade and commerce in the new administration, was offered the Department of Agriculture. He declined Pearson's offer because he knew his hands would be tied by the minority government, and to accept would have been political suicide. He did, however, agree to continue as minister of forestry with responsibility for ARDA. The forestry department was running smoothly, which allowed him to concentrate on rural development, and he was supported by a succession of outstanding young executive assistants, among them Peter White (who went on to become appointments secretary for Prime Minister Mulroney), Harold "Sonny" Gordon (now a prominent Montreal lawyer), Claude Frenette (who became a senior business executive), and John

Roberts (who was subsequently a Liberal cabinet minister in his own right).

Owing to the redistribution of electoral boundaries in 1964, Maurice knew that the Magdalen Islands were destined to disappear as a constituency in the next election. This meant that he would have to find another riding. Maurice's home constituency, the Montreal riding of Outremont, was the logical choice because the incumbent, Maurice Lamontagne, was about to be elevated to the Senate. Also, Outremont was so solidly Liberal that it was said that you could run a cow there and get it elected, provided it was a red one.

Lamontagne resigned his seat in the House of Commons on 6 April 1967. The next day a three-column story appeared in *La Presse* saying that Maurice Sauvé was resigning his seat in the Magdalens to contest the Outremont seat vacated by Lamontagne. On the following day, Maurice received this telegram:

"DISTURBED BY REPORT IN LA PRESSE THAT YOU ARE RE-SIGNING YOUR SEAT IN ILES DE LA MADELEINE TO CONTEST OUTREMONT BYELECTION STOP THIS SHOULD BE DENIED AS IT CERTAINLY HAS NOT BEEN AGREED BY ME AND IT WOULD CAUSE DIFFICULTIES

L B PEARSON"

The use of the word "difficulties" was an allusion to the precarious state of the Liberal minority government. Pearson was certain that the Liberals would retain Outremont, but if Maurice resigned his seat in the Magdalens the Tories might easily win that by-election. Maurice understood this, but it did nothing to alleviate his problem. He still wanted a chance to run in Outremont. A compromise was reached at a meeting in Pearson's office attended by the hierarchy of the Quebec caucus: Senator Bob Giguère, Maurice Lamontagne, Jean Marchand, and Pierre Trudeau. Maurice Sauvé took the pre-caution of bringing Sonny Gordon along as a witness. It was agreed that a "seat-warmer" or temporary candidate would be found to occupy Outremont until the next election. At that time, because Outremont had a substantial Jewish population, the party would seek a Jewish candidate. If a suitable Jewish candidate was not forthcoming, and if Trudeau was not rejected by his Mount Royal constituency, then the Liberal party would support Maurice's candidacy in Outremont. This arrangement was confirmed by Prime Minister Pearson in a letter dated 11 April to his Quebec lieutenant, Jean Marchand.

In mid-December 1967 Mike Pearson rose in the House of Commons and announced his intention to retire as Leader of the Liberal party, adding that he would remain in office until his successor was chosen at a leadership convention. During the second week of January 1968, Eric Kierans, Paul Hellyer, Allan MacEachen, and John Turner entered the leadership race. The following week Mitchell Sharp, Joe Greene, and Paul Martin also tossed their hats in the ring. At this juncture Paul Martin was the front runner, backed by most of the Quebec caucus as well as Quebec Premier Jean Lesage.

A month later, on 16 February, Pierre Trudeau announced he would run for the leadership. Buoyed by a massive ground swell of support, Trudeau immediately became the odds-on favourite.

However, by this time Maurice had already declared himself for Paul Martin. Jeanne, Sonny Gordon, and Claude Frenette all pleaded, without success, to get him to shift his allegiance to Trudeau. Or even to Mitchell Sharp, because Sharp would be knocked out early in the contest and his delegates were slated to go to Trudeau. But Maurice refused to budge, because he didn't think a French prime minister would be able to make the tough decisions needed to handle Quebec, and he had twice told Trudeau that he shouldn't run for the leadership. Martin, a Franco-Ontarian, who was fluently bilingual and an old pro at politics, was in Maurice's opinion the best man to lead the party. (Cynics said that Maurice's reason for backing Martin was that, if Martin won, he would get a senior cabinet post, and probably end up as Quebec lieutenant.)

Martin's backers defected in droves after the entry of Trudeau and Robert Winters. Three days before the April leadership convention, Maurice knew that Martin didn't stand a chance. As an eleventh-hour convert he went to Trudeau's campaign manager, Marc Lalonde, and, after pocketing two Trudeau buttons, asked Lalonde to tell Trudeau that he was going to support him when Martin dropped out. Martin was eliminated on the first ballot, and Maurice, with Jeanne in tow, made a bee-line for Trudeau's box. When Maurice arrived, he pulled out his button and said, "Pierre, pin it on me!" Trudeau barely acknowledged his presence, nor was room made for him in the front row. In the eyes of the Trudeau camp, Maurice's move was an empty gesture. He had committed political heresy by backing Martin, and he was now an outcast.

This became obvious when Trudeau called a general election for 25 June. Maurice assumed, in view of the agreement, that he would be running in Outremont, as there was no Jewish candidate, and Trudeau had again been nominated in Mount Royal. However, he was told by Marchand that Outremont was no longer available because the temporary incumbent, Aurelien Noël, had decided to run again.

This was an unexpected blow. Shifting his sights from Outremont, Maurice accepted an invitation to try for the nomination in Gamelin, a constituency in the east end of Montreal. Busy with a rural-development project in the Gaspé, he made a half-hearted attempt to get the nomination but lost out to Arthur Portelance, an underwear salesman. Throughly disenchanted, Maurice decided to quit politics.

At a meeting outside St. Viateur church after the funeral of André Laurendeau, Pierre Trudeau and Jean Marchand made Maurice a proposition. (In the political world, especially in Quebec, funerals are considered useful occasions to do business.) The Liberals needed a new candidate in St. Hyacinthe to challenge Théogène Ricard, the popular Tory incumbent who had represented the riding since 1957. If Maurice would run in St. Hyacinthe, and was defeated, they would see that a safe seat would be opened for him after the election. Remembering the Outremont agreement, Maurice was understandably sceptical, and declined their proposal. Some days later, after persistent telephone calls from Marchand, he changed his mind and accepted their offer. With only two weeks left in the campaign, Maurice entered the race in St. Hyacinthe. On the afternoon before polling day, Trudeau dropped in by helicopter to address Maurice's final rally at the Royal 22nd Regiment's armoury in St. Hyacinthe. The main benefactor of this brief visit was Maurice's nine-year-old son, Jean-François, who was given an exciting ride in the Prime Minister's helicopter.

Maurice lost the election by a scant 788 votes. He would have won had it not been for a massive turnout of the clergy, who voted against the Liberals because of the Omnibus Bill. Ironically, this Bill, which legalized abortion and permitted homosexuality between consenting adults, had been introduced to the House of Commons a few months earlier by the Minister of Justice, Pierre Trudeau.

Quebec's two leading French papers, La Presse and Le Devoir, both ran complimentary articles on Maurice's career and lamented his disappearance from the federal scene. For his part, Maurice was comforted by the assurance that another seat would be opened for him in the near future.

After the election Maurice met with Trudeau, who suggested that he consider becoming Canada's ambassador to France. Maurice gave the matter serious thought, and then arranged another appointment to see Trudeau in Ottawa. At this meeting Jean Marchand, to Maurice's intense irritation, was also present. After exchanging pleasantries with Trudeau, Maurice said, "I've decided to stay in politics and I'd like that seat you said you'd open up for me." There was a long silence before Marchand replied blandly, "We never told you *when* we'd open up a seat." Barely able to control his temper, Maurice suggested that, if it was going to be a long wait, he could be appointed to the Senate until a seat became available. Trudeau rejected this proposal on the basis that he didn't want to begin his mandate by making patronage appointments. (In fact, during the next few weeks a raft of defeated candidates and party hacks were appointed to the Senate.) With his options dwindling, Maurice brought up the Paris offer. Trudeau said he'd changed his mind, because Maurice was unsuitable for the post because of his strong Quebec bias. However, he would agree to give Maurice a permanent rather than a temporary appointment to the Senate or to make him ambassador to Italy. At this point Maurice lost his temper and terminated the meeting with these words: "Pierre, j'ai mon voyage!" (I've had it!).

Maurice left Trudeau's office with his pride intact, but with a feeling of bitterness that lingered for months. Jeanne, when she heard the story of the denouement, also felt that he'd been treated shabbily. Both agreed, however, that the parting had been inevitable, and it was now time for Maurice to seek another career.

From Trudeau's point of view, had Maurice been brought back into the House he could have been a divisive force within the party. Maurice had opposed Trudeau's leadership, he was barely on speaking terms with Marchand, Trudeau's Quebec lieutenant, and he had always been a political maverick. For these reasons it's not surprising that Trudeau blocked Maurice's re-entry into politics. Trudeau was ruthless, but he did offer Maurice the choice of an ambassadorship or a seat in the Senate — by Trudeau's standards, reasonable compensation.

That summer Maurice received job offers from a number of Canadian corporations. After weighing his alternatives he accepted a position as vice-president of administration with Consolidated-Bathurst, a large Canadian pulp-and-paper company. When a cabinet colleague told Mike Pearson of Maurice's new position, Pearson quipped, "He'll either be fired within the year, or end up as president!" Neither happened. Maurice stayed with Consolidated-Bathurst for thirteen years, and retired at the end of 1981 with a handsome pension.

During this period his main political concern was national unity. In this connection, from June 1978 until May 1980 he was president of the Quebec-Canada Unity Group, the largest and most influential association in the province to support the "NO" faction in the Quebec Referendum.

Maurice, who is now in his early sixties, is still active in business as a consultant, and he is a director of ten major companies.

Chapter 6

JEANNE: A PUBLIC PERSONALITY
1952–72

When the Sauvés returned from France in 1952, Jeanne gave little thought to her career until she and Maurice were settled in St. Hyacinthe. Being both a reformer and a devoted wife, she wanted to help Maurice with his union activities as well as have time to look after their home. This ruled out a nine-to-five job. Her most outstanding qualifications were her speaking and writing skills. She was also well organized, she got along with people, and she enjoyed communicating with an audience. After careful consideration, she decided to try free-lance broadcasting.

With this in mind she took the bus to Montreal and registered for work at Radio-Canada. Her name was added to the talent pool and she was told, "Don't call us, we'll call you." A few weeks later she was phoned by a Radio-Canada producer who offered her a trial assignment on "Fémina", a public affairs program for women. Her role was to explain in simple terms recent developments in the news. When she arrived at the studio she learned that, owing to the serious nature of the program, to entice women to listen to it the show would begin with an eight-minute cooking lesson. This patronizing format had an unexpected consequence. She had planned to broadcast under her maiden name, Jeanne Benoit, knowing that Maurice would go into politics, but by coincidence the person giving the cooking lesson that day happened to be Madame Jehane Benoit.

As a result, she had no alternative but to go on the air as Jeanne Sauvé, the name she used throughout her career.

Following her successful debut on "Fémina", Jeanne was given a regular slot on the show, which in turn led to a long relationship with Radio-Canada. Even more important, her radio work opened the door to television — her ultimate goal.

Television had just been introduced to Canada by the Canadian Broadcasting Corporation. The public was so entranced with the new medium that people who owned television sets (and many went into hock to buy them) slavishly watched everything that was shown on the tube. During the fifties, the golden age of television, the CBC was a creative mecca that attracted the best talent in the country. Because television was new, there were no guidelines to follow; everything was improvised. This element of spontaneity applied not only to the producers and directors but also to the performers, as all the shows were "live" productions. A further attraction of the CBC was that it had a Canadian monopoly; hence its programs were watched by one hundred per cent of the viewing audience.

In December 1952 Jeanne received a call from a producer on the CBC French TV network, Yvette Pard, who said she was looking for someone who could inform women about summer camps. Jeanne replied, "You couldn't be talking to a better person — I wrote the Quebec directory on summer camps." She was given the assignment, which went off without a hitch. Jeanne did a number of other television shows for the same producer, and she was so enchanted with the medium that Maurice used to tease her by saying that she would pay the CBC to let her appear before the cameras. One day she was asked if she would like to do a sewing show in which she would demonstrate how to make a pair of boy's short pants. Her desire to be on television got the better of her judgement, and she agreed to do it. Unfortunately for Jeanne, although she was proficient at sewing by hand, she had no mechanical aptitude. While the cameras were rolling she encountered a problem with the sewing machine, which flustered her, and the show turned into a disaster. After that fiasco, she was a great deal more selective in her assignments.

Early in her television career Jeanne spotted a women's program that she desperately wanted to do, and that she thought would be ideal for her. To look her best for the audition she made a stylish new dress. The audition went flawlessly, but to her chagrin she was turned down by the producer. The reason he gave was that the black-and-white camera "washed out" her blue-green eyes. This problem was eliminated when the camera lenses were improved. Then, later on when her hair went prematurely white, the cameras created a "flare" or halo around her head. (This fetching effect disappeared, and the colour of her eyes became an asset with the advent of colour television.)

As her career developed, Jeanne kept encountering colleagues from her JEC days. During the fifties, discussion programs were very popular on the French network. She often appeared as one of the four high-powered guests on "Les Idées en Marche", a discussion show hosted by her old friend Gérard Pelletier. Another frequent guest was Pierre Trudeau, who at that time was typecast as "the official intellectual leftist". Trudeau's presence was appropriate because the subjects selected for discussion by Pelletier (and later by Jeanne, when she hosted the program) had a strong left-wing bias: topics such as "The right to strike in the civil service", "Free university tuition", "NORAD", and "Free medical care". On several occasions Premier Maurice Duplessis, whose policies were a favourite target, attempted to get the program taken off the air. When this failed, he tried to have Pelletier and Jeanne removed from the show. At one point the CBC yielded to Duplessis and asked Jeanne to modify her stance, but she responded with a sharply worded telegram, and stood her ground.

As Secretary of the Canadian Committee for the World Assembly of Youth, Jeanne was also deeply committed to the youth movement. While Maurice was working in Ottawa on the Gordon Commission, she made the rounds of government offices trying to raise money for student travel and student assemblies in Canada.

She believed that travel would broaden the students' horizons, while the assemblies would provide a forum to discuss their problems. In her words, "It would have been marvellous for national unity, and it would have killed rabid nationalism in the Province of Quebec." However, the federal government wouldn't touch the scheme because it smacked of youth regimentation, conjuring up the memory of the Young Fascists and the Hitler Youth movement.

Having been rebuffed by the government, Jeanne hit upon another idea: she would use television to reach young people. Although she had no experience on English television, she went to one of the bright young CBC producers in Ottawa, Michael Hind-Smith, and presented him with a proposal for a discussion show for young people which she would host. As she would also write the script and select the participants, it was a neat package. Hind-Smith, who knew Jeanne by reputation, bought the idea. What impressed him most was Jeanne's empathy with her young guests, and the way she could draw them out. "She was never too solemn; she always had a twinkle in her eye and a gay sense of humour." Only once did she lose her sense of humour. This happened just as her program was going on the air. On live TV a floor director normally does a count-down and, when zero is reached, points a finger at the performer to indicate the cameras are rolling. On this occasion the floor director, Pierre Bourgault, whipped out a banana and pointed it at Jeanne. She was momentarily flummoxed, but managed her opening lines. After the show, she gave Bourgault a dressing down and threatened to have him removed from the program if he ever tried a stunt like that again. (Bourgault later left the CBC for politics and was elected president of the Rassemblement pour l'indépendence nationale, a separatist organization that merged with the Parti Québécois in 1968.)

Jeanne's weekly half-hour show in Ottawa was produced at the Lanark Avenue studio, for local broadcast. Initially it was only going to be aired for four weeks, but it was so successful that its run was extended to three months.

Encouraged by her reception on English television she went to

Montreal and proposed a similar show to Fernand Doré, the Director of Youth Programming on the French network. As her idea — a discussion program for teenagers — had never been tried on French television before, Doré was somewhat wary but agreed to air it on a trial basis in the Montreal area for one month. The program, called "Opinions", was such a hit that it was soon beamed over the entire French network.

"Opinions" was entirely Jeanne's creation. She chose the topics, researched and wrote all the material, and selected the participants. As hostess of the show she would introduce the topic to her four student guests and deftly guide the discussion. A further attraction was the presence on stage of a psychiatrist, Dr. Denis Lazure, who would interpret the responses of the boys and girls. The topics included such taboo subjects as teenage sex, parental authority, premarital relations, and student discipline. Because of the sensitive nature of many of the programs, Jeanne took care to select articulate and clean-cut young people for the show. To do this she regularly toured colleges, schools, and convents where she interviewed scores of students. These visits gave her an extraordinary insight into the concerns of the younger generation.

Jeanne's empathy with young people was a major reason that Fernand Doré, her director, kept accepting her presentations. Recollecting her show, Doré said, "She projected a responsible, intelligent image, and she expressed herself well, in a mellow voice which carried authority but was pleasant to the ear. She was also nice to look at — sexy, but in a ladylike way".

Because she understood teenage problems, Jeanne had a close rapport with her guests. On stage, she took delight in drawing a shy student out with a disarmingly simple question. The element of surprise, combined with the candid replies she provoked, added much to the program's appeal. Although "Opinions" was aimed at a young audience, CBC surveys revealed that many adults watched it too. Some of the more controversial programs caused the CBC switchboard to light up with calls from irate parents, but most of the adult fan mail was complimentary. Indeed, "Opinions" was so popular that it went on for seven years, from 1956 to 1963, and it was the show that made Jeanne famous. Looking back on those days, she recently remarked, "The show was fun, it was never work. I left it on my own volition because I was tired of doing it — I was crazy, the money I made was incredible!"

While Jeanne was becoming a household name in the province of Quebec, she was also gaining fame in English Canada. Broadcaster and columnist Charles Lynch, who was on a television series with her in 1956 celebrating the completion of the national network, considered her an exceptional performer. In his words, "She had two things: she had the intense curiosity of the journalist, but she also had a genteel quality — class. There weren't many people then, and there aren't many people now, with that quality. I was enormously taken with her."

By 1956, not only was she busy as a commentator, interviewer, and moderator on French and English television, but she also was active on radio in both languages. Increasingly she was drawn to politics and public affairs — two subjects that in broadcasting were traditionally a male preserve. At that time conventional wisdom decreed that a woman commenting on either of these topics wouldn't be taken seriously. Jeanne was one of the first women in Canada to destroy this myth. Starting in 1956 she became a regular contributor to "Trans-Canada Matinée", a CBC English-network radio program on public affairs and political commentary. This assignment, which paid forty dollars per broadcast, lasted until 1964. During this period she was on "Trans-Canada Matinée" as frequently as twice a week. She also did a similar program in French on radio station CKAC in Montreal. Her first heavy-weight public affairs programs on English and French television were guest appearances on "Viewpoint" and "Les Idées en Marche". In addition to her work on television and radio, she began writing editorials for French and English newspapers such as *La Presse* and the *Montreal Star*. By 1959 Jeanne was a full-fledged media celebrity, known from coast to coast.

In 1959 she was also pregnant, for the third time. Because her two previous pregnancies, in 1949 and 1954, had ended in miscarriages, her family and friends were very concerned that she would lose this baby as well. Jeanne, who wasn't obsessed with having a child, made a conscious effort not to worry, knowing that if she did it could easily precipitate another miscarriage. To everyone's relief, she had a routine pregnancy that went full term. Her baby, a healthy boy, was born on 30 July 1959. Although she was thirty-seven, she chose to have him by natural childbirth, using controlled breathing instead of anaesthetics. For Jeanne it was a "marvellous and satisfying experience — and at my age I thought it was quite a feat." Maurice, who wasn't allowed in the delivery room, saw his son shortly after he was born. "He was all grey and greasy, but he was beautiful!"

They christened their son Jean-François, knowing that when he got older his friends would probably nickname him "J-F". From the moment he was born, Jean-François was the apple of their eye. In Jeanne's words, having a child "was just extraordinary, it opens up the span of your emotions, it's a different love. You do lots for them, but they do lots for you."

When Jean-François was born, Maurice was working for the Quebec Liberal party, and the Sauvés were living in a rented duplex on rue Michel Bibaub, just below St. Joseph's Oratory. Although they had a full-time housekeeper, in preparation for the baby they had also engaged a nurse. While Jeanne was in hospital she had been exhilarated by the experience, but two weeks after she got home she suffered a severe bout of post-partum depression. To add to her unhappiness she found herself in conflict with the nurse, who insisted on looking after the baby exclusively. This made Jeanne, who wanted to learn how to care for her son, feel inadequate. The situation in the nursery eventually deteriorated into a battle of wits. It was resolved when the nurse was fired. From then on, Jeanne looked after Jean-François herself.

Three months after her son was born, she resumed free-lancing on a limited basis. Even then, most of her time was spent at home working on scripts and editorials. Jean-François was never out of her sight; when she was writing at her desk, he would be in his crib by her side. Her devotion — and her priorities — were put to the test in November 1959 when she got an offer from a CBC producer to host a one-hour television special on the English network. To do the show she would have to travel across the country to interview a number of prominent Canadian intellectuals. This, of course, meant that she would have to leave Jean-François. She was sorely tempted by the offer, and knew that passing it up might jeopardize her career, but she decided to turn it down. Expecting the producer to understand, she said to him, "I'm sorry, I can't accept it, I'm nursing." The producer, who was dumbfounded, retorted, "Are you crazy? Just give the kid a bottle!"

Jeanne needn't have worried. In addition to her weekly "Opinions" program, she had a new radio show, "Jeu de Dame", on CKAC in Montreal, and she was also writing editorials. The following spring, in May 1960, she received another tempting offer: the post of editor of the newly established *Châtelaine — La Revue Moderne*, the French edition of *Chatelaine* magazine. Lloyd Hodgkinson, the publisher of *Chatelaine*, and Doris Anderson, its managing editor, twice travelled from Toronto to Montreal to try and persuade Jeanne to take the job. She considered it seriously, but declined because Jean-François was only ten months old. Once again it was a question of priorities. Motherhood came first.

A month later, in June 1960, "Opinions" celebrated its one-hundredth program with a special retrospective show. In an interview marking the occasion Jeanne was asked, "Are our young people happy?" She replied, "An adolescent is never very happy because of the problems of adapting to life. Posing questions does not in itself make them unhappy, but it is the anguish and anxiety that lies behind these questions that can make them unhappy. However, they are happier than the previous generation; their parents understand them better."

For a number of years Jeanne and Maurice attended the annual Couchiching Conference at Geneva Park on Lake Couchiching. This conference, sponsored by the Canadian Institute on Public Affairs, was a forum for critical discussion on national and international issues. Maurice was an active participant and often a panelist, while Jeanne usually covered the proceedings as a journalist. However, at the winter conference in February 1961, she was chosen to head one of the panels—the only woman among nine discussion leaders. The *Globe and Mail* recognized this achievement by publishing a feature article on her. When asked by the *Globe* how women in Quebec differed from those in English Canada, Jeanne responded, "Differences between French- and Anglo-Canadian women are merely a matter of cultural and social habit. We have the same ideals." Then, as an afterthought, she added, "I do think, though, that we are more feminine, perhaps more withdrawn, than U.S. women."

In May 1961, Jeanne attracted less welcome publicity as a result of questions raised at the hearings of the Commons Broadcasting Committee. Traditionally these hearings are a bear-baiting exercise, with the bear being the president of the CBC. One may judge the tenor of the proceedings, and the cultural sophistication of some of the participants, by noting that Jack Horner, Conservative member for the Alberta riding of Acadia, castigated the CBC for using an American announcer at the Calgary Stampede. Warming to the subject of imported talent, Mr. Horner went on to dismiss the Irish playwright Brendan Behan as "just another crackpot".

Jeanne was singled out for criticism by Jean-Noël Tremblay, the Tory member for Roberval, a man with a fine classical education and a mercurial temperament. Tremblay objected to Jeanne's being employed by the CBC for two reasons: she was the wife of a prominent Liberal organizer in Quebec, and she had allowed René Lévesque to appear on "Opinions". These activities, he said, were "a danger", without specifying to whom. Alphonse Ouimet, the president of the CBC, acknowledged that Lévesque had taken advantage of his appearance on "Opinions" to make a political speech, but defended Jeanne by pointing out that she had been a free-lance broadcaster long before her husband had entered politics, and, in any case, guest performers were the responsibility of the producer.

When Tremblay criticized Jeanne in the Commons Broadcasting Committee the matter had already been righted by the appearance on "Opinions" of Jean-Jacques Bertrand, a former Union Nationale minister. Nevertheless, it was front-page news in both the French and the English press, and it brought into question Jeanne's objectivity as a political commentator. The irony in this story is that, sixteen years later, after Jean-Noël Tremblay had left politics and Jeanne was a Liberal cabinet minister, he joined her staff as a speechwriter. Today they are good friends, and he is still writing speeches for her as Cultural Attaché at Government House.

Jeanne feared that her career would suffer from the Lévesque incident, but a few weeks later she received a plum from the CBC, an assignment to interview the former leaders of the three national political parties for a television special on the program "Inquiry". She was chosen for the job by the show's producer, Patrick Watson, who had watched her on English and French television and thought she was "dazzling". In Watson's words, "As an interviewer, she asked questions that had a line and a direction. She had a marvellous sense of humour, and could be quite twinkly and deft in getting a tough question in. She's wasn't beautiful in a conventional way, she had pouchy cheeks like a chipmunk, but I thought she was stunning. The outstanding thing was her presence. To me she had that quality that any star has, whether it's Barbra Streisand or Alec Guinness — when she was on the screen you had to watch her."

The first interview of the series was done with M. J. Coldwell, the former leader of the Co-Operative Commonwealth Federation (CCF), the forerunner of the New Democratic Party. The interview was filmed at his apartment in Ottawa, and Jeanne enjoyed it immensely, finding Mr. Coldwell "charming and sincere". The next interview, with George Drew, the former leader of the Progressive Conservatives, was postponed and subsequently cancelled because of Drew's failing health.

The key interview, and the most difficult one, was with former Liberal Prime Minister Louis St. Laurent. It was filmed in July at his summer residence at St. Patrice on the south shore of the St. Lawrence. Annoyed that his holiday was being interrupted, St.

Laurent refused to allow the CBC crew in the house and insisted that all the filming be done in the lower garden near the stables. During the course of three mornings, Jeanne recorded a total of seven and a half hours of conversation with him. At the outset he was very brusque, but after he realized that she was well prepared, he gradually thawed into the patriarchal character that had earned him the nickname "Uncle Louis". For Jeanne, though, "it was a struggle all the way."

Maurice accompanied Jeanne to St. Patrice for that week. When the crew wasn't filming, the Sauvés toured the countryside with Patrick Watson in Maurice's new Peugeot. Watson, who had recently had his left leg amputated and was on crutches, was touched by their concern for him. As an example of their kindness, Maurice persuaded him to drive the Peugeot, which had an electric hand-operated clutch. It was the first time Watson had driven a car since he lost his leg, and the experience was a great boost for his morale.

That September, while he was in Montreal being fitted for an artificial leg, Watson stayed with the Sauvés for two weeks. Having lived in rented quarters since they were married, they had bought a large brick house on McDougall Avenue in Outremont the previous June. At that time it was modestly furnished, but over the years Jeanne and Maurice have transformed it into a showplace of Quebec pine furniture, exquisite old silver, and fine Canadian art. What struck Patrick Watson when he crossed the threshold was the welcoming atmosphere of the house. Rather than being treated as a guest, he was made to feel one of the family — a family whose attention was focussed on the youngest member, two-year-old Jean-François. When Jean-François cried, Jeanne would cuddle him and murmur endearments such as "Mon petit trésor d'amour", whereas Maurice would deal with his son on a man-to-man basis, sitting him on his knee and saying, "Eh bien, mon ami, pourquoi tu t'agites?"

The house on McDougall, which the Sauvés still own, was built in the twenties. One of a row of upper-middle-class dwellings on a quiet side street, it is Maurice's castle. Although it is undistinguished from the outside, its spacious and elegant rooms are ideal for entertaining — one of Jeanne's greatest pleasures. It was here that she began a tradition of informal get-togethers where friends could drop in for a drink and good conversation. These "salons" invariably attracted a mixed bag of French and English friends from the media, the professions, politics, and the business world. Remarking on Jeanne's hospitality, an old friend recently observed, "She'll give a dinner party at the drop of a hat, and she's the best hostess I've ever known." Her favourite number for a dinner party is eight, even though the long refectory table in her dining room can seat more than a dozen. When Maurice was in politics, she would sometimes entertain for two — and not be present at the table. Patrick Watson remembers Mike Pearson coming to have lunch *à deux* with Maurice. For this important occasion Jeanne cooked one of her specialties, steak *flambé*: filet mignon in a delicate butter sauce, set alight with brandy and sprinkled with freshly ground pepper. While Maurice and the leader of the Liberal party discussed politics over their steak *flambé* in the dining-room, Jeanne and her house guest enjoyed the same meal in the kitchen.

The St. Laurent interview was broadcast on the national network in October of 1961 and drew mixed reviews. *Time* magazine said, "Unfortunately, in the 30-minute sample chosen for *Inquiry*, interviewer Jeanne Sauvé probed little deeper than if she were inquiring the time. Even so, *Inquiry* provided a rare glimpse of St. Laurent as Canadians remember him — a courtly, patrician, eminently discreet gentleman who still seems faintly surprised that he ever entered politics at all."

Jeanne, who did all the biographical research, as well as the interviews, was paid approximately ten thousand dollars for the series on the leaders — a hefty sum in those days. In addition, she established a precedent by negotiating a residual-rights clause in her contract, which meant that she would be paid each time excerpts were shown. Maurice used to chide her for being too soft in her business dealings, but the insertion of the residual clause shows that she was a shrewd negotiator.

Jeanne's ability at the bargaining table was recognized in 1961 when she was elected to the board of the Union des artistes. This union represented most of the performers on the CBC French network, as well as many other artists who worked in the theatre and on commercials. The union played a vital role in their lives because it negotiated minimum rates of pay and working terms with their employers.

When Maurice emerged from the political back rooms to run for Parliament in the spring of 1962, Jeanne rescheduled her broadcasting activities so that she could be with him. Up to this point, she had rarely been away from two-year-old Jean-François, and quite often she even brought him to the studio with her. Leaving him for more than a week was hard for her, but while she was in the Magdalen Islands he was perfectly happy in the capable hands of Madame Lambert, the Sauvés' long-time housekeeper. Although she missed her son, as soon as she arrived in the Magdalens Jeanne was swept up in the excitement of the election. Pitching into the campaign with gusto, she toured the constituency speaking to women voters, she helped with the organization and strategy, and she fed Maurice and the members of his team at the end of each long day. When the election results were announced, it was a toss-up as to who was more pleased with the victory, Jeanne or Maurice. In this connection, friends who have known the Sauvés for years unanimously agree that not only are they an extraordinarily close couple, but they are also each other's greatest fans.

After Maurice's election to the House of Commons, he and Jeanne often shared the same podium speaking on behalf of Canadian unity. At a public meeting in Toronto in January 1964, sponsored by the Committee for Canada (whose patrons included Claude Bissell, the president of the University of Toronto, and Murray Ross, the president of York University), Maurice warned his audience that Quebec's separatist movement would soon be too big to stop unless action was taken immediately. Jeanne told her listeners that there was also a danger that the young French Canadians awaiting trial for the death of a night watchman in a bomb explosion could become martyrs. She had heard that students at the University of Montreal were planning a sympathy demonstration for the accused terrorists, and said, "I hate to think what would happen if this wave of sympathy rose so that it would be difficult to distinguish between what was actually done, and the way in which the young men were treated."

A month later Jeanne was back in Toronto to address the Junior Board of Trade at its annual Ladies' Night dinner. One of the points she made in her speech was that she knew Canadians were fed up with the endless talk about biculturalism, but biculturalism must be supported as long as there was separatism in Quebec. "If you start discussing in terms of two nations, then there will be two nations."

Following this engagement she returned to Montreal, but barely had time to unpack before she was off again on a speaking tour of western Canada. On this trip she was one of a three-member panel that discussed the question "Quebec — Revolution or Renaissance?" before audiences in major western cities. The other two panelists were Claude Ryan, editor-in-chief of *Le Devoir*, and Guy Beaugrand-Champagne, consultant to the Quebec Ministry of Youth. Sponsored by the Canadian Association for Adult Education, the purpose of the panel was to promote understanding between westerners and the people of Quebec. The trio received a surprisingly warm reception from large audiences in Regina, Winnipeg, Edmonton, Calgary, and Vancouver. Their success was partly due to the fact that, while their topic was a serious one, they often used humour to get their message across. In Edmonton, for instance, the panel agreed that Canadians should never be forced to become bilingual. Pursuing this conclusion with tongue in cheek, Jeanne observed that there was even some concern in Quebec that too many English-speaking Canadians might learn French, adding, "If they do, we'll never get a job on the basis that we're bilingual!"

At the conclusion of the tour she flew back to Montreal, and then went on to Ottawa for the opening of Parliament. The opening was an auspicious event for the Sauvés because Maurice had just been appointed minister of forestry. As a result of his entry into the cabinet, which meant that he would have to spend more time in the capital, Maurice rented a stone house on King Edward Avenue and moved his family to Ottawa. Not only did this change their life-style (previously he had lived in bachelor quarters and gone home to Montreal on the weekends), but Maurice's new status as a cabinet minister spelled trouble for Jeanne's broadcasting career.

At that time she had two weekly programs on the French CBC television network and she was also wrapping up a thirteen-part television serial on women in the work-force. With these assign-ments in hand, and a number of new proposals to consider, she was at the peak of her career. Asked by the *Ottawa Journal* about her role as wife of a cabinet minister, Jeanne said, ''Women must fight the notion that all they have to do is sit at home and look pretty. I work — and I hope to continue. I think that it's important that women get out and do things.''

Her view was not shared by Louis-Joseph Pigeon, the Conserva-tive member for Joliette-L'Assomption-Montcalm. In early June 1964, three months before Maurice cut the ground from under him, Pigeon denounced Jeanne in the House of Commons. Possibly owing to the lateness of the hour, his speech was a rambling and repetitious diatribe. The following excerpts from Hansard indicate the gist of Pigeon's complaints:

> "Mr. Speaker, the wife of the Minister of Forestry (Mr. Sauvé) is the moderator of many programs of opinion for the C.B.C. I cannot do otherwise than denounce this family compact. The Minister of Forestry has emoluments of $35,000 a year and his wife receives from the C.B.C. approximately $15,000 a year. Moreover, she is a member of the Na-tional Centennial Commission."

> "Mr. Speaker, the wife of the Minister of Forestry embarrasses the employees of the C.B.C. and her presence in that corporation represents another type of blackmail for the authorities of the C.B.C., who do not dare dismiss her. In fact, what would happen if the head of the service

concerned would dare dismiss the wife of a minister of the crown? The C.B.C. is wrongly considered as a den or the Mecca of the Liberal party on account of the wife of the Minister of Foresty."

"Mr. Speaker, Caesar's wife must be beyond reproach . . . Caesar's wife should not be open to suspicion, even if these suspicions amount to $15,000 to $20,000 per year collected from the C.B.C. while her husband, Caesar Sauvé, gets $35,000 a year as minister of the crown."

J. B. Stewart, Parliamentary Secretary to the Secretary of State, responded, noting that while it was difficult to identify Pigeon's question, it had originally concerned the propriety of Jeanne's appointment to the Centennial Commission. Stewart explained that the commission was made up of sixty people, representing a cross-section of Canadians, each of whom had made a contribution to the country. The members of the commission were paid nothing except a daily expense allowance when they attended meetings. He concluded:

"Madame Sauvé was appointed to the conference on October 15, 1963. She had participated actively in numerous regional and national organizations. She had been active in radio, television, and other forms of communications. She has a good knowledge of Canadian public affairs and, Mr. Speaker, she is bilingual."

Following Pigeon's accusations in the House, Jeanne told an interviewer from the Canadian Press, "I gave up making political commentaries two years ago when my husband was first elected to Parliament. However, there is no reason why I can't continue broadcasting and express an opinion on other subjects. After all, a wife is still free as an individual to hold an opinion, is she not?"

Jeanne's defiant attitude drew howls of rage from a few radical journals in Quebec. One of these, *La Frontière*, published a scurrilous article in July titled "Jeanne Sauvé Clings to Radio-Canada". Citing Louis-Joseph Pigeon's speech as gospel, this editorial decried the "scandal" at the CBC, and demanded that she cease working for the Crown corporation. Jeanne ignored these pot-shots, but Pigeon's attack in Parliament caused a temporary setback to her career. "When you got a critique like that and you were a free-lancer, they'd forget your number for a month."

Frustrated by the political strait-jacket she was in, she seriously considered leaving the airwaves for a career in journalism. At the height of the furor she was offered a position as one of the three senior editors at *La Presse*. She would have taken the job, but at the last minute the offer fell through because it was feared that the paper's militant union would rebel at an outsider's being brought in.

In that same year, 1964, Jeanne became the first woman to be elected president of l'Institut canadien des affaires publiques, the French equivalent of the Couchiching Canadian Institute on Public Affairs. The principal difference between these two prestigious institutes, aside from language, was the ambience of their conferences. The Couchiching conferences were held in Spartan surroundings where members shared communal bathrooms and the food was distinguished chiefly for its blandness. The French institute, on the other hand, convened at a plush resort in the Laurentians where members enjoyed luxury accommodations, gourmet food, and vintage wines. For this reason, the members of l'Institut canadien des affaires publiques used to taunt their English colleagues, telling them they didn't have to be uncomfortable to discuss national and international issues.

In 1966, Jeanne was elected general secretary to the Fédération des auteurs et des artistes du Canada. This union, composed of French-speaking authors and artists, was formed to deal with local problems and to work in concert with ACTRA, the Alliance of Canadian Cinema, Television and Radio Artists. Jeanne, who was the general secretary and main spark-plug of the union for six years, was concerned not only with the welfare of its members but also with the standard of the industry. Writing in the ACTRA magazine in 1967, she acknowledged that television had gone through its pioneering stage with flying colours, but then went on to say:

Fifteen years later, Canadian TV seems to be unable to catch its second wind. The infatuation of the public has relapsed not only because the novelty

of the medium has worn off, but because the public are genuinely disappoint-
ed that television is not offering a sufficient quality of entertainment....

In the field of information where I have always had a great interest, I
feel that television, i.e., the C.B.C. — because only C.B.C. has made a
significant contribution in this respect — has not yet been able to decide
how to treat news and information. The news is still a newspaper that is
read to you by a nice voice and an acceptable picture. Its on-the-spot
reporting is still very poor. Its coverage falls short of what TV should do:
allow the public to see the events as they occur so they can make their
own interpretation of the facts and not have to rely on someone else's
reporting. The news is still a cheap show. More money should be thrown
into it so that it may rise to TV standards.

The summer of 1967 was a milestone for Jean-François, who at
the age of eight showed his independence by going off to Camp
Ahmek. Located on Canoe Lake in Algonquin Park, this camp was
founded by Taylor Statten in 1922 as "a gathering place for boys
and young men who give promise of high attainment". Despite its
excellent reputation and fine facilities, Jeanne and Maurice didn't
want Jean-François to go because they thought he was too young,
and they also worried that he would feel out of place among the
other campers, most of whom were English. (In fact, although it's
a bastion of the Anglo establishment, the camp has always had a
small contingent of French Canadians.) Jean-François, who had been
sold on the idea by a schoolmate, insisted that he be allowed to go.
Reluctantly they agreed, on condition that he must stay the full
four weeks. Expecting him to be dreadfully homesick, at the end of
the second week they made the long drive from Montreal to Algonquin Park to visit him. To their surprise and dismay he didn't appear to be particularly pleased to see them. Driving home that evening
they were so upset by his indifference that Maurice had to stop the
car because he couldn't see through his tears, and Jeanne was also
crying so hard that she couldn't take the wheel. As soon as they got
back to Montreal, Jeanne asked Dr. Denis Lazure (the psychiatrist
who had worked with her on "Opinions") about her son's behaviour

and was told that it was perfectly normal — it was just a case of his being unable to relate to his parents in that environment. Jean-François enjoyed Ahmek so much that he was a camper there for eight years, and worked as a counsellor for a further five years. He made many close friends at Ahmek, and is very much part of the "network" of ex-campers.

In 1968, the year she attended a conference for film and television writers in Moscow, Jeanne was elected vice-president of the Union des artistes. Her greatest achievement for the union was a deal she made with the CBC that guaranteed how much the corporation would spend on production versus administration. As this had never been done before, the CBC was leery of stipulating the amount in a formal contract but agreed to do so in a letter of intent, which is not as binding. In its letter, the CBC made an error that overstated the amount by a million dollars. A week or so later, when Jeanne was flying to Montreal for the funeral of André Laurendeau, she met the head negotiator from the CBC at the Ottawa airport. He said to her, "Jeanne, we need that letter back." Feigning surprise, she replied, "Why do you want it back?" Losing patience, he said, "You know damn well why; we made a mistake!" Jeanne let the corporation stew for a bit but eventually returned the letter. Even with the extra million dollars lopped off, it was still a healthy production commitment.

A few months after this incident, Maurice left politics and the family moved back to Montreal. Jeanne was upset by the machinations that led to his downfall, but relieved that he would no longer be subject to the stress and buffeting of political life. She was also happy that, for the first time in six years, they would no longer have to commute to Ottawa.

The following year Jeanne gained a new perspective on labour/management relations when she was elected to the boards of three broadcasting concerns: radio station CKAC, Telemedia, and Bushnell Communications Limited. As a director of these private-sector companies she found the profit motive stimulating, and she enjoyed formulating policy, but she was bored by administrative details —

Madame Sauvé completing her inspection of the RMC Guard of Honour. (Department of National Defence)

Their Excellencies arriving at Rideau Hall in the state carriage following the investiture. (John Evans)

Front view of Rideau Hall. (M. S. Heney)

An ambassador being escorted to Government House in the covered landau to present his Letters of Credence. (RCMP photo)

Entrance to Rideau Hall. (M. S. Heney)

Her Excellency's study, Rideau Hall. (M. S. Heney)

Dinner invitation to Government House with presentation card.
(M. S. Heney)

Madame Sauvé chatting with the guest of honour, United Nations Secretary
General Pérez de Cuellar, at a state dinner. (Government House)

One of the drawing-rooms on the second floor of the Governor
General's residence at the Citadel. (M. S. Heney)

Entrance to the Governor's Wing, the Citadel, Quebec. (M. S. Heney)

Madame Sauvé, flanked by her sister Berthe and her brother Jean, leaving the Church of Saints Donatien and Rogatien, Prud'homme, October 1984. (Saskatchewan Protocol Offic

Madame Sauvé with the dancers who performed for her at the Silver Age Hall, Prud'homme, October 1984. (Saskatchewan Protocol Office)

Their Excellencies with Prime Minister Mulroney at Rideau Hall. Portrait of General Vanier in background. (Canadian Government Photo Centre)

Madame Sauvé escorting the Pope to her study. Behind them is Jean-François Sauvé. Rideau Hall, September 1984. (Government House)

The Queen after being greeted at the
Fredericton airport by the Governor
General, September 1984. (Department
of the Secretary of State)

Her Majesty leaving Rideau Hall,
September 1984. (Government House)

particularly the endless hours spent going over the securities prospectus for Bushnell Communications. She remained an active director in all three companies until 1972, when she went into politics.

The autumn of 1970 was marked by terrorist violence in the province of Quebec. On 5 October, FLQ (Front de la Libération du Québec) terrorists kidnapped James Cross, the senior British Trade Commissioner, from his Redpath Avenue house in Montreal. After abducting Cross, the FLQ demanded five hundred thousand dollars in gold bullion, the release of twenty-three political prisoners, and the national airing of its manifesto. The "political prisoners" included five people awaiting trial on manslaughter charges, three convicted murderers, a man serving a life sentence for bombings, and a man convicted of seventeen armed robberies. The prisoners weren't released, but on 8 October the CBC broadcast the FLQ manifesto on the national television network. Two days later the FLQ kidnapped Pierre Laporte, the Quebec Minister of Labour and Immigration, while he was throwing a football with his son on their lawn. As soon as Laporte was abducted, the situation suddenly became deadly serious. Premier Bourassa and his key ministers moved into a heavily guarded suite in the Queen Elizabeth hotel. Anarchy was in the air, and rumours were rife that the provincial government would be usurped by a separatist junta.

On the night of 12 October, Jeanne participated in a CBC television special hosted by Norman DePoe. This one-hour program, titled "Kidnapping", consisted of a live hook-up with correspondents in Ottawa, Montreal, and Toronto. Among those interviewed were Pierre Trudeau, Robert Stanfield, Réal Caouette, and Robert Lemieux, the lawyer for the FLQ. Jeanne, as a free-lancer, provided political commentary from the CBC studios in Montreal. Immediately after the show, which was watched by a huge audience, she was driven to New York by one of Maurice's former campaign workers. She napped for most of the journey and arrived at five-thirty the next morning. After checking into a hotel for a quick shower and a change of clothes, she then took a cab to the CBS studio, where she appeared on the "Morning Show". Interviewed by Barbara Walters, she gave American viewers a first-hand report on the FLQ crisis. She returned to Montreal the same day.

Jeanne agonized over the FLQ crisis. When it started, most Quebecers had thought it was just a prank by some youngsters to gain attention for the separatist movement, which they viewed with tolerance, and even with sympathy. But with the abduction of Laporte the situation became truly alarming. Jeanne felt she should speak out — and many of her colleagues urged her to do so — but she wasn't clear in her mind what she wanted to say. The kidnapping of Laporte was a personal blow, because the Laporte and the Sauvé families were friends who saw each other often, and had even spent an Easter holiday together in Florida. After much soul-searching, she wrote several editorials on the crisis, including one (which she stayed up most of the night to write) for *Le Monde* in France and another for the *Montreal Star*. In the *Star* article, which was published on 13 October, Jeanne reviewed the startling events of the past week and then said:

> *We are going through this crisis in the only way we know how: with traditional strategy and reasoning. Force calls for force; terrorism must be met with outright courage. In this particular scenario, two men have to play the part of the symbols of the values we want to preserve. It is their lives against our sense of authority and our moral stature. Somewhere the equation is phony. It bears the mark of what might be arrogance. . . .*
>
> *If the government resists the terrorists, will they understand its code? If we apply firmness, are we sure that the message we are trying to convey will reach them? . . .*
>
> *We do not understand the F.L.Q.'s philosophy. They do not accept ours. We are confronted with an organized form of violent protest. More will follow. But we will have no less if the two hostages go to a useless death. The practical view is that such deaths will achieve nothing.*
>
> *Therefore, let us pack these young men off to Cuba or Algeria where they can live out their revolutionary theories and sort them out. . . .*

Prime Minister Trudeau was intensely irritated by this editorial

because of Jeanne's soft approach to the terrorist problem. At a
dinner party months later, Jeanne learned from Paul-André Bis-
sonnette, a senior Ottawa mandarin and mutual friend, that Trudeau had succinctly described her *Star* article as "bullshit".

Two days after it was published, Premier Bourassa asked for military aid from the federal government. Within an hour of his formal
request, a battalion of the famous Royal 22e Régiment moved into
Montreal and took up strategic positions in the city. At dawn the
next morning Prime Minister Trudeau invoked the War Measures
Act, which gave the government sweeping powers to deal with the
turmoil in Quebec. On 18 October, Pierre Laporte's body was found
in the trunk of a parked car on the outskirts of Montreal. Laporte
had been strangled to death. Terrorist violence crested with his murder
and then subsided. Cross was released in December and the terrorists were given safe passage to Cuba.

In 1971, shortly after the FLQ crisis ended, Jeanne was one of a
small group of Canadians who went on a speaking tour of the United
States. The tour was sponsored by an American public affairs body,
and its purpose was to explain what Canada was, and what Quebec
wanted from Confederation. It attracted small audiences, and in
Jeanne's opinion "it didn't accomplish much." One of the participants, former NDP member and journalist Douglas Fisher, remembers
Jeanne well because he often clashed with her in the public discussions.
Being a socialist, he didn't like either of the Sauvés on principle
(assuming erroneously that they had inherited their wealth), but he
admired the strength of their marriage. "At the core of their
relationship was a tremendous amount of affection. When Jeanne
was on the tour with us and she arrived at her hotel, there would
always be flowers in her room from him. Before they started the
day they would always speak on the phone, and there would always
be a call waiting for her at the end of the day."

By the middle of 1972 Jeanne was anxious for a fresh challenge.
For the past twenty years she had been primarily an observer and a
commentator on the passing scene. Now she wanted to take a more
active role in shaping events. Politics seemed the obvious answer.

The first time she had been asked to enter politics was in 1966, when Jean Lesage had made an indirect approach to see whether she would run for the provincial Liberals. Jeanne had asked René Lévesque (who was a minister in Lesage's government) what he thought of the idea and he had said, "You and Maurice had better decide which bed you're going to sleep in, the federal or the provincial." Slightly puzzled, Jeanne replied, "You think there's a conflict?" Lévesque answered, "Oh yes!" His vehement reaction made Jeanne wonder why he was in the Liberal party. "That's when I realized that René Lévesque and I weren't on the same frequency."

In 1970, Lesage's successor, Robert Bourassa, telephoned Maurice at his office in Montreal and asked him whether Jeanne would run in the forthcoming provincial election. Maurice said, "Ask her." When Jeanne found out about the call she was furious ("Can you imagine that guy phoning my husband!"), but she was also tempted to accept the offer. Again she decided against it because she felt her son was too young. It was simply the wrong time.

However, when the federal Liberals approached her in the early autumn of 1972 to run in the riding of Ahuntsic, she didn't take long to make up her mind. Jean-François was now thirteen, she had an excellent housekeeper, and Maurice — who was all for her going into politics — was firmly ensconced with Consolidated-Bathurst. The time was right. She agreed to run for Parliament.

Looking back on his long career as a journalist and television commentator, Charles Lynch said in a recent interview, "René Lévesque and Jeanne Sauvé were the two best broadcasters I have seen in any language." After this pronouncement he took a few puffs on his pipe, blew out the smoke, and then added, "Jeanne's entry into politics was a grave loss to broadcasting."

Chapter 7

THE POLITICAL ARENA
1972-80

Jeanne had her work cut out for her when she ran for election in Ahuntsic in the autumn of 1972. Even though the Liberal party had asked her to be a candidate in the Montreal riding, her first problem was to win the nomination. She squeaked by her opponent, a leading figure in the local Liberal association, by a mere twenty votes. Her next hurdle was to get elected by the public. Ahuntsic was a Liberal stronghold, but after four years of Prime Minister Trudeau's government, the public's honeymoon with the party was over. To add to the challenge, no woman had ever been elected to Parliament from the province of Quebec.

"I felt uneasy for the first time in my life when I was campaigning. I felt people were taking a second look at me and wondering whether a woman was adequate for the job. They were terribly suspicious that I would be sitting in a parliament located in another city. They wondered what would happen to my husband and my son. I must say I had qualms about it myself."

In this and subsequent contests, Jeanne campaigned as though she were the underdog. She needn't have. Because of her personal popularity and her solid reputation as a broadcaster, support poured in from every direction. More than twenty lawyers volunteered to serve on her legal committee, when two at most were required. Financing her campaign was incredibly easy; one of her organizers summed up the fund-raising drive for Jeanne's campaign in these words: "Six phone calls and we had all the money we needed." She was also fortunate to have Roméo Beaupré, one of the shrewdest and most efficient campaign managers in the province. His strategy was to establish a personal bond between Jeanne and the voters. Television was used sparingly, and there were no mass rallies. Instead, she spoke to small gatherings, visited shopping malls, attended coffee parties, and spent endless hours shaking hands with people after church.

This approach paid off. When the ballots were counted on election night, 30 October, Jeanne won by more than fifteen thousand votes. She was one of only three women from the province to be elected to Parliament. On a national basis, the Liberal party dropped forty-six seats to end up with 109, the Progressive Conservatives under Robert Stanfield gained thirty-five to come second with 107, while the NDP rose to 30 and the Social Credit added one for a total of 15. Once again it was a minority Liberal government.

After a party is elected to power, anyone with the slightest hope of being included in the cabinet waits expectantly for a call from the Prime Minister. Many take elaborate precautions to ensure that they can be reached by phone at any hour of the day or night. Jeanne didn't think she had a chance of being included in the new cabinet, and dismissed the idea from her mind. On the day that the calls went out to the new ministers, she spent the early part of the morning on the phone to her campaign manager. Then, because she wanted to write some letters, she took the phone off the hook. While she was attending to her correspondence the Prime Minister's Office tried repeatedly to reach her. Finally, one of Trudeau's staff called Maurice at his office and explained that the Prime Minister urgently wanted to speak to his wife. Maurice bolted out of the building, took a cab home, and told Jeanne. A few minutes later the telephone rang, Pierre Trudeau came on the line, and she was invited to be the new minister of state for science and technology.

Jeanne was the lone woman in Trudeau's cabinet, and the third in Canadian history to be a federal minister (the first being Ellen Fairclough, the second Judy LaMarsh). When she was sworn in as a member of the Privy Council, a lifetime appointment, she and Maurice became the only husband and wife in Canada, and one of very few married couples in the history of the Commonwealth, to be Privy Councillors.

Jeanne's appointment was lauded by both the French and the English press. Soon after it was announced, the *Hamilton Spectator* published an editorial titled "She made it on her merits". Interviewed by the *Toronto Star* after her first cabinet meeting, Jeanne said she hoped she hadn't been appointed as a token woman, adding, "I think it's very important for a woman to be put in the cabinet, because it will bring to women the knowledge that they can aspire to positions of power." Asked if she was referring to women's liberation, Jeanne, who has always believed in equal rights for women but has little sympathy for radical feminists, told the reporter, "I've exercised power so far in my life and I've never sacrificed my femininity. I had to fight to maintain myself in my career and it wasn't easy. But I fought with the proper tools — good preparedness and good performance. They're the tools we must all use."

At the conclusion of this interview she was asked about her political goals. "I've got a general goal in politics," she said, "to keep this country together. It's very important for Quebecers to stay in Confederation. And it's a very deep motivation for me. It's one of the main reasons I ran."

Her ministry, Science and Technology, was a minor department with a small staff and a small budget. Still in its infancy, the ministry had only been established the previous year. Its mandate was to develop a national research policy so that money (more than one billion in 1972) being spent on research would produce the maximum social and economic benefits for Canadians. Co-ordinating a national policy, however, was a ticklish problem, because the ministry had no executive powers and could only act in an advisory capacity. To further complicate matters, government, university, and industrial research fields overlapped each other.

Although Trudeau had been at a loss to explain why he appointed

Jeanne to Science and Technology, she was well suited to the port-folio. The future fascinated her. An avid reader, she once said that reading about what was happening in scientific research was "bet-ter than reading a novel". Added to this, she had a sound knowl-edge of social and technological trends. While she was a broadcaster, she had written, researched, and hosted a twenty-two-part science series for the CBC titled "The 1980s". Prior to her election, as co-founder of the government-sponsored Institute for Research on Public Policy, she had advised the cabinet on future policy. In her words, working with the Institute had given her "a chance to get in touch with research around the world".

Jeanne, a stickler for efficiency, found the first few weeks as head of Science and Technology a nightmare. Like all cabinet ministers she had two offices: one in the Parliament Buildings and the other in her department in the Confederation Building. Initially she couldn't get into her department office because it was still occupied by Alastair Gillespie, the former minister. As a result, she had to run her ministry from cramped quarters in the Parliament Build-ings. Through a bureaucratic mix-up, one night all the telephones in this office were removed and given to a Social Credit member. She eventually moved into a newly renovated office in the Confed-eration Building, but it too lacked telephones. Her only contact with the outside world was by foot messenger — an inauspicious beginning for the minister concerned with communications research.

In Ottawa, Jeanne lived with her widowed sister Berthe on Alta Vista Drive. Whenever she had a free weekend, she went home to Montreal. While she was in the capital, Maurice took over the re-sponsibility of looking after thirteen-year-old Jean-François. This arrangement, which they had agreed upon before the election, worked out well for everyone. Jeanne knew that Jean-François was in good hands, Maurice was happy for the chance to forge a closer bond with his son, and Jean-François established a strong rapport with his father. Reflecting upon his mother's political career, Jean-François could only remember one minor drawback: "When I was around sixteen and wanted to speak to Mom during the day, it was sometimes difficult because I had to go through two or three secretaries.''

The Sauvés spent many of their weekends at their country house on the Richelieu River near the village of St. Charles, a thirty-minute drive east of Montreal. Famous as the site of a *patriote* defeat during the Papineau Rebellion, St. Charles was part of the St. Hyacinthe riding. While he was campaigning in 1968, Maurice had noticed a charming old farmhouse outside St. Charles. Built of stone in 1804, with a summer kitchen and an outside hearth, it was a classic example of early French-Canadian architecture. Both Jeanne and Maurice were captivated by it. Learning that the house might be for sale, Maurice contacted the owner, Simon Lusignan. However, it took three and a half years of conversations, negotiations, offers, and counter-offers before M. Lusignan finally agreed to sell.

The Sauvés bought the house, which was sadly in need of repairs, intending to restore it. But, after talking to friends who'd restored old houses, and after doing some research on the subject, they realized they couldn't do the job themselves. Maurice, who never does anything by halves, engaged Gilles Vilandré, an architect, and Michel Lessard, an historian, who were specialists in restoration. Because the dwelling had been altered several times since it was built, considerably research was required to determine its original dimensions. Once the dimensions were established, it was stripped to the bare stone and faithfully reconstructed. Without detracting from the heritage aspect, electricity and indoor plumbing were skilfully incorporated into the house. When it was finished, Jeanne and Maurice took pleasure in furnishing it with period pieces of pine, old pottery, and artifacts they had collected. The former owner, Simon Lusignan, agreed to act as caretaker of the house and outbuildings, which include a small stable for riding horses and a barn. Over the years Maurice has bought additional land, and the property now encompasses more than five hundred acres.

For Jeanne, St. Charles is a retreat where she can escape from the pressures of her hectic life. She treasures it for its tranquillity and the pastoral beauty of the surroundings. One of her main pleasures there is tending her rose garden. She is also sensitive to the historic legacy of the dwelling. In her introduction to *La Maison traditionnelle au Québec* by Michel Lessard and Gilles Vilandré (Les Éditions de l'Homme, Ottawa, 1974), which features the Sauvé house and five others, she wrote, "Old houses have a soul. . . . With the building one must take all the lives which it has sheltered. These are retained in an old house. This we must respect."

Jeanne, who was fifty when she entered Parliament, took the responsibility of running a government department in her stride. Accustomed to authority since her early twenties, she found that her greatest challenge was understanding the intricacies of scientific and technological research. In the words of her first deputy minister, Dr. Aurèle Beaulnes, "She grasped a number of complex issues very quickly. It didn't take us long to get on the same wavelength." Her ability to comprehend and retain complex information surprised her staff, most of whom were professionals with numerous degrees. They were also left in no doubt as to who was boss — Jeanne was soft-spoken, but she demanded high standards of performance.

At cabinet meetings Jeanne wasn't intimidated by the fact she was the only woman minister, but, being a neophyte, she kept a low profile. Always well briefed, she only spoke if she had a point to make, unlike some of her more garrulous colleagues who loved the sound of their own voices. John Turner, Minister of Finance from 1972 until his resignation of 1976, said recently, "I remember Jeanne's interventions in cabinet as being very precise, well articulated, well organized and elegantly delivered." She spent relatively little time in the House of Commons, preferring to concentrate her efforts on her own department. However, when she did speak in the House, in Turner's opinion "she handled herself with a lot of flair and a lot of confidence."

Within a month of assuming the Science and Technology portfolio, Jeanne was invited to go to England. The invitation came from her opposite number, Margaret Thatcher, Minister of Education, whose portfolio included science and technology. Uncertain what she should do, she was advised by External Affairs to accept the invitation. In February 1973 she flew to England, her first official trip abroad.

Jeanne was enormously impressed with Margaret Thatcher. "A remarkable woman intellectually and very strong. Although she was hard-line, we hit it off." Thatcher organized four days of full briefings, which for Jeanne were very satisfying. They also found time for some good private discussions. During the visit they established a friendship that was reinforced by the many things they had in common — including their solitary positions as the only women in all-male cabinets. Before Jeanne left, Thatcher gave a dinner for her at Marlborough House, the former residence of the Queen Mother. When Jeanne returned to Canada, she told friends that Margaret Thatcher was "made of steel", a view shared by the press, who later nicknamed her "The Iron Lady".

In the ensuing year Jeanne led a number of scientific missions to other parts of the world. One of these was a month-long trip to China, where she visited universities and government research laboratories. (She made such a hit in China that, for years afterwards, whenever a Chinese delegation came to Canada they always asked to pay their respects to Madame Sauvé.) She also made similar journeys to France and to Belgium. These missions opened the door for future exchanges of scientific information between Canada and the host countries.

In May 1974, the NDP withdrew their support and Trudeau's minority government was defeated on a want-of-confidence motion. Once again, for the third time in six years, the country was faced with a general election. Having looked after her constituents diligently, Jeanne felt sufficiently secure in her riding to spend most of her time touring the province on behalf of other Liberal candidates. Her campaign was so well organized that the day before the election her staff shut up shop and went swimming. On polling-day, she was returned with a majority of more than eighteen thousand votes. Nationally the Liberal party won a clear majority with 141 seats, compared to 95 for the Tories, 16 for the NDP, and 12 for the Social Credit.

Jeanne was appointed minister of the environment in Trudeau's new government. Formed in 1971, Environment was a sprawling department with diverse responsibilities. Among its components was what is now the fisheries department, along with waste-disposal groups, water-study and environmental-impact agencies, the Canadian Wildlife Service, forestry units, and weather-monitoring establishments. With administrative offices occupying two large buildings in Hull, it operated a string of meteorological establishments (the main one being in Toronto), ships on Canada's inland waterways and both coasts, and research laboratories across the country. Compared to Science and Technology, which had fewer than two hundred employees, Environment had twelve thousand employees, more than two thousand of them with doctoral degrees. Because of its size, Environment was a promotion for Jeanne. But it was still a junior portfolio, with little clout in cabinet.

Historically, the Minister of the Environment has had to function with formidable handicaps. In some respects it's a no-win game. Differing jurisdictions make it difficult to take decisive action on many environmental problems. Air and water pollution are typical examples. Quite often these issues end up in court and take years to resolve. Then there is the political reality of the portfolio. The attitude of Canadian politicians (with the possible exception of the NDP) toward the environment is an even greater handicap than the jurisdictional dilemma. Politicians have traditionally paid lip service to the quality of the environment, but when it comes to the crunch, and the question is clean air or jobs, short-term economic considerations win every time.

At the end of August 1974, less than two weeks after she'd been sworn in as minister of the environment, Jeanne represented Canada at a world-population conference in Bucharest. One of the main topics of the conference was birth control. Even though she was a devout Roman Catholic, because of the population explosion Jeanne was in favour of birth control. After the conference she told a reporter:

"The first question that came to my mind was: my God, are we going to one day say to people how many children they can have?

"Yet we have to say that in some way, because we can't keep growing as we are now. We've got to face the problem. I'm not sure that Canadians are conscious at all that there is a population problem in the world.

"You only become conscious of that when you visit a country that is overcrowded. It's incessant; a constant flow of people moving up and down the street. If you are a Canadian, you think there must be some opera or circus that is just over and the crowd is going to disappear. But it doesn't."

Jeanne's views on birth control, in a somewhat different context, made the papers again in February 1975 when she addressed the wind-up dinner of the second annual conference on Women and the Law at the University of Manitoba. She worked at her office in Ottawa that morning and after lunch took a government plane to Winnipeg. En route, having been told that it was a formal affair, she changed into an evening gown. When she arrived at the dinner, she was embarrassed to see that most of the delegates — all militant young women — were wearing blue jeans. Jeanne's long dress served to underline the generation gap, and did nothing to endear her to them. In her speech, which reviewed government initiatives to improve women's rights, she said that she had "grave misgivings about any proposals to liberalize abortion laws". This brought a chorus of hisses and boos from the audience of five hundred, who, earlier that afternoon, had voted for abortion on demand and a removal of abortion from the federal Criminal Code. At the end of her speech she was challenged by one of the audience, who said, "You should have the right to decide for yourself whether you want an abortion." Jeanne responded, "But you are deciding for the fetus as well. The fetus is not yourself."

This was the only time that Jeanne faced a genuinely hostile audience. Although she didn't enjoy the experience, she wasn't unduly upset by it. Indeed, she'd been warned to expect a rough reception. But she believed she had something to say, and for this reason she had accepted the invitation.

Throughout her political career, Jeanne was fortunate to have a succession of able deputy ministers. A deputy minister is a senior civil servant whose job is to manage the department for the minister. Ministers are elected officials, whereas deputy ministers are government employees who provide an element of continuity in the department. For the first five months that she held the Environment portfolio, Robert Shaw, who had been deputy commissioner of Expo 67, was her deputy minister. At the end of 1974, Shaw left the civil service to return to private industry, and was replaced by Blair Seaborn.

Seaborn, a slim man with sandy hair and an astute mind, had previously been with the Department of Consumer and Corporate Affairs. Having just been promoted to the rank of deputy minister, he was somewhat apprehensive when he presented himself to Jeanne. Welcoming him to her department, she said, "We haven't met before but I've heard some good things about you." Seaborn replied, "Thank you, ma'am; I hope you can put up with me for a while because I really don't know anything about Environment."

"Splendid!" she exclaimed, breaking into a big smile. "This will probably be the only time in my ministerial career that, for a few months at least, I'll know more than my deputy does. I shall enjoy it! I'm just about to travel across Canada to meet my provincial counterparts — why don't you come along?"

Seaborn protested that he wouldn't be of much use, but Jeanne brushed this aside: "Don't worry, you'll learn on the job, and you'll meet the key provincial players. Come along — we'll have fun!"

By accompanying her on the trip, Seaborn gained valuable insights into his responsibilities, and made some useful contacts with his provincial counterparts. In the ensuing months he worked closely with Jeanne and was particularly impressed by her warmth and openness with her staff. "She had none of that built-in scepticism of public servants, nor did she believe, as politicians of all parties do, that 'they're out to get us'. She worked me hard, and she was demanding of the quality of the work, but she was never unpleasant.''

Jeanne's diplomacy was a special asset in the Environment portfolio because so many issues required the co-operation of the provinces or the municipalities (often both levels of government). Her diplomatic skill was also useful within her department, because the fisheries section was a separate realm with its own minister of state, Roméo Leblanc. Although Jeanne was the senior minister, Leblanc had a large staff which reported to him, causing an element of tension. Able and ambitious, Leblanc constantly pushed for more funds and a higher profile for fisheries. While Jeanne headed Environment it was an ongoing struggle for her to maintain a balance between the demands of the fisheries section and the needs of the other components in her ministry. This problem was eventually resolved in 1979 when Fisheries — quite rightly — was re-established as a separate department.

One of the first environmental problems Jeanne tackled was pollution in the St. Lawrence River. Earlier efforts to clean up the river had been frustrated by a lack of co-operation between the various levels of government. Co-operation was essential, because, while the St. Lawrence came under federal jurisdiction, several tributaries in the province of Quebec poured effluents into the river, and a number of cities, especially Montreal, dumped raw sewage into the St. Lawrence. The river is still badly polluted, but Jeanne's negotiations with the Quebec Minister of the Environment, Dr. Victor Goldbloom, resulted in the first constructive measures to clean up the St. Lawrence.

In a similar vein, while she was minister of the environment her department warned the public of the dangers of polychlorinated biphenyls (PCB's). PCB compounds have a variety of commercial applications as lubricants, as heat-transfer fluids, and as ingredients in protective coatings for wood and metal. They are also highly toxic, and resistant to decomposition in water and soil. For this reason, they pose a serious threat to humans and to wildlife. When Jeanne's department issued its warning ten years ago, it was ignored. Today people take the PCB threat more seriously.

At the end of March 1975 Jeanne led a diplomatic mission to Washington. During two days of negotiations with top-level U.S. officials she was able to win important points on a number of controversial environmental issues. The most dramatic was agreement to refer the Garrison project to the International Joint Commission. The Garrison project, at a cost of hundreds of millions of dollars, was intended to divert waters from the Missouri River. This would have seriously affected the quality of water over a huge area in Canada. As a result of being referred to the IJC, the project was put on hold while it was scrutinized by experts from both sides of the border. Recommendations by the commission to safeguard Canada were subsequently accepted by the U.S. government. Thus, for Canada the Washington conference was a major environmental victory. Blair Seaborn, who attended the conference (and later served on the International Joint Commission), remembers that Jeanne made a very good impression on senior U.S. negotiators. "Her obvious qualities of character, intellect, and social capacity played well for us there when she was doing both a diplomatic and a ministerial job."

On the last day of October 1975 the Commons approved Third Reading of the Environmental Contaminants Act. This Bill, which put legislative teeth into pollution control, had dragged through the House for more than a year. Just before it came up for Third Reading the Opposition threw up yet another roadblock by proposing nine amendments. Anxious to get the Bill passed, Jeanne phoned Joe Clark, the Environment critic for the Opposition. She told Clark, who was in Toronto for the day, that she couldn't accept six of his amendments but that she would agree to three of them. On this basis they struck a deal. Just before hanging up she asked Clark why he was in Toronto, and learned that he was preparing to run for the party leadership. When she wished him good luck, Clark responded, "I don't need luck, I need money."

A few days after the Contaminants Act was passed, and the House was once again in session, Jeanne put fifty dollars in an envelope and sent it across the floor to Clark. Handing the envelope to a parliamentary page, she nudged her seatmate and whispered, "Watch this!" Clark broke into a wide grin when he opened the envelope and sent back a note: "Do you need a receipt?"

It was also in October that Jeanne attended the annual conference of the Water Pollution Control Federation in Miami, Florida. In her keynote speech she stressed the need to clean up the Great Lakes, a major point she had made earlier in Washington. Reminding U.S. delegates that their country was behind in its commitment to build sewage-treatment plants, she said, "Canadians are naturally disappointed that slippage has occurred in the schedule. Several Canadian communities are wondering why they are spending their money on sewage-treatment plants when completion of plants across the border is significantly behind schedule." This speech received wide press coverage and was lauded by environment groups across the continent.

At the beginning of December 1975, after sixteen months in the Environment portfolio, Trudeau asked Jeanne to take over the Department of Communications. The following day the *Toronto Star* published a half-page critique headed "Sauvé Switches Jobs Instead of Fighting". The article, written by *Star* staff writer Mary Janigan, began:

> She'll never be a fighter. Tough, maybe. Firm, some of the time. But never a no-holds-barred fighter.
>
> Her critics say Jeanne Sauvé failed in her environment portfolio precisely because she didn't go to battle: A minister without dedication. . . .
>
> Behind her she leaves an unwieldy department still plagued by lack of real clout and little public support. Her performance in the future can only be guessed on the basis of the widespread dissatisfaction with her past political record.

But the article wasn't totally negative. John Fraser, who replaced Joe Clark as Environment critic, was quoted as saying, "It was really a grab-bag department. When it was brought together, none of the groups was a real environmentalist and it would have taken any minister a lot of time to bring it together.'' Kenneth Hare, director of the Environmental Studies Institute at the University of Toronto, pointed out, ''She had an incomplete set of powers, since the British North America Act assigns resources of all kinds — land, water, wood, and soil — to the provincial governments.'' One of her most outspoken critics, Kit Vincent, executive secretary of the Arctic Resources Committee, was also quoted. He put his finger on Jeanne's dilemma: ''The real problems came with the energy crisis. The real environmental questions today are about trade-offs between industry and the environment. And that's when the government retreated to such an outstanding extent.''

Jeanne wasn't a fighter. At least not in a pound-the-table sense, and she's always been the first to admit it. However, those who have worked with her know that she's an exceptionally determined woman, and she pursues her goals relentlessly. Her aggressiveness is masked by the fact that she tries to avoid confrontation and prefers to negotiate solutions. This strategy, combined with her courteous manner, has led many people to underestimate her strength. In a *Weekend Magazine* profile, Pierre Nadeau, one of her special assistants, defended Jeanne's gentle approach: ''There are many ways to win, are there not? You can kill your opponent and win. You can maim him and win. You can also charm him and win. If the object remains to win, you are wise to use the method that suits your style.''

The charge that Jeanne lacked dedication in the Environment portfolio wasn't shared by her staff. When she was transferred to Communications, they were genuinely disappointed. In the words of one of her senior officers, ''Most of us felt 'Damn it, we've lost a good minister — if she'd been allowed to stay longer, she would have changed things.' ''

Jeanne's extensive broadcasting experience was one of the main reasons Trudeau chose her for the Communications portfolio. The Department of Communications was both a promotion and a challenge. As minister she was responsible for the orderly operation and development of all forms of communication throughout the country. Among the agencies, institutions, commissions, and Crown corporations that reported to Parliament through her were the National Film Board, the National Museums of Canada, the Canada Council, the National Library, Telesat Canada, and the Canadian Radio-television and Telecommunications Commission (CRTC). The CRTC, with whom Jeanne was sometimes at odds, was a highly independent operation. Its mandate was to regulate and supervise all aspects of the Canadian broadcasting system, and to approve rates charged to the public by the national telecommunications companies, such as Bell Canada.

By coincidence, Jeanne followed in the footsteps of two of her former JEC colleagues, Gérard Pelletier and Pierre Juneau. Pelletier had been minister of communications until the end of August 1975, when he resigned from Parliament to become Canada's ambassador to France. He was succeeded by Juneau, who had previously been chairman of the CRTC. Juneau held the portfolio for only six weeks before he was defeated in a by-election. He was forced to step down after failing to get a seat in Parliament and was appointed a special adviser to Trudeau. Noting Juneau's background, and his position in the Prime Minister's Office, some journalists speculated that he rather than Jeanne would pull the strings in the Department of Communications.

Among those who dismissed the idea was Guy Cormier, another former JEC colleague (and admirer), who wrote an editorial in *La Presse* in which he said:

> *One can be sure that Madame Sauvé is not the type to serve as a figurehead. Nimble spirited, she has an acute sense of responsibility and she is strong willed, which does not exclude her from resorting to diplomacy when the need exists. Setting aside her unconditional loyalty to Mr. Trudeau's politics, Jeanne Sauvé has for all the rest a very personal style and retains an autonomy of thought and opinion on a vast range of subjects.*

After the swearing-in ceremony at Government House, Jeanne told a reporter that she found the notion that Pierre Juneau would have an undue influence on her department to be offensive — especially to her deputy minister, Max Yalden, who would be her chief adviser on policy matters. As it turned out, the whole thing proved to be idle speculation. Years later she recalled, "Juneau never bothered me. Undoubtedly he had his own opinions which he voiced to the PM, but I was never aware of them."

A few months later, in March 1976, Jeanne made her first major policy speech. Its purpose was to reopen the dialogue between Ottawa and the ten provinces on a national broadcasting policy. The previous July discussions at a federally sponsored communications conference had been so rancorous that the meeting had ended in a shambles. Making it clear that the federal government would never abandon its predominance in the area of communications, she urged the premiers to return to the bargaining table, and to push Ottawa to the limit to negotiate a new power-sharing deal. Her appeal broke the deadlock, and paved the way for a successful conference in Edmonton the following year — a significant accomplishment.

Pay television was a burning issue when Jeanne took over the Communications portfolio. Speaking to the Canadian Cable Television Association in June 1976, she announced, "Pay TV is inevitable." Jubilant to hear this, the industry made it their rallying cry. Not only did she believe pay television was inevitable, but she wanted it introduced as soon as possible. Jeanne wasn't convinced that pay TV would enrich the viewing hours of the public, but she knew that Canadian-content requirements would provide a tremendous financial boost to the Canadian movie industry. The longer it was delayed, the less funding it would attract, because of the increasing availability of American channels and foreign television transmitted by satellites.

There were, however, a number of stumbling-blocks to the swift implementation of pay TV. First, the Department of Communications had to formulate a national policy, and licence applications had to be approved by the CRTC. This was easier said than done.

The CRTC, possibly feeling that Jeanne had impinged on its mandate by announcing that pay TV was inevitable, insisted on receiving briefs from interested parties before considering any licence applications. While the CRTC was engaged in this leisurely process, the provinces jumped into the act by demanding that they should have control of pay TV within their boundaries. Jeanne tried to prod the CRTC into speedy action, but the commission refused to budge until the submissions were heard the following year. Meanwhile, Jeanne was delayed in formulating a federal policy because she had to work out agreements with the provinces. After hearing the briefs, the CRTC concluded that it was premature to introduce pay television. (Most of the briefs submitted were from conventional broadcasting companies who feared competition, and from citizens' groups concerned that American programs would destroy Canada's cultural sovereignty.) Another round of pay TV hearings by the CRTC in 1978 produced a similar verdict. The issue dragged on for years. When pay TV was finally implemented, an incalculable amount of funding for the Canadian film industry had been lost.

After living with her sister Berthe for the first few years in Ottawa, Jeanne rented a small apartment on the Driveway. She found her new quarters lonely, and casually mentioned this over lunch one day to her recently widowed sister Annette. A few weeks later, Jeanne moved to Annette's high-rise apartment on the MacArthur Road. This apartment was large enough that they weren't continually tripping over each other, and Jeanne was able to furnish her room with some of her own pieces and to hang a few favourite pictures. The arrangement worked out beautifully, except for one minor incident. One night Maurice came to visit and picked up the phone on Jeanne's bedside table, not realizing that it was a special telephone that sent a signal to the RCMP as soon as the receiver was lifted (one of a variety of "panic button" devices issued to senior government officials). When Jeanne told him what he'd done, Maurice tried to explain to the RCMP who he was and what had happened, but within minutes three burly plainclothes officers appeared at the apartment. Knowing her husband's compulsive telephone habits, as soon as the Mounties had gone Jeanne took some adhesive tape, fastened the receiver in place, and put the phone under her bed. From then on, the only purpose it served was to gather dust.

In the spring of 1976 Jeanne became embroiled in the air-traffic controllers dispute, an issue that touched all French-speaking Canadians. It had been simmering since 1975, when a government committee had recommended bilingual air-traffic control within the province of Quebec. On the grounds that it would endanger air safety, bilingual service was rejected by the Canadian Air Traffic Control Association and the Canadian Airline Pilots Association. These associations were opposed by the newly formed francophone air-traffic controllers association, les Gens de l'Air. At the end of June, just before the start of the Olympics, the English air-traffic controllers and pilots went on strike. The air-traffic controllers were swiftly legislated back to work, but the pilots stayed out. A week later, Otto Lang, the federal Minister of Transport, capitulated and signed an agreement with the Canadian Airline Pilots Association that for all practical purposes maintained the status quo.

French Canada was outraged. Jean Marchand, who had succeeded Jeanne as minister of the environment, was so incensed that he resigned. Jeanne was also appalled by the agreement, fearing that Quebecers would lose faith in the federal government. In a telephone interview from her home she accused the Liberal administration "of falling on its knees before a bunch of fanatics".

Seizing on this quote, Claude Wagner, the Tory member for St. Hyacinthe, gleefully rose in the House to ask the Prime Minister if, in view of Jeanne's denunciation of Otto Lang, he intended to ask for the resignation of both the Minister of Transport and the Minister of Communications. After Trudeau chopped him off with a monosyllabic "No", Wagner addressed a supplementary question to the Speaker:

"I therefore put my question to the Minister of Communications and ask her whether, in the light of the well known principles of cabinet

solidarity the Prime Minister chooses to ignore today, she persists in accusing the government of having knelt before a bunch of fanatics? If so, does she intend to resign, thus imitating the courageous gesture of the hon. member for Langlier?"

Hon. Jeanne Sauvé (Minister of Communications): "Mr. Speaker, several of us feel that the agreement is bad, but still the best possible we could conclude under the circumstances.

"I said in my statement that we could not denounce collectively what one of our colleagues, in the normal exercise of his duties, had felt he should accept. . . . We have to live with an agreement that is not perfect. We remain united behind our colleague who supported the agreement, but I still feel that, faced with a bunch of fanatics, we were forced to accept an agreement that will be difficult to live with, but which in no way calls in question again the policy of bilingualism within the federal government."

The backlash Jeanne feared from the air-traffic controllers dispute contributed to the victory of the Parti Québécois that November. In the wake of the Parti Québécois triumph, few federal politicians dared to comment publicly on the spectre of separatism. Jeanne was one of the few who did. Six weeks after the Quebec election, *The Gazette* quoted her in an article titled "Federalism — Only Sauvé Seems to Have Found the Faith":

I have unshakable faith in the gamble my country is taking that two great cultures bound by history and geography will join their destinies in a logical and fruitful association. . . .

Péquiste ideology backs away from the challenge of taking hold of this new country, of its vast horizons, of its more ambitious, more numerous social, economic and cultural projects, of a wider market for our ideas as well as our merchandise.

Canadian federalism is not immutable. The important thing now is to regroup all reforming federalists, to arm them intellectually and morally so they can keep their Canadian heritage as they keep the country together.

In March 1977 Jeanne tabled a package of legislation containing sixteen policy objectives. Her proposals, designed to give firm direction to communications in Canada, were to be discussed at a federal-provincial conference the following month in Edmonton. Just before the conference began, Louis O'Neill, the Quebec Minister of Communications, stated that he wouldn't attend because the proposed legislation opened the door to political interference, and he wasn't prepared to negotiate with a "foreign government". Jeanne refuted his charge of political interference by pointing out that all the bill did was to impose on the federal government and the CRTC the obligation to reserve radio frequencies and cable channels for "the broadcasting and distribution of educational programs for those provinces which wished to do so". The conference in April was attended by ministers from all the provinces except Quebec.

O'Neill's intransigence, which was meant to show that Quebec was a sovereign state, came as no surprise. Not only was it Parti Québécois strategy to have nothing to do with the federal government, but the previous provincial administration under Bourassa had also refused to acknowledge federal control of communications. In December, however, O'Neill unbent a little and agreed to negotiate, providing, among other things, that control of cable TV and Bell Canada's operations within Quebec were ceded to the province. "I'm willing to negotiate with Mr. O'Neill and I'm delighted that he has recognized that this is a useful exercise," Jeanne said, "but I obviously cannot accept all the proposals — they don't leave the federal government an important role. It's very important to have a large, effective telecommunications network across Canada." Having known O'Neill for years and worked with him in the JEC, Jeanne knew the game he was playing. "I just sat around and waited for him to cool off. We never settled anything, but we kept talking."

In July 1977 Jeanne was attacked in the Commons by one of her own party, Pierre DeBané, the Liberal member for Matane. DeBané charged that the proposed purchase by the CBC of three private radio and television stations in Rimouski had been engineered by Jeanne to help her old friend Philippe deGaspé Beaubien. Beaubien was the president of Télémédia, the company that owned the stations. (DeBané carefully refrained from mentioning the long-standing rivalry between Matane, which was in his constituency, and Rimouski, which at that time was a Social Credit riding.) Jeanne was furious at his accusation, because the purpose of the takeover was to improve CBC coverage in the Gaspé and western New Brunswick. Moreover, the decision to acquire the stations, which had been independently approved by the CRTC, was out of her hands: the CBC at that time reported to a different minister, the Secretary of State.

Aside from championing the interests of his constituency (Matane had previously had the only CBC station in the Gaspé), DeBané may have been trying to get even with Jeanne. One night in Ottawa she had sat him down and given him a lecture, saying, "You're always complaining about the party. If you use the name of the Liberal party to get elected, then you owe something to the party — there is such a thing as party discipline. If you don't agree with Liberal policy, you should resign."

DeBané's charge that Jeanne had arranged the purchase of the Rimouski stations for the benefit of her friend got a big play in the Quebec press. Jeanne not only explained her position formally in the House, but also told Le Soleil:

"The accusation is absolutely unfounded. I find that Mr. DeBané, a self-appointed defender of the poor, wants to take from me something that you don't take from the poor or from the rich — their reputation."

The spat between DeBané and Jeanne died as quickly as it had begun. They later became friends and DeBané, after serving as a cabinet minister, was subsequently called to the Senate. Jeanne's reputation emerged unscathed from the fracas.

Indeed, by 1977 she was immensely popular not only in her constituency but throughout the entire province of Quebec. She was also highly respected in the cabinet. Richard Gwyn, author of The Northern Magus (McClelland and Stewart, Toronto, 1980), wrote that no matter how well briefed, only a handful of ministers could hold their own with Trudeau, and he named Jeanne as one of the few. Edgar Gallant, who was chairman of the Public Service Commission (which is responsible for appointing qualified people to positions within the federal civil service), remembers, "Unlike most ministers, I never heard any criticism of her. She was highly regarded by public servants." Her deputy minister at that time, Bernard Ostry, who is now head of TVOntario, recalled, "I don't know of a minister who was more in command of her department. She had knowledge in depth and she operated in a highly democratic manner. In my experience in Ottawa her tenure as minister was just about the only time I saw it was possible to have a ministry with no real tensions." The absence of tension was due to her openness and frankness. Pierre Lafleur, her executive assistant in Communications, was impressed by the high morale of her staff. "She was tough, but she gave us a lot of latitude so long as we produced results. We would have killed for her!"

Susan Cornell, who is now a cable-television executive but who was then a junior assistant in her office, remembers Jeanne's thoughtfulness. "She inspired loyalty because she respected her staff and she cared about them. If we had a problem she was always accessible. She was also very generous. I used to like to wear shawls, and one day she wore a stunning shawl to the office which I admired. That afternoon when the mail was delivered to me, there was the shawl with a note 'This will look much better on you than on me. Please have it.' She often made spontaneous gestures like that."

While she was minister of communications, Jeanne continually goaded the broadcasting industry to improve the quantity and the quality of Canadian content in their programs. Addressing the Broadcast Executives' Society on this subject in February 1978, she quoted Mavor Moore (former chief of programming for the CBC), who had said some years before, "We have a chance to do something freshly Canadian." After pausing to let his words sink in, she added, "Well, we had a rare chance, and we used it — but then we discovered imports are cheaper." Admitting that she couldn't force the industry to increase its Canadian content, she reminded her audience that the CRTC had this power and would take it into consideration when granting licence renewals.

Among her duties as a Liberal cabinet minister was responsibility for two political regions in Quebec: the south shore of the island of Montreal, and the Gaspé peninsula up to the city of Rimouski. One weekend in February 1978, Jeanne attended a heated nomination meeting in Rimouski. The contest was between a man from Montreal, who worked for Consumer and Corporate Affairs in Ottawa, and a local woman, Eva Côté, vice-president of the riding's Liberal Association. Although nominally neutral, privately Jeanne favoured Eva Côté. At the meeting, the male candidate made a wild, demagogic speech in which he promised, among other things, that if elected he would make the Gaspé as prosperous as Alberta. (To which a heckler yelled, "Well, you'd better find some goddamn oil!") When the vote was taken on Sunday, Eva Côté won by a landslide.

It was so windy in Rimouski that day that Jeanne's plane, a government Viscount, had to be anchored to the tarmac. Although the wind continued to howl, it abated sufficiently after dark for the plane to take off for Ottawa. Crossing the St. Lawrence River the plane bucked and pitched so violently that everyone, especially Jeanne, was terrified. Making a joke of the situation, one of the passengers, John Welch, ran up and down the aisle crossing himself and loudly reciting mock prayers of contrition. Joining in the fun, others left their seats and knelt in the aisle. While this travesty was unfolding, Jeanne sat rigidly in her seat with a death grip on Pierre Lafleur's arm. Finally she could stand it no longer. Turning around, she said through gritted teeth, "Get back in your seats. If we're going to die, we'll die with dignity!"

They landed safely in Ottawa two hours later. The next day the defeated candidate, who was Jewish and the son of a prominent Marxist professor, accused Jeanne on a Montreal radio program of rigging the Rimouski convention and of being a Nazi and an anti-Semite. She could have sued him, but it was beneath her dignity. Eva Côté lost to the incumbent Social Credit member in the next election, but later won the Rimouski seat.

In September 1978 Jeanne obtained twenty-four million dollars for the expansion of the David Florida space laboratory on the outskirts of Ottawa. This was a coup, because the government was in an austerity phase, and the cabinet considered money spent on space technology to have no political value. Jeanne, however, wasn't concerned with short-term political gains — she believed that to develop Canada's space industry one had to take the long-term view. In this connection she encouraged manufacturers to specialize in components rather than to try and build complete space vehicles. One example of the success of this approach is the CANADARM, a remote-manipulator system used in the U.S. Space Shuttle program, which is manufactured by Spar Aerospace Limited.

She also obtained funding, some nine million dollars, for the development of Telidon, which employs television, telephone, and computer technology to store, retrieve, and transmit information. It has many applications and may be used in a number of ways, including by householders to call up information on their TV sets. Although Telidon has been recognized as the standard system for the world, to date it has been a commercial failure. Many authorities consider it to be at least ten years ahead of its time.

Jeanne's interest in high technology encompassed all forms of communication, including the telephone. Her interest was far from academic; she wanted to create jobs in the private sector, and she wanted Canadian companies to win their share of foreign business. To this end she rolled out the red carpet for a delegation from Saudi Arabia who subsequently signed a multi-billion-dollar contract with Bell Canada and Northern Telecom. The latter company, a world leader, recently won a widely publicized contract to install a sophisticated telephone exchange system in the White House. Fibre optics, which utilize the principle that light entering a glass fibre is conducted from one end to the other without loss of energy, was another area of research that Jeanne promoted. Fibre optics have exciting applications in medicine, photography, and television.

The satellite program, which fascinated Jeanne, was her top priority. The twenty-four million dollars she wrung from the cabinet for the expansion of the David Florida Laboratory was used to equip the establishment so that it could assemble and test satellites. During her time in the ministry she presided over the launching of the second generation of Canadian satellites, including the "Hermes" satellite. This communications satellite, named for the messenger in Greek mythology, was the most advanced in the world.

On another front, in June 1978 Jeanne warned a meeting of Canadian and U.S. broadcasters that the government would step in if the industry didn't clean up its act and tighten advertising codes. She was particularly concerned with three issues: ads aimed at children, advocacy ads (for example, you can't have a good party without beer), and the stereotyping of women in commercials. In the case of women, she considered their stereotyped portrayal to be ludicrous. "Such advertising is degrading to women, since it treats women as servile beasts of burden whose every happiness lies in pleasing their men with cleaner floors or whiter whites—but women know that removal of ring around the collar is no guarantee of a happy home life."

Although Jeanne is not a militant feminist, and has often said she didn't believe in "throwing her bra to the breeze", she has staunchly defended women's rights. In the summer of 1978, on her way to be guest of honour at a luncheon, she refused at the last minute when she learned the lunch was being held at the Rideau Club. This prestigious Ottawa club, founded by Sir John A. Macdonald in 1865, didn't allow women to be members. Not only did she refuse to darken the club's door, but she also ensured that under the government's discrimination policy, until the club admitted women members it was denied any further government patronage. As the club was running a deficit and depended heavily on government business, this was a telling blow. The following year, after more than a century as a haven for men, the Rideau Club elected Jean Pigott, a former Conservative MP, as its first woman member. Few people were aware of Jeanne's role in this historic breakthrough. Since then, many women have been admitted to membership, the club's fortunes have improved, and there is even a long waiting list.

At the end of November 1978, Jeanne addressed the Montreal Chamber of Commerce on the pending Quebec referendum. Her audience applauded warmly when she told them the Parti Québécois government was trying to "trap people by engaging in a conscious and intentional obstruction of the democratic process." Jeanne's speech was also praised in an editorial by the *Calgary Herald*, a paper that rarely tossed bouquets to Liberals, especially those from Quebec:

> *Jeanne Sauvé, federal minister of communications, has said what other cabinet ministers appear afraid to state: that the Parti Québécois leaders "persist in talking about the issue without spelling it out."*
>
> *Her statements that Quebec premier René Lévesque and his ministers are "inventing soothing formulas" to reduce the impact of their proposals for the coming independence referendum are a breath of freshness and surprisingly honest simplicity.*
>
> *The question of Quebec separation has been clouded in so much rhetoric and pussyfooting around by both the PQ and federal spokesmen that the ordinary Canadian would have trouble these days even knowing what was being said, let alone making a judgement.*

Jeanne was the only federal cabinet minister, but not the only member of the Sauvé family, to take a public stand on the referendum issue. Earlier in the year Maurice had been appointed president of the Quebec-Canada unity group. This organization, which had more than one hundred thousand members, was a dynamic force in Quebec for national unity.

In December 1978 Jeanne was appointed Francophone Adviser to External Affairs Minister Donald Jamieson. She replaced Jean-Pierre Goyer, former Minister of Supply and Services, who was dropped from the cabinet. Because Jamieson didn't speak French, her job was to represent him at the Paris-based Organization for Cultural and Technical Cooperation and to stand in for him in diplomatic negotiations with francophone countries. She didn't have a chance to do any travelling, however, because Trudeau, who was preparing to call an election, told her not to leave the country.

After trying for two years to persuade the advertising industry to mend its ways, in the spring of 1979 Jeanne mobilized the CRTC to put pressure on advertisers to change their stereotyped portrayal of women. Tom Blakeley, president of the Association of Canadian Advertisers, told the *Globe and Mail* that advertisers "would cooperate to the utmost with the CRTC." But he cautioned, "I sincerely think that if a product has a target audience of women from age 18 to 35 and they are homemakers, it's dumb as hell to show a man in that situation."

Before the CRTC hearings got under way, Prime Minister Trudeau announced a general election for 22 May. Because of her federalist stance, and the fact that through redistribution her old Ahuntsic riding had been doubled in size, Jeanne wasn't sure how she'd fare. Her constituency, renamed Laval-des-Rapides, now encompassed a number of communities that had voted for the Parti Québécois in the 1976 provincial election. By coincidence her main rival, the Tory candidate, was a thirty-two-year-old lawyer named Pierre Trudeau.

Nevertheless, as in past campaigns, she toured the province on behalf of other candidates. And, as usual, she ran a low-key campaign in her own riding. When she was interviewed on election night after being returned with a majority of more than thirty-one thousand votes, the greatest of her career, she told *The Gazette*:

"It's fantastic! I feel just great. It was nearly like a first election because two-thirds of my riding was new."

The results for the party, however, were less joyous. The Tories, led by Joe Clark, won 136 seats compared to 114 for the Liberals, while the New Democratic Party picked up 26, and the Social Credit trailed with 6 seats.

Jeanne returned to Ottawa as the Communications critic for the Opposition. "I immediately got very active in the House. I enjoyed that but found the Parliamentary Communications Committee frustrating because I only had ten minutes to question whoever was appearing — and what can you do in ten minutes? Once you start probing and asking questions you only get to the guy in twenty minutes.''

As it turned out, she served a short stint in Opposition. The House convened in October 1979, and on 21 November Pierre Trudeau announced his resignation as leader of the Liberal party. Three weeks later, on 13 December, the Tories fulfilled a death wish by going through with a vote of confidence on the Crosbie budget, which they could have avoided. As Jeanne entered the Commons for the vote she told a reporter, ''I don't know why we're doing this.'' Unlike most of her Liberal colleagues, Jeanne wanted to give the Conservatives a chance — a chance to make more mistakes. By ten-thirty that night it was all over; the Tories had lost the non-confidence motion.

The following morning the Liberal caucus convened to work out their strategy for the 18 February election. Without a leader, or a platform, they were in total disarray. The first thing they had to decide was who would lead the party. Jeanne and many other Liberals were all for bringing back John Turner from his self-imposed exile in Toronto. The caucus broke up into regional caucuses and then reconvened after lunch. Both Trudeau and his right-hand man, Allan MacEachen, addressed the joint caucus several times. In Jeanne's words, ''MacEachen kept concluding things for us we hadn't agreed upon, and then it would start all over again.'' The meetings dragged on until nearly midnight. When they ended, nothing had been decided, except that Trudeau would be asked to lead the party. In this connection, Jeanne later referred to MacEachen's performance as ''the rape of the caucus''. Three days later Trudeau announced that he would lead the Liberals in the election.

Although Jeanne was opposed by five other candidates in her riding (including Alain ''Bugs'' Bonnier of the Rhinoceros Party), she won by a margin of nearly twenty-nine thousand votes. On a national basis, the Liberals won 146 seats to the Conservatives' 103, the NDP took 32 seats, and the Social Credit party was wiped out. Once again the Liberals were in the driver's seat.

After the election Jeanne wasn't sure what she would be offered

Madame Sauvé presenting Jonathan Carter with the Medal of Bravery at an investiture in the ballroom of Rideau Hall. July 1984. (John Evans)

Her Excellency departing for Halifax in a Canadian Forces Challenger jet.
Man in the white sweater is Madame Sauvé's son, Jean-François.
(M. S. Heney)

En route to Halifax Madame Sauvé reviews one of her speeches.
(M. S. Heney)

Reviewing the Royal Newfoundland
Company of the Signal Hill Tattoo,
St. John's, Newfoundland,
July 1985. (author)

Madame Sauvé and Mayor Jean Drapeau share a joke at a civic luncheon in
Montreal. (Government House)

Madame Sauvé inspecting the cockpit of a CF-18 fighter at CFB Baden, West Germany, July 1985. (Department of National Defence)

Investing Pierre Trudeau with the Order of Canada, Rideau Hall, October 1985. (Ottawa *Citizen*)

The Tent Room at Rideau Hall set up for a children's party, December 1985. (M. S. Heney)

Madame Sauvé carving the first piece of turkey at the Governor General's annual children's Christmas party. (M. S. Heney)

Flower bouquet presentation to Her Excellency by three-year-old Christine Dewell at City Hall, Halifax, May 1985. (Sid Barber, *The Daily News*)

in the cabinet. While she waited for the Prime Minister to phone, she kept hoping that it would be the External Affairs portfolio. But she knew that her reluctance to participate in the non-confidence vote, and her open support of John Turner (Trudeau's arch-enemy), hadn't helped her standing in the Trudeau camp. When the Prime Minister called and told her that he wanted her to be Speaker she was aghast, and exclaimed, "Oh no. Not that!"

Trudeau countered by telling her it was a very important position, but Jeanne didn't believe him. Then he took a different tack and said, "Jeanne, as a minister you're going to be forgotten once you leave politics, but you'll never be forgotten as the first woman Speaker." This argument didn't impress Jeanne, who said to herself, "The hell with it, who wants to be remembered — I just want to do something I like."

They talked a bit more and then Jeanne asked, "If I say no, will I be in the cabinet?" Trudeau said, "Yes, you will be."

"What portfolio?"

"That I'm not telling you."

The conversation ended on this inscrutable note. Before they hung up, Jeanne agreed to phone Trudeau with her decision by noon the following day.

Chapter 8

MADAME SPEAKER
1980–84

Jeanne didn't phone Pierre Trudeau the next morning. Instead, she took the early train to Ottawa and met with him at his office. During their conversation the Prime Minister explained why he wanted her to be Speaker. It was the turn for a francophone, and he believed it was time a woman occupied the Chair. She was the logical choice because she had both the temperament and the presence for the role — and as she hadn't been overly partisan, she would be acceptable to the Opposition.

Jeanne was in a dilemma. If she didn't accept the job, she knew the opportunity for a woman to be Speaker would be lost. On the other hand, if she accepted, she couldn't take sides on political issues, and she wanted desperately to participate in the Quebec referendum. Trudeau, who shared her feelings on national unity, solved her problem by saying that if she agreed to be Speaker she could take a public stand on the referendum issue.

As a precautionary measure Jeanne then went to Joe Clark, the Leader of the Opposition, and to Ed Broadbent, the leader of the NDP, to get their blessings. Clark agreed immediately to her participation in the referendum, but Broadbent hedged on the question. Suspecting that one reason for Broadbent's reluctance was that many separatists were also socialists, and hence supporters of the NDP, Jeanne confronted him with her suspicion and eventually obtained his consent.

The Speaker's job is essentially that of a referee. Trudeau once said that the Speaker has to be "a tightrope-walker, a juggler, and, occasionally, a lion-tamer". More precisely, to quote *Speakers of the House of Commons* by Gary Levy (Library of Parliament, Ottawa, 1984), the Speaker

> . . . presides over proceedings in the House. The Speaker's control over question period is all pervasive. He calls on members to speak, rules on points of order, decides whether a matter of privilege should take precedence over other business, represses disorder should it arise, decides whether or not an emergency debate can be granted and generally interprets the Standing Orders in accordance with precedent. While a legal background may be a definite asset in sorting out the intricacies of parliamentary procedure, personal characteristics are even more important than professional training. Speakers must be authoritative without being overbearing: dignified but not lacking in wit or humour, capable of maintaining a distance from other members without appearing aloof. Above all the Speaker must remain completely impartial between members and between parties.

The office carries great prestige — the Speaker ranks fifth in the order of precedence after the Governor General, the Prime Minister, the Chief Justice, and the Speaker of the Senate. The office is also well paid. The Speaker receives the same salary as a cabinet minister, a private apartment in the Centre Block, and the use of "The Farm" (Prime Minister King's former country residence in the nearby Gatineau hills). In addition, there are generous travel and entertainment allowances because one of the duties of the Speaker is to entertain guests on behalf of the government.

There are, however, drawbacks to being Speaker. Accepting the Chair is normally the kiss of death to a political career — most Speakers go on to the Senate, the bench, or an ambassadorship. Although "first among equals" in the Commons, the Speaker is the servant of the House and can't effectively represent his constituency. The only time the Speaker has a vote is in the event of a tie, and in this case the Speaker is required to vote in such a way as to prolong consideration of the issue. It can also be very lonely in the social sense because one is isolated from one's former party and political cronies. Added to this, the work-load is heavy and there are periods of excruciating stress.

Public reaction to Jeanne's appointment was highly favourable, except for a sour comment from Laura Sabia, the former chairperson of the Ontario Status of Women Council. Ms. Sabia, addressing a conference on Women in Politics, told her audience that Jeanne had been ''emasculated'' by accepting the job of Speaker. This statement revealed the hostility of the women's movement towards Jeanne (and also brought into question Ms. Sabia's knowledge of anatomy).

To prepare for the speakership, Jeanne, who was then fifty-seven, began a crash course in parliamentary procedure under the tutelage of Beverley Koester, the Clerk of the House of Commons. Having been a cabinet minister from the day she entered the Commons, she had very little experience in the House. Among other things, she had to learn the 116 Standing Orders of the Commons, as well as to familiarize herself with countless rulings and precedents, many of them couched in the most arcane language. To add to the challenge she also had to memorize the faces of all 282 members of the House and their constituencies. Koester, her right-hand man, started his tutorials in early March. It was a tight schedule (Parliament was due to convene in six weeks), but Jeanne might have pulled it off had she not been a trifle over-confident and taken a short holiday. While she and Maurice were in Europe, Koester was hospitalized for major surgery. When she returned she found that she was missing her most valuable adviser, and to make matters worse, most of his assistants lacked experience. Thus, partly through circumstances, and partly owing to her own fault, she was ill-prepared when the House convened on 14 April.

The ritual of electing the Speaker goes back to the early days of the British Parliament. In the seventeenth century two Speakers ended their careers with their heads on the block. For this reason, the ceremony of leading the Speaker to the Chair is accompanied by a feigned show of resistance on the part of the candidate. In the

Canadian Parliament the ritual has always been an occasion for levity, particularly as the Speaker is usually speeded on his way by kicks in the pants from his escort. When Jeanne was led up the Commons aisle by the Prime Minister and the Leader of the Opposition, Trudeau whispered, "Don't resist too much, we don't want to have to kick you!"

The Speaker sits in a raised, ornately carved chair at the end of the chamber. Parliamentary pages sit on the steps at the Speaker's feet, and rise with arms crossed every time the Speaker addresses the House. On the Speaker's right are the government benches, on the left the Opposition benches. The centre aisle is by tradition two sword-lengths in width. The Clerk of the House and his assistants sit at a table in the aisle directly in front of the Speaker. While the Speaker is in the Chair, the Mace, a gilded club signifying the authority of Parliament, rests on the table.

The Speaker's chair is so massive that when Jeanne, who is only five feet four inches, first sat in it her feet didn't touch the ground. Occupying the chair was an extraordinary experience. "The feeling that you're above everybody makes you realize that you have to be impartial — you're in the middle of both sides. The physical location gives you the message immediately. It's quite overwhelming!"

Speakers wear black court dress with a black gown (complete with wig bag), a black tricorn hat, and white gloves. Always fashion-conscious, Jeanne decided against this uniform because she didn't want to look like a transvestite. Instead, she had her couturier, Serge et Réal of Montreal, design her a costume that closely resembled the original made of black wool, trimmed with silk, and a black felt hat.

On 15 April, the day after she was elected Speaker, she participated in a gigantic referendum rally at the Montreal Forum. This rally was in reaction to a remark by Lise Payette, the Parti Québécois Minister of Social Development, who had contemptuously referred to Claude Ryan's wife Madeleine as an "Yvette". (Yvette is a stereotyped character, a passive daughter, who appears in some Quebec primary-school books.) Payette's insult reverberated through the province, and pushed many uncommitted women into Ryan's federalist camp. Spontaneous meetings of "Yvettes" were held in a number of centres, the largest being the "Yvette" rally at the Forum attended by fifteen thousand women. In Jeanne's words the atmosphere in the Forum was "sweet and soft — some women held flowers in their hands — it was like a sweet breeze. The applause was genuine but it wasn't hysterical, there was no element of militancy in the audience. Just quiet determination."

Jeanne shared the platform with a number of outstanding Quebec women, including her role model, Thérèse Casgrain. Senator Casgrain, the mother of four, had led the struggle for woman suffrage in Quebec. In the thirties she had been a radio broadcaster, hosting the program "Fémina". During the war, she served as a member of the Women's Surveillance Committee for the Wartime Prices and Trade Board. Active in politics, and staunchly opposed to Duplessis, she later became leader of the CCF in Quebec. In the sixties she founded the League of Human Rights and the Quebec branch of the Voice of Women. She was appointed to the Senate in 1970, and died in 1981.

Jeanne's speech at the Forum that night, and the others she made on behalf of the federalist cause, was carefully worded. "I only gave written speeches so I wouldn't get carried away!" The "Yvette" phenomenon proved to be the turning-point in the campaign. When the votes were cast on 20 May the "NO" faction won by a substantial margin.

On the day Jeanne was installed as Speaker she was given a standing ovation. What she didn't realize was the fleeting nature of this accolade. Beneath its show of goodwill the House was in an ugly mood. The Tories were bitter at losing power, while the Liberals were vindictive, thirsting for revenge after their unaccustomed stay in the wilderness.

Because the business of the Commons is conducted through the Speaker, Jeanne found herself in the thick of the fray. Members may not address each other directly, nor may they use personal names. Members are identified by their position or by their constituency, for example, "The Minister of Finance" or "The honourable member for Mouse Chop". Despite this protocol, insults fly back and forth and the elected representatives often behave like rowdy schoolchildren — especially during the forty-five-minute Question Period or during a heated debate.

She was soon in trouble. Not only did she have difficulty recognizing members on both sides of the House, but she was accused of favouring the Liberals. When she recognized members, she often got their constituencies wrong. Without the advice of the Clerk, who was still in hospital, she also fumbled procedural rulings. Being one of only two Speakers in the history of Parliament who didn't have a legal background made her competence even more suspect. Normally, for the first few months a new Speaker is treated with tolerance. But these weren't normal times.

On one occasion, seven NDP members walked out of the chamber in a huff. On another, a group of Liberal backbenchers became so angry at being ignored that they gave Jeanne a pair of opera glasses. (She thanked them by inviting them to dinner, and she still uses the opera glasses.) Because of her years as a broadcaster her instinct was to make her rulings brief and to the point, which provoked more resentment. For example, an Opposition member who had spent several days preparing a Point of Order resented having it dismissed in a couple of sentences. Had she given a long-winded ruling, she would have achieved the same end but salved the member's pride. The recent introduction of television in the House, which made MP's sensitive to the fact that they were playing to a national audience, added to her problems. Television improved the standard of dress, but encouraged posturing and "showboating" in front of the cameras.

Another cause for hostility was the fact that Jeanne was a woman. The Commons had previously been a male preserve; even in 1980 there were only fourteen women in Parliament. Some male chauvinists undoubtedly thought to themselves, "First there was my mother, then a succession of female schoolteachers, later my wife— and now there's a woman Speaker telling me what to do!"

Jeanne's problems in the House were quickly picked up by the press. In mid-May she explained to Pamela Wallin of the *Toronto Star* that most of the criticism was from backbenchers "who come into the House once a week and expect to be recognized". At the end of July, an article by Stewart MacLeod, syndicated columnist for Thomson News Service, titled "Recess Would Help Speaker" appeared in the Charlottetown *Guardian and Patriot*; it began:

> *Apart from the fact that Parliament had become cantankerous and unco-operative, there is another good reason why the institution is in need of a summer recess: It will give Speaker Jeanne Sauvé an opportunity to catch her breath, perhaps make a few adjustments and return in the fall to make a fresh start.*
>
> *That's what football teams do at half time.*
>
> *And while it might be indelicate to compare Mme. Speaker with a football team, I think it's fair to say she has had her share of difficulties trying to cope with the opposition in the Commons. Half-time adjustments would appear to be in order.*

In addition to being responsible for procedural matters, the Speaker is also responsible for the administration of the House of Commons. Occupying five buildings, the Commons has an annual budget in excess of one hundred million dollars and a staff of more than three thousand. It has been likened to a small town, because it has its own post office, its own "newspaper" (*Hansard*), its own police force, a liquor store, a barber shop, a beauty salon, first-aid facilities, even its own fleet of mini-busses to transport people from one building to the other. The staff encompasses people of many disciplines, including *maîtres d'hôtel*, hordes of chefs (there are seven restaurants as well as a number of private dining-rooms), computer experts, locksmiths, librarians, carpenters, language translators, tour guides (hundreds of thousands of tourists troop through the Parliament Buildings each year), and a carillonneur who performs on the Peace Tower bells. There is also a sculptress who, with a half-dozen assistants, continually works on the stone interiors of the buildings.

Two weeks after she was installed as Speaker, a confidential report by the Auditor General on the administration of the House landed on Jeanne's desk. It had been requested by the previous Speaker, James Jerome, on the recommendation of the all-party Standing Committee on Management and Members' Services (MMSC). Summarizing the findings of his 118-page report, Auditor General James Macdonell wrote, "the quality of general and financial administration is significantly below a minimum acceptable standard."

During the previous fifteen years the Commons budget had increased tenfold — from $9.6 million to $96 million — and the number of staff had tripled to over three thousand. Although the size of these numbers was surprising, everyone knew that administration on the Hill was a shambles. In 1964, a year before the budget started to skyrocket, a Civil Service Commission study had unearthed 170 administrative problems in the House of Commons.

With everyone aware of the situation, why had it been allowed to continue?

There are several reasons. The overriding one was that while some members were genuinely concerned, and others paid lip service to the idea of a shake-up, most people on the Hill didn't want any major changes. Equally important, many parliamentarians believed that running the nation entitled them to service at any cost. This stemmed from their concept of parliamentary privilege. Members of Parliament enjoy special exemptions from the law. For example, they can't be sued for libel for anything they say in the House, nor can they be arrested for civil offences within the precincts of Parliament. By the same token, they don't have to appear in court as witnesses, nor do they have to serve as jurors.

To preserve the institution's special status, Parliament has always functioned as an independent entity, separate from the rest of the government. Parliament is not, and never has been, a part of the federal bureaucracy. Even the staff on the Hill have special status; most don't come under the Civil Service Act but report to Parliament. In essence, Parliament runs its own shop and doesn't tolerate outside interference.

Indeed, the Auditor General, the country's financial watchdog, couldn't have set foot on the Hill had he not been invited to do so. However, as Parliament had requested him to investigate the administration of the Commons, it could hardly ignore his findings. Macdonell's interim report was given to Speaker Jerome on 31 October 1979 and tabled in the House the next day. The report recommended, among other measures, separating procedural and administrative responsibilities. As the Clerk was responsible for both, but his priority was to advise the Speaker on procedural matters — a full-time job — the Auditor General recommended the appointment of a top-flight administrator to look after the administrative function. When he tabled the report, Jerome announced that, owing to the urgency of the situation, Rhéal Chatelain, Senior Deputy Auditor General, had agreed to act as interim administrator. Responding to the Speaker's announcement, Walter Baker, the House Leader for the Government, commended Jerome and concluded, ''I say on behalf of the government that we support the action you have taken with respect to this matter.''

Thus, in November 1979 the administrative clean-up appeared to be launched. But a few weeks after Chatelain took up his duties, the Conservatives were defeated in the House and Parliament was dissolved. Rather than contesting the election, Speaker Jerome accepted an appointment as Associate Chief Justice of the Federal Court of Canada. With Jerome's departure, Chatelain lost his sponsor, and the fall of the government deprived him of much of his authority. Working under these handicaps, Chatelain did his best but encountered suspicion, mistrust, and hostility wherever he went. Later, recalling his stint on the Hill, he told a CBC interviewer, ''I was there for eight or nine months and my gosh it could have been eight or nine years and it would not have been worse!''

When Parliament convened in April 1980 it was widely assumed that the administrative review would be scrapped, that Chatelain's services would no longer be required, and it would be business as usual on the Hill. Representations were made to Jeanne, the newly appointed Speaker, to shelve the report.

For Jeanne, who was already in trouble on the procedural side, it would have been the easy way out. After all, it was a new Parliament (the Liberals, who hadn't officially endorsed the report, were now in power) and the study had been commissioned by the previous Speaker. She could also have avoided dealing with it by making a few token changes and then letting the matter drop.

But, after studying the report, Jeanne was so outraged that she decided to clean up the mess.

Among other things, she discovered that patronage was rife; hiring wasn't done on the basis of competence but on the basis of whom a person knew. Patronage was a tradition on the Hill that went back as far as anyone could remember. In 1880 Sir John A. Macdonald observed, "The system [of hiring staff at the House] for so many years was admitted by all to be a vicious one, many . . . were quite ignorant and untrained, and unfit for their work. . . ." Aside from flaunting the merit principle, patronage led to nepotism and petty fiefdoms on the Hill. In one instance, a senior manager who was a grade seven drop-out dispensed overtime payments, extra holidays, and other goodies to his friends, but froze out those who didn't toady to him. Depending upon the personal connection, new employees were often hired for the same salary as workers with ten years' experience.

While hiring practices were deplorable, spending was also out of control. Most areas were grossly overstaffed, especially the maintenance section and the cafeterias. Don Boudria, a former Hill employee, and the only one in history to be elected to Parliament, recollected that when a request would come for a desk to be moved, instead of sending two or three men, six or seven would be dispatched to do the job. Maintenance workers were paid for a seven-and-three-quarter-hour day, of which four and a half hours were taken up by coffee breaks, a lunch break, and one hour for which they were paid but didn't work. On a cost-per-square-foot comparison, the housekeeping costs were two or three times the norm for commercial or government buildings.

It was the same story in the purchasing area: most goods and services were bought without tender, often on a retail rather than a wholesale basis. One example was the purchase of refrigerators for members' offices. If a Member of Parliament was a diabetic he could have a refrigerator to store insulin. All he had to do was to write the Sergeant-at-Arms stating that he suffered from diabetes. In consequence it was revealed that nearly 100 of the 282 members of the Commons had diabetes (a startling medical statistic). Nearly all of their refrigerators were bought in small lots, from retail outlets.

Management also left a great deal to be desired. Policy manuals and job descriptions were virtually non-existent. There were no training programs for managers or for blue-collar workers. The payroll office couldn't account for those on staff, nor could it reconcile the staggering overtime payments — which mysteriously increased when the House was in recess. Because eighty per cent of the hiring was done without consulting the personnel office, the people in this department spent most of their time playing cards.

For years Members of Parliament had ignored the situation on the Hill, even though taxpayers were footing the bill. Prior to Jeanne's arrival, nobody had dared to challenge the system. To do so meant confrontation with a self-serving, deeply entrenched culture.

Jeanne knew that if she followed through on the Auditor General's report, she was in for a battle, that she would make enemies, and that her life would become even more difficult. Nevertheless, she went ahead.

The first thing she did was to convene the Executive Committee and advise them of her decision. The Executive Committee, which she chaired, was responsible for the policy of the House. This small committee consisted of Jeanne and four of her senior officers: the Deputy Speaker, C. Lloyd Francis; the Clerk, Beverley Koester; the Sergeant-at-Arms, Major-General M. G. (Gus) Cloutier; and the interim Administrator, Rhéal Chatelain. At this meeting she received full support for her plan to reform the House, and it was agreed that a permanent Administrator would be engaged as soon as possible.

She then informed the Board of Internal Economy and the Management and Members' Services committee of her intentions. The

Board of Internal Economy, chaired by the Speaker and consisting (at that time) of four cabinet ministers, had the power to act on all financial and administrative matters pertaining to the Commons. The Management and Members' Services committee (MMSC) was composed of members from both sides of the House, but it had no executive authority, being advisory in nature.

At the beginning of July 1980, after screening a number of candidates, the Executive Committee unanimously selected Arthur Silverman as administrator. Thirty-five-year-old Silverman had previously been an assistant deputy minister in the Department of Communications. A dedicated public servant with a passion for efficiency, he was a sound choice for the job. His lack of tact, however, would subsequently nettle many people on the Hill. In mid-July, Silverman's appointment was sanctioned by the Board of Internal Economy and, two days later, endorsed by the MMSC. With her key player in place, Jeanne was now ready to start the clean-up.

Silverman quickly recruited a team through the Civil Service Commission and started to work. One of his senior lieutenants, who joined him a week after his appointment, said recently, "We had no idea of the conflicts and the culture on the Hill, it was really weird." Silverman's crew, after assessing the management procedures (which they considered medieval), began issuing policy bulletins to bring some order into the situation. The next step was to sort out the staff. Four managers were transferred or given a "golden handshake". A dozen employees were fired for cause, such as repeated drunkenness or fighting. One was prosecuted for the theft of $65,000 and subsequently sentenced to six months in jail. Many were retired on pension, including several cleaning-women who were in their eighties. Others quit when they realized the good old days were gone forever. No blue-collar workers were laid off. From this point on, the policy was to reduce the staff through natural attrition.

The personnel department, renamed "Human Resources", was increased fivefold. Every job on the Hill was screened and classified. Training programs were designed and implemented at all levels.

Budgetary controls were tightened and improved dramatically. Hiring was done on the merit principle — which resulted in a head-on collision with the old patronage system.

The changes on the Hill were unsettling for everyone. Members of Parliament, used to arranging jobs with a simple phone call, were frustrated by the new hiring practices. Other MP's were concerned that the authority of Parliament was being usurped by bureaucrats, who they dubbed "Pollyannas with stopwatches". Soon there were mutterings of discontent, and a rising ground swell of complaints against the Speaker and her "hatchetman", the Administrator.

Many employees were confused as to what was going on and feared for their jobs. A significant number of middle managers not only felt insecure, but were angry at losing the power they had previously held. At the senior level, Beverley Koester, the scholarly Clerk, was in favour of the appointment of an administrator, but some of his staff believed that it undermined the importance of his office and that of the whole Procedural Branch. Gus Cloutier, the personable Sergeant-at-Arms, bore the brunt of the changes because he was responsible for most of the support functions and patron to almost one thousand blue-collar employees — including the maintenance division, security, the cafeterias, and the messenger service. Jeanne's reform measures eroded the Sergeant-at-Arms' traditional rights in the area of hiring, personnel policy, and financial management. To make matters worse, although Cloutier had been one of the Executive Committee who had selected Silverman, the two men soon developed a healthy dislike for each other.

Several influential people on the Management and Members' Services committee were also unhappy. The MMSC had started the whole thing by recommending the study, but they had not wanted the Auditor General to undertake the task; he was merely to be consulted for the names of private firms. Not only were civil servants intruding in their business, but they were, in their view, threatening the independence of Parliament.

During the autumn of 1980 pressure mounted to stop the reforms. Damaging rumours were planted in the House by a dedicated group who lobbied tirelessly to turn back the clock. This made the situation increasingly tense for Jeanne, who knew that her campaign could be nullified by a simple vote in the Commons. On weekends, she often held strategy meetings with Art Silverman at her house in Montreal. Sonny Gordon, Maurice's former executive assistant (now the Sauvés' lawyer), frequently sat in on these sessions. Not only was the integrity of the House at stake, but so were Jeanne's and Silverman's careers. If the clean-up were halted, Silverman would be out on his ear, and Jeanne couldn't, in conscience, remain as Speaker. She would have to resign.

The conflict became public knowledge on 18 November when the *Globe and Mail* published a report by John Gray titled "The Old Guard resisting new broom on the Hill". The next day the *Toronto Star* ran a story by the Canadian Press headed "Irate MPs fight for their rights". In its article the *Star* quoted Marcel Lambert and Charles Turner:

> *"The Hill is not a government department," said Marcel Lambert, Conservative MP for Edmonton West and a speaker in the Diefenbaker years.*
>
> *He said Parliament was being turned into another branch of the public service.*
>
> *"I see a good deal of people coming here out of the civil service," he said, referring to the new managers. "Some of them will have to be taken on a shakedown cruise."*
>
> *Charlie Turner, Liberal MP for London East, warns that he, for one, is prepared to defend his MP rights and says the issue could explode soon.*
>
> *"He [Silverman] has gone too far," he said.*
>
> *"The administration should be asking MPs how to do things instead of telling them what to do," he said.*

Both of the MP's quoted in this article sat on the Management and Members' Services committee, and both were consistent critics of Jeanne.

Marcel-Joseph-Aimé Lambert, born in Edmonton, had been a Tory member of the Commons for twenty-four years. A Dieppe veteran and a former prisoner of war, he was a Rhodes Scholar and a lawyer by profession. For a period of five months, from September 1962 until February 1963, he had been Speaker of the House. While Jeanne was Speaker, he occupied a front-row Opposition bench and often contradicted her rulings — usually without bothering to stand up. In the words of one observer, "When he wasn't sleeping, he was always mumbling." One day Jeanne grew tired of his needling and said to him out of the corner of her mouth, "Shut up — I'm Speaker now!" Her *sotto voce* remark had no lasting effect, but it brought a laugh from those within earshot.

Charlie Turner, a big, bluff railway engineer, had been the Liberal member for London East since 1968. He was appointed Government Whip in 1980, and his job was to ensure that Liberal MP's attended committee meetings and turned up for votes in the House. Not being a student of parliamentary procedure, he rarely challenged Jeanne in the House, but he frequently harassed her from his position on the Management and Members' Services committee (irreverently known by some of Jeanne's staff as "The Hot Stove League").

With flak coming from two directions — from both the administrative and the procedural sides of the House — Jeanne had little time to do anything but react to problems. She did, however, manage to squeeze in further study. To better recognize members she had an assistant flash pictures of MP's in front of her while she ate lunch, and she would match the face with the constituency. A foolproof system, except for the day a new MP shaved off his mustache — "I looked at him in despair. I had no idea who he was!" To avoid charges of partiality, she devised a simple score-card to ensure that she recognized an appropriate number of MP's from both sides of the House during Question Period. "If by ten to three I hadn't heard from my third NDP member, I knew I was in trouble!" At night, if she didn't have to entertain, she would bone up on parliamentary procedure by reading the tomes of May, Bourinot, and Beauchesne. Gradually she developed more confidence, and a surer hand in the Chair.

The tide of opposition to Jeanne's reforms crested at the end of

November 1980. On 9 December, the Victoria *Times-Colonist* printed an editorial headed simply "Hear, Hear!"

Since her appointment last March as the first woman Speaker of the House of Commons, Jeanne Sauvé has had her problems and her share of criticism. . . .

The criticism may or may not have been deserved. From this distance it is hard to tell. But recent indications are that Madame Speaker is grasping more firmly that part of her job which entails general supervision of Commons administration, especially in cracking down on bureaucrats whose spending ambitions are equalled only by their sense of self-importance.

Last week Sauvé announced she had vetoed a proposal by Maj.-Gen. M. G. Cloutier, sergeant-at-arms of the House of Commons, to establish a super security force on Parliament Hill.

Among the special equipment proposed to protect MPs and staff from bombs, riots and the like were, believe it or not, protective vests, a 12-gauge shotgun, handcuffs and riot gear. The sergeant-at-arms is obviously a fan of those S.W.A.T. television programs, and in any case seems to have lost touch with reality.

Now the Speaker is turning her jaundiced eye on a posh new restaurant that dishes up subsidized meals — similar to the fancy fare available in the parliamentary restaurant — to senior bureaucrats. A splendid tuck-in apparently costs as little as $3.

Go to it, Madame Speaker. . . .

On 10 March 1981, Ronald Reagan, the recently elected president of the United States, paid his first state visit to Canada. During his busy round of events in Ottawa, he and his wife Nancy impressed everyone with their warmth and relaxed good humour. When he visited Parliament, Jeanne, as Speaker, welcomed Reagan on four different occasions: on the steps of the Centre Block, at the entrance to the House of Commons, at the entrance to the Parliamentary Library, and at an official reception she hosted and in her suite. Encountering Jeanne for the fourth time, Reagan joked, "We can't go on meeting like this — people will start talking!"

Reagan's visit provided Jeanne with a brief respite from the pressures of the House. For weeks a bitter debate had been raging over patriation of the Canadian Constitution. As the days passed, tempers grew shorter and it became increasingly difficult for Jeanne to maintain control. Aside from having to monitor proceedings in both French and English, she was constantly required to make decisions. "You have to put together all the rules and the precedents, and you have to do it very quickly — it's instant judgement all the time." She also had to gauge the mood of the House. "I was often puzzled what I should do — should I be cross with them, should I be patient, or should I try and humour them out of the situation?"

At precisely 1.57 p.m. each day Jeanne would leave her office for the Chamber. Preceded by the Sergeant-at-Arms with the gold mace on his shoulder, and followed by the Clerk with two of his black-robed assistants, the little procession would wend its way along the marble corridors, its path cleared by three uniformed security guards marching ahead. Jeanne quite enjoyed this ritual, but during the constitutional debate, when she approached the oak doors of the Commons she often felt as though she was entering a lions' cage.

She had good reason to be apprehensive. In the last week of March the Liberal House Leader announced that he was going to move a motion to limit debate on the constitutional issue. Under the rules of Parliament, at the end of the time limit a vote would be taken on the bill. The Tories, knowing they would lose the vote, resorted to a filibuster to frustrate the government's plan. A filibuster is a legitimate tactic designed to take up time and thereby prevent the motion from being put to a vote. It is orchestrated by having a series of speakers raise Points of Order and Questions of Privilege. The longer each member of the Opposition can hold forth, the better. A truly successful filibuster causes chaos, and can ultimately force an election.

During a filibuster, one of the Speaker's jobs is to rule on the length and the relevancy of the Points of Order and the Questions of Privilege. This puts the Speaker in a dreadful position, because the government obviously wants the Opposition muzzled, while the Opposition feels just as strongly that it should be allowed to proceed unfettered.

At the beginning of the filibuster, Jeanne allowed Opposition speakers twenty minutes to make their case. After five days, she reduced it to ten minutes. For some, this wasn't enough. Frank Oberle, a Tory MP from British Columbia, when urged by Jeanne to get to the point, lost his temper. Flailing his papers about he yelled at her, "I want the right to speak and I do not want to be interrupted fifteen times just because it takes me a little longer than the next guy to make my point." Jeanne listened to his tirade in silence. Oberle's outburst, however, brought a protest from NDP member Bob Rae, who described it as "primal scream therapy".

As the filibuster dragged on, Jeanne progressively shortened the length of time for Questions of Privilege. Eventually she told the House, "If in the first two sentences you don't convince me that you have a Question of Privilege, I won't hear you any further." This news was greeted with open hostility by the Opposition. Meanwhile, the government was carping at her for allowing the Commons to degenerate into what Trudeau called "an absolute state of disorder".

The government forced a vote in the second week of April by invoking a motion of closure, which ended the stalemate. (A year later, almost to the day, the new Constitution Act was signed by the Queen on Parliament Hill.) For Jeanne, the filibuster was the harshest test of her speakership. Not only was it nerve-wracking, it was also physically exhausting. Had she wished to, she could have turned over the Speaker's Chair to her deputy, but throughout the crisis she stayed in the Chair from two in the afternoon to ten o'clock at night.

Jeanne's conduct in the House drew praise from many sources. Richard Gwyn wrote a column titled "Sauvé wins spurs as Speaker". The Brockville *Recorder and Times* published an editorial which began:

Who won and who lost the constitutional debate . . . will be a matter for

history to decide. What is evident is the affair produced a new Canadian
heroine.

Jeanne Sauvé, the first woman Speaker of the House of Commons,
by her patience, wit and skill controlled one of the most difficult situa-
tions any Speaker has had to face.

The *Cape Breton Post* wrote a similar editorial with the heading
"Even Handed Lady":

If there is one person who has emerged with honours through the proce-
dural turmoil of the House of Commons during the sometimes riotous
Conservative filibuster on the constitutional resolution, it is the Speaker
of the House, Mrs. Jeanne Sauvé. She has displayed equanimity, even-
handedness in rulings and even at times a touch of humour in most
trying circumstances for a presiding officer. . . .

When it was all over, Jeanne told a reporter, "I always said it
would take a year to make a Speaker. I feel very confident now.

"The fire does make you stronger, there's no doubt."

While the House was in session, Jeanne led a Spartan existence.
Rising at seven, she would do a half-hour of calisthenics and then
eat a quick breakfast of orange juice, dry toast, and coffee. At her
desk by eight, she would spend the morning on procedural and
administrative matters. After a light lunch in her quarters, she would
change into her Speaker's costume and proceed to the Commons. If
the House didn't sit late, or if she didn't have official guests to
entertain, she would dine alone. After dinner, it was back to the
books. And so it went, day after day. Her weekends in Montreal
were her salvation, and sometimes, when the House wasn't sitting,
she'd slip home to Montreal for the night. What used to infuriate
her was when friends would ask how "poor Maurice" was adjust-
ing to her being Speaker — "They never asked me how I was doing!"

In June of 1981 Jeanne flabbergasted the government benches
when she ruled that ten items — worth $1.2 billion — were im-
properly included in the spending estimates. Among the items she
threw out were the home insulation and off-oil programs. What

the government had hoped to do was to finesse these through the Commons in a non-debatable motion. Now it had no alternative but to dismantle the package and present the disallowed portions for debate. The Tories considered Jeanne's ruling a major victory. Because of its ramifications and the staggering amount of money involved, her ruling was front-page news. The *Winnipeg Free Press* made it the subject of an editorial titled "Integrity in the Chair" which began:

> *No House of Commons speaker since René Beaudoin in the pipeline debate has taken the beating from the Opposition that Jeanne Sauvé endured in her first few months on the job. The members of Parliament, whom she was supposed to keep in order, complained not only of her inexperience and unfamiliarity with the House but of a tendency to favour her old colleagues in the Liberal party.*
>
> *No such complaints are being heard these days. Mrs. Sauvé has been carrying out her duties as Speaker with a degree of integrity and independence which has caused acute embarrassment to the government and which ought to win her the thanks of all Canadians who care about the future of Parliament.*

In July 1981 Jeanne issued a terse press release announcing that she was closing a restaurant for senior Commons staff in the South Block. When she had learned of the restaurant, which had been opened by the Sergeant-at-Arms without her authorization, she immediately ordered an audit of its books. The audit revealed that, except for Friday nights (when people took their friends for dinner), the restaurant was operating at twenty-per-cent capacity — and losing more than twelve dollars on every meal. The closure of the restaurant was the second time she had publicly rebuked the Sergeant-at-Arms.

All the restaurants and cafeterias on Parliament Hill were, and still are, subsidized by the taxpayer. When Jeanne took over as Speaker, they were running at a deficit of more than $3.5 million per year. Not only were the meals priced far below cost, but thousands of unauthorized people were taking advantage of these bargain prices. Tour companies routinely fed busloads of customers in the cafeterias. To cut the deficit, Jeanne restricted access to the cafeterias, reduced the staff, instituted cost controls, and raised the prices.

These innovations were not greeted with joy. Such minor changes as having cafeteria customers remove their own dishes (which reduced the need for casual staff, and resulted in an annual saving of $150,000) brought squeals of outrage. Liberal MP Marcel Dionne told Canadian Press, "We're not here to clear the table or wash the dishes. We're here to do services for our constituents." To which *The Gazette* replied: "It seems to have escaped his attention that saving tax money, even if it involves 30 seconds a day of mild physical effort by Mr. Dionne, is surely one key service his constituents would like him to perform."

In this connection, Jeanne's reforms were designed not only to save money, but to enhance the level of support for Members of Parliament. Yet, even when she was trying to help them, some MP's went out of their way to fight her. One of her innovations, providing members' offices with word-processors, was a good example. On 30 July she was criticized in the House by several MP's for choosing Micom word-processors over those made by AES Data Limited. Robert Coates, Conservative member for Cumberland-Colchester, and long-time chairman of the MMSC, said that he had written to Jeanne voicing the concerns of several MP's over her selection. At the same time, AES Data had complained in writing to many members, and suggested that Arthur Silverman had acted improperly in securing the contract for Micom.

At first glance, it appeared that Jeanne and her Administrator had played favourites, and ignored the advice of the special parliamentary committee appointed to choose the equipment.

In fact, the Department of Supply and Services (the purchasing arm of the federal government) had assessed the various suppliers and recommended Micom. Silverman had in turn presented this information to the committee and answered questions to their satisfaction. The committee, which was chaired by Robert Coates, had then unanimously approved the selection of Micom, and instructed Jeanne to enter into a contract.

The following day, Coates confessed in the House that indeed his committee had unanimously approved the contract with Micom, which ended the controversy. It is difficult to explain Coates's behaviour, other than to note that he was one of Jeanne's most stubborn antagonists. This incident also shows the length to which some of her opponents would go to discredit her. (Coates later became minister of national defence in the Mulroney government, a post he resigned amid a storm of controversy following charges of improper conduct.)

Another innovation that took place in 1981 was the introduction of an information-retrieval system, similar to Telidon. Called Oasis (Office Automation Service and Information System), this piece of electronic wizardry would eventually do everything but mix drinks for the members. Among the services it provides is video coverage in French and English of House debates and committee meetings, electronic mail within the House and outside it, regular cable television, word-processing linked to the member's constituency, information from a host of data bases, and a transcript of *Hansard*. It is also hooked up to the Commons security and alarm systems, and will even turn off the lights. Oasis is so advanced that legislators from all over the world have come to Ottawa to admire it.

In December Jeanne unveiled plans to establish a day-care centre for children of MP's, senators, and Hill employees. It was a project dear to her heart, for she had long been concerned about the plight of working mothers. To be effective, she knew the centre must be on the Hill—a requirement that drew objections from a number of MP's, who feared that it would be too noisy, and an affront to the dignity of Parliament. Notwithstanding these complaints, Jeanne was able to obtain the consent of the three caucuses. The centre, designed to accommodate forty children, was to be located on the ground floor of the Confederation Building. Renovations to meet Ontario government standards would cost $240,000, but after this initial outlay it would be self-supporting. Opened in April 1982, the day-care centre has proved to be a great success. Jeanne considers it one of her most important achievements.

On 2 March 1982 the business of the House came to a noisy halt. The Liberals had been trying to ram through an omnibus bill that incorporated twelve different pieces of legislation. The Tories objected, insisting that the bill must be dismantled and dealt with piece by piece. When Jeanne ruled that the omnibus bill was valid, the Tories moved that the House adjourn. Then they left the Chamber. When the bells rang, summoning members to vote on their motion to adjourn, the Tories refused to return to the House. Under the rules of Parliament, a vote can't be taken unless both the government Whip and the Opposition Whip are present in the Chamber. As the Opposition Whip was absent, the vote couldn't be held. The bells continued to ring. They rang all night and throughout the next day. The Tories ignored them.

Parliament ceased to function.

Meanwhile, the Chair had to be occupied round the clock by Jeanne or one of her deputies. On the third day, for humanitarian reasons, she silenced all the bells except for a single symbolic bell outside the government House Leader's office. As the walkout continued, pressure mounted from all sides for her to end the crisis. The government wanted her to force the Opposition back into the House. The Opposition, however, knew that there was no precedent to justify this action. Indeed, there was no clear-cut solution. After searching fruitlessly for a precedent to justify her intervention, Jeanne decided that she would do nothing. Her philosophy, which infuriated everyone, was quite simple. "The House gets itself into a mess, the House must get itself out of the mess." Once she'd set her course, she said, "I just waited for things to fall in place."

She was treated as a pariah for her decision (even former colleagues turned their backs when she passed them in the corridor), and she was also pilloried in the press. Canada's largest newspaper, the *Toronto Star*, wrote a series of scathing articles, among them "Sauvé shirks her duty" and "Why the bells can't save Jeanne

Sauvé", the latter illustrated with a hilarious cartoon by Duncan Macpherson. One of Ottawa's best-informed political columnists, Frank Howard, wrote in the *Citizen*:

> *On the face of it, one would have to assume that Jeanne Sauvé's days as Speaker are numbered.*
>
> *Already there are voices, including that of the quasi-Parliamentarian Charles Lynch, saying that she will have lost the confidence of the House, or at least of the official Opposition, no matter what happens during the coming week to end the impasse brought on by the Tory boycott.*
>
> *I hope they are wrong, but I'm afraid they might be right.*

Each morning Jeanne would summon the House leaders to her office and ask them, "Where are we today?" Invariably they would answer that no progress had been made to resolve the deadlock. It was a frustrating exercise for everyone, including the press who waited expectantly outside. Being a former journalist, Jeanne was very generous to the media. During the walkout she held several press conferences and also granted a number of personal interviews. At the end of one of these sessions the young woman who was interviewing her said dolefully, "I wouldn't want to be in your shoes." Bloodied but unbowed, Jeanne retorted, "Nobody has asked you to be."

The stalemate lasted fifteen days. It ended when the government made a deal with the Opposition to split the omnibus bill in return for time limits of debate on the pieces. The next day, Jeanne made an impassioned plea to the House for a review of the rules so that the same thing wouldn't happen again. As a result, a special parliamentary committee was formed and the rules were changed to prevent a similar stoppage.

The bell-ringing crisis proved to be the turning-point in Jeanne's speakership. She won grudging admiration and new respect for her steadiness in a situation that had threatened the viability of Parliament. When the Commons resumed its business, everyone knew she was there to stay. For the next few months a more co-operative spirit prevailed in the Chamber. By this time, experience had given her what all good Speakers possess, an instinctive "feel" for the mood of the House. "You have to be able to read the mood of the House — God help you if you don't read it right!"

Modifications to the Speaker's chair also made her days physically more comfortable. The chair was changed after her deputy, Lloyd Francis, began to suffer severe back pains. (Because of its height and width, it was also very uncomfortable for Jeanne, who could neither touch the floor, nor reach both arms. In consequence, she had to perch like a sparrow in one corner.) The Department of National Health and Welfare, called in to examine the chair, recommended the seat be replaced with a first-class Boeing 747 seat which combined comfort with excellent support. This was done, and, as an added refinement, a hydraulic lift was installed so that it could be raised or lowered at the touch of a concealed lever. The new seat was covered with the same material as the original, and no one noticed the difference. For Jeanne, "it was a godsend."

One day while she was presiding in the Commons, she heard rustling noises and tapping behind her chair. As soon as the House adjourned, two plainclothes security men came up to Jeanne and reported that there had been a bomb scare.

"Where was the bomb meant to be?" she asked.

"Behind your chair," was the reply.

"But I was sitting in it! Why didn't you tell me?"

"We always work discreetly, Madame."

In the autumn of 1982 Jeanne was asked by the UN if she would head the World Refugee Commission. She was so intrigued by this proposal that she flew to New York to discuss it with Javier Pérez de Cuellar, the Secretary General of the United Nations. When she returned to Canada she had pretty well made up her mind to accept the offer.

Her husband Maurice, however, was strongly against it. He believed she would be unhappy in the role. Not only would the job be depressing, and hard for her emotionally, but her nerves would be frayed by the constant travelling. Although she knew that Maurice had her best interests at heart — that he was her greatest promoter

— she was still tempted to accept the challenge. They talked it over at length and also sought Sonny Gordon's opinion (which was the same as Maurice's). Still undecided, she went to see Pierre Trudeau.

Trudeau said to her, "Jeanne, you can't leave now. The House needs you — you control it. It's going to be rough, but you've got to stay another year." The Prime Minister made no mention of any future appointment.

Reluctantly Jeanne turned down the UN offer. Gritting her teeth, she accepted the fact that she would have to continue for another year as Speaker. It was not a prospect she relished, because the pressure was beginning to take its toll. A mediator by nature, she couldn't understand why members chose to attack the Speaker, and she was upset each time it happened. "I hated it. I wanted to walk out of the Chair. I kept asking myself, 'Do I need this?' " Despite her luxurious quarters and personal servants, living over the shop meant that she couldn't escape from the Commons — she was surrounded by it twenty-four hours a day. Indeed, it was so confining that she once told a reporter that she felt like "a bird in a gilded cage". She was even tired of her uniform; she loved bright colours, and wearing black all the time reminded her of the convent.

Jeanne's morale received a boost in December when Richard Gwyn made her the subject of one of his syndicated columns. After citing examples of abuses on the Hill before she took over, Gwyn wrote:

> For decades, every Speaker knew about all of this, and looked deliberately the other way. Each waited out their time until they became an ambassador or a judge.
>
> Of the 30 Speakers since Confederation, Jeanne Sauvé is the first who has dared to be different. Since becoming Speaker in March, 1980, she's cut spending by a cumulative $18 million and has reduced the payroll by 305.
>
> Administrative efficiency is a dry subject, something that Canadians favour when public funds are involved, but don't care to know much about.
>
> Still, it is interesting that Sauvé, while trimming spending, has improved services. . . .

*The real story of what Sauvé has done, though, isn't about adminis-
trative efficiency, but about personal courage. The courage, that is, to
take on the most powerful private club in the country and to force it to
practice what so many of its members preach about economy and efficiency in public spending. . . .*

*By the standards by which Speakers usually are judged, and quite
correctly so, of reigning over the daily Question Period and of coping
with crises like the affair of the bells, Sauvé will rate only a brief line in
Parliament's honor roll. But by another standard, her name will stand
apart from those of all her predecessors: She's the first Speaker in 115
years to care enough and to dare enough not to look the other way.*

In May 1983, Jeanne entertained Mikhail Gorbachev, the Soviet
Minister of Agriculture, on his first official visit to Ottawa. It escaped most people's notice that it was she rather than Gorbachev's
counterpart, the Canadian Minister of Agriculture, who hosted the
visit. However, there was a good reason for this. Gorbachev, a member of the Politburo and Secretary of the powerful Central Committee, was expected to be the next leader of the Soviet Union.
Trudeau wanted to have private talks with him, but because of the
sticky rules of protocol the only way this could be done was if
Gorbachev was invited as a parliamentarian by the Speaker. Had
Gorbachev come as a guest of the Minister of Agriculture, protocol
would have prevented him from meeting anyone above ministerial
level. However, as a guest of the Speaker, he could stay at 7 Rideau
Gate (a stone's throw from Rideau Hall and the Prime Minister's
residence) and meet both the Governor General and the Prime
Minister — which he did. Jeanne got along well with Gorbachev,
whom she found more affable and relaxed than most Russian officials. Before he left, it was agreed that she would make a goodwill
visit to Russia as his guest in August.

On 8 May, Jeanne flew to Halifax to give the Convocation address at Mount St. Vincent University. Because Mount St. Vincent
is a women's college, she chose to speak on feminism and the role of
women in modern society. This speech is especially significant be-

cause it reveals her personal views, views that she still holds today. The following excerpts capture the essence of her message:

> *In their denial of the profound, complex, human relationship between men and women, the feminists only succeeded in polarizing the sexes, alienating men and women, and destroying all hope of complicity in accomplishing the more legitimate objectives of the campaign.*
>
> *Feminists argued at the time that this rejection of mutualism was a necessary, but only temporary aberration in the natural order, believing that when women's rights were won, the relationship between the sexes would heal itself. Their reactionary fervor seemed to blind them to the immediate implications and logical outcome of their actions; that in rejecting and defaming men they gained a jilted and powerful adversary.*
> . . .
>
> *My own career took place at a time when it was not socially acceptable to have one. I fought an uphill battle for myself and to promote women, or help them, as I was helped, to make breakthroughs. I pride myself in having established what I believe to be a most essential service if women are to participate fully in society and the workplace: a day care centre in the House of Commons, the only such facility in the entire government apparatus.*
>
> *Was I too moderate in the Sixties when I would not condone the rejection of family and femininity espoused by the movement? Was I anti-feminist to refuse to be caught up with the misguided missile of sexual politics? In this, as in many other areas of endeavour, I remained loyal to my deepest instincts. . . .*
>
> *I was always convinced that women could reconcile career and family, because I was never prepared to sacrifice one for the other or to accept that one's sex determined a woman's whole life. . . .*
>
> *If I had a contribution to make to feminism in its early stages, it was in fulfilling my duties as Minister as competently as possible, and supporting the efforts of those Canadian women determined to rectify the irregularities of the system through the appropriate legal and political avenues. . . .*
>
> *We can have it all! We can embrace the fullness of life derived from*

*love and work, and we need not do it at the expense of femininity,
children or family life; but, we cannot, and we should not, do it alone!*

*The superwoman phenomenon, spawned by the fierce independence
of the early feminists' approach to women's liberation, has created an
agenda for the working mother that is clearly exhausting and impracti-
cal. To continue to cope by shouldering alone both domestic and career
responsibilities will inevitably be self defeating. Clearly we must put
aside this misbegotten pride in our own self sufficiency and begin to take
a more practical approach to accommodating our ambitions. . . .*

*Ironically, the true liberation of women lies not in rejecting men, but
in offering men a more liberated role; not in destroying the institutional
framework of the family but in strengthening and moulding it to meet
our needs. We must create a new alliance with men, instil in their
minds the idea that they too have a stake, that they can share their
responsibilities with women, and can profit equally from women's liberation. Once having gained a vested interest in our progress, we can begin
the work of redefining the nature of our relationship which has traditionally been one of male dominance, to one of complicity, mutual respect,
and support.*

A few weeks after she gave this speech an incident in the House
showed that Jeanne meant it when she spoke of mutual respect.
Tory MP Mike Forrestall had risen on a Question of Privilege and,
while he was roasting the government in his preamble, Jeanne interrupted him to ask, "Does the honourable member have a question?" Without thinking, Forrestall replied, "I certainly do, my
dear." On her feet in a flash, Jeanne snapped, "Don't call me 'my
dear', call me Madam Speaker!" After the House adjourned he apolo-
gized, explaining that it was a slip of the tongue, that he'd been
thinking of his wife. With a smile Jeanne said, "That's what I
thought." Charles Lynch was so amused by the interchange that he
wrote a column on it.

That August, before going to Russia, Jeanne and Maurice visited a resort in Switzerland and then went on to Italy. While they

were in Italy, Jeanne caught what she thought was a chill—she had a low fever — and she consulted a local doctor. He too thought it was a cold, when in fact it was the harbinger of a much more serious illness. He prescribed some pills, the ''cold'' cleared up, and Jeanne continued on to Russia. On her arrival in Moscow she was met by her host, Mikhail Gorbachev, and given the red-carpet treatment. The highlight of her visit was a private two-and-a-half-hour conversation with Gorbachev (now the leader of the Soviet Union).

When she returned to Canada in September, she fell ill again, and went into the hospital for tests. Stories in the media suggested that she had picked up a nasty Russian virus. After a couple of weeks in hospital she went home to Montreal to convalesce.

It was mid-October when she resumed her duties in the House. The Commons was in the final throes of the Crowsnest Pass debate, which had been festering since the spring. The Tories, who knew they couldn't stop the proposed legislation, tried every trick in the book to delay it, including a short-lived walkout. Jeanne terminated the second bell-ringing episode in a matter of hours. At one point she was also compelled to rule seventy-eight amendments out of order. The ''Crow Bill'' was finally passed, and Parliament was prorogued at the end of November 1983.

This session, which had lasted three and a half years, was not only the longest, but one of the most contentious, in Canadian history.

In the third week of December, Jeanne had lunch with Prime Minister Trudeau at 24 Sussex Drive. The purpose of their meeting was to discuss her future. Since she had followed his advice and served another year in the Chair, she hoped he would now offer her an ambassadorial post. Paris, which had once been offered to Maurice, was her first choice.

All thoughts of Paris vanished when Trudeau asked her if she would consent to be governor general.

''It was such a great honour, there was no way I could refuse. I didn't even say, like you would about a cabinet post — I'll think about it, or I'll see if I can handle it — I accepted immediately.''

Trudeau was delighted with her reaction, but suggested that she might like to talk it over first with Maurice. Jeanne, who knew that Maurice would be totally in favour, waved this aside, saying:

"No, I don't think I should delay my answer — it's such an honour, I will say yes right away."

Happy to have the question settled, Trudeau said that he would announce her appointment before Christmas. Hardly able to wait to tell Maurice, she left the Prime Minister's residence in a state of euphoria. In Jeanne's words:

"It was a leap into something totally unexpected."

Chapter 9

A TIME OF ANXIETY
January–May 1984

The appointment of Jeanne Sauvé as governor general was announced on 23 December 1983. The news made headlines across Canada as well as the front page of the *New York Times*. Smiling radiantly, Jeanne told reporters, "It's a terrific opportunity to serve the country and I'm really quite delighted to have been asked to do it."

Maurice, beaming at her side, said, "I'm very happy for my wife, my son, and me." When asked what his role would be, and what he would do about his corporate directorships, Maurice said it was too early to tell, but that "we have to adjust to a new reality." Defending his autonomy, Jeanne interjected, "One member of the couple shouldn't eat the other up — we've always lived that way."

Twenty-four-year-old Jean-François, who didn't attend the press conference, later told a friend that he'd been hoping his mother would be ambassadress to France, but that the viceregal appointment was even better, explaining, "There are lots of ambassadors, but only one governor general!"

For nearly a century the office of governor general was filled by a succession of British peers, who were proposed by the British Colonial Office and approved by the Canadian Prime Minister. This tradition changed in 1952 when the first Canadian, Vincent Massey, was appointed governor general. Since then the Prime Minister has chosen the governor general, and put forward his choice to the

Queen for her approval. Because the Prime Minister now makes the selection, there is an inherent risk that the candidate will be chosen for political reasons. However, once appointed, the governor general must be above politics and completely non-partisan. Success in the viceregal role depends largely upon the public's perception of the incumbent.

Both the public and the press reacted enthusiastically to Jeanne Sauvé's appointment. The *Globe and Mail* wrote, "Mme. Sauvé will bring not only a history of public service and high intelligence to Rideau Hall, but an air of elegance that it needs and deserves." The *Edmonton Journal* said, "Jeanne Sauvé is an inspired choice for Canada's 23rd, and first female, Governor General." The *Winnipeg Free Press* noted, "By any measure, Jeanne Sauvé has the qualities which will ensure her a constructive and distinguished term." Both *La Presse* and *Le Devoir* published lyrical editorials by distinguished academics. Columnist Charles Lynch wrote, "This time, Pierre Trudeau got it right. He gave the nation a marvellous Christmas present in the person of Jeanne Sauvé, our new governor general."

On a brasher note, *Vancouver Sun* columnist Jamie Lamb commented:

> *Madame Sauvé will likely prove to be a fine governor-general. She has grace, charm, and wit, and if she carries some mouldy baggage from her former days in the Trudeau cabinet, well, at least it's less luggage than the trunks Ed Schreyer lugged into Rideau Hall. . . .*
>
> *Mr. Schreyer's tenure as governor-general can only be called a flop. He may be a charming and interesting chap in private, but in public he has all the vice-regal charm of a sack of potatoes. . . .*
>
> *So, a cynical choice for governor-general, but one that should work out for the best. Here's to Her Excellency Jeanne Sauvé, and perhaps the return of dignity to a post in desperate need of it.*

William F. Gold of the *Calgary Herald* was even more flippant:

> *The wave of acclaim following Jeanne Sauvé's appointment as Governor-General is a classic national suspension of disbelief.*

For no discernible reason other than that she is a woman there has been an outpouring of praise.

This tells us more about the reluctance of people to appear anti-feminist than it does about Sauvé herself.

Of course it is a "good thing" to have a woman, at last, in this highly visible national office.

But by the same token it might be a good thing to appoint a stuffed owl to occupy this nest of largely irrelevant ceremonial hokum. Goodness knows the departing incumbent, Ed Schreyer, came pretty close.

The last word, however, came from Stewart MacLeod in the Charlottetown *Guardian and Patriot*:

While Mme. Sauvé's appointment has been cheered lustily by women's groups as a breakthrough . . . the real satisfaction lies in the fact that we are not dealing, to the slightest degree, with tokenism.

The more you think about the Sauvé appointment, the more convinced one becomes that there simply wasn't a better candidate, male or female, in the entire country.

Never one to go into a new situation ill-prepared, the first thing Jeanne Sauvé did after her appointment was announced was to ask her future Secretary, Esmond Butler, for a briefing on the viceregal office. Armed with a binder of notes, he presented his briefing to her at the Speaker's chambers in the first week of January. As they had known each other for years, it was a friendly meeting.

Both had a chuckle remembering how they'd worked together the previous June during the visit of Prince Charles and Diana, Princess of Wales. A reception had been given at Rideau Hall, in the Tent Room, for the royal couple to meet special guests invited from all parts of Canada. The hosts, Ed and Lily Schreyer, instead of staying with the Prince and Princess, drifted off to chat with friends. This put Butler in a difficult position because it was his job to round up guests for presentation — but he was also painfully aware that the royal couple shouldn't be left unattended. Jeanne, spotting his dilemma, told him to stay with Charles and Diana while she ferreted out the people he needed. After each sortie she would materialize at his side and quietly ask, "Who do you want next?"

Among the subjects the Governor General-designate and her future Secretary discussed were the changes involved with a woman in office and the role her husband would play. Butler also reviewed the staff positions in the Household, and noted that by tradition she could bring a reasonable number of her own people. In this connection, Rideau Hall has a staff of approximately one hundred, including three military aides-de-camp and six footmen. Madame Sauvé indicated she would bring some of her staff with her, but she would not require a lady-in-waiting. Another topic for discussion was the design of a personal coat of arms to be used on Governor General's Medals, on the Privy Seal, and for stamping on picture frames and other viceregal gifts.

Madame Sauvé was animated and enthusiastic throughout their two-hour meeting. Although she looked frail from her recent illness, Butler was confident she was firmly on the road to recovery. However, when he brought up the question of her Installation date, she told him that she needed to have more medical tests, and the date would depend upon the results.

Jeanne Sauvé's official term as Speaker ended on 16 January 1984. The following day she suffered a relapse of her respiratory illness and was rushed to Ottawa General Hospital. Treatment proved difficult because she was allergic to certain antibiotics. Despite the efforts of a top team of doctors headed by John Henderson, a specialist in respiratory diseases, her condition grew steadily worse. A week later she was transferred to the intensive-care unit.

Being seriously ill was a totally new and frightening experience for her. Throughout her life she had taken good health for granted. Now, at the age of sixty-one, with the highest office in the country before her, Fate had intervened and she was suddenly faced with the prospect of early death.

Maurice remained steadfastly optimistic, even when she went into intensive care. It was only after his brother, Dr. Gaston Sauvé, spoke to him that he accepted the fact that his wife was in critical condition. As soon as he realized the gravity of the situation he phoned Jean-François in Toronto, who took the first plane to Ottawa. For the next week Maurice and Jean-François spent most of their time at Jeanne's bedside. Never having known his mother to be ill, Jean-François was shocked to see her lying semi-conscious in a hospital bed with a breathing-tube down her throat, being fed intravenously, and wired to monitoring equipment. When he first saw her, he tried to hide his dismay by joking that it was a good thing she couldn't speak or she might call him "Boo Boo", his childhood nickname.

The media learned of her illness at the end of January. On the thirty-first the *Globe and Mail* published a report with the headline "Condition of Sauvé is Listed as Serious". Both this article and others in the press mentioned unconfirmed rumours that she was suffering from cancer. In its story the *Globe and Mail* quoted Renée Langevin, Madame Sauvé's personal secretary, who said, "Yes, it is serious, but she's not dying."

Many people, however, thought differently. Renée Langevin was offered a lucrative job by a senior government official. When she turned it down, explaining that she was happy where she was, the mandarin told her callously that Madame Sauvé would be dead within a few days. A number of eager reporters gave their home telephone numbers to Marie Bender, Madame Sauvé's Press Secretary, and asked her to call them, no matter what the hour, as soon as her employer died. The Canadian Press updated its obituary on Jeanne Sauvé and had it ready to send over the wires at a moment's notice. The CBC was also standing by with a hastily assembled half-hour obituary film of her career. During this harrowing vigil, her staff tried to comfort one another but were frequently reduced to tears.

Jeanne was convinced she was dying when she was transferred to intensive care. Not only was she under medication but she was heavily sedated to reduce the pain of the breathing-tube. As she slipped in and out of consciousness, the days became a blur. At one stage she thought she was dreaming when she heard a voice ask, "Madame Sauvé, do you pray for your recovery?" Moving her head with difficulty, she saw a man in a white jacket standing near her bed. Unable to speak, she could only nod. He said, "I pray for you every day." Then he disappeared as quietly as he had come. Later, she learned that her anonymous well-wisher was one of the hospital orderlies.

He was one of literally thousands of Canadians who prayed for Madame Sauvé's recovery. While she was ill, her office was deluged with mail, and Ottawa General Hospital also received a flood of calls, letters, cards, and flowers from well-wishers. Half the mail came from the province of Quebec, which in recent years has shown indifference to the Crown. (Indeed, she is so popular in Quebec that when she was appointed, the Quebec National Assembly, led by René Lévesque, an avowed separatist, passed a unamimous resolution presenting its respects.) The knowledge that others were praying for her, combined with her own faith, unquestionably contributed to her recovery.

The turning-point came on 1 February. That day her condition stabilized and showed some slight improvement. By this time the breathing-tube has been in her throat for a week and Dr. Sauvé, fearing permanent damage to her vocal chords, suggested that the tube be removed. But, as she was still in serious condition, he was overruled by his colleagues on the basis that it was more important for her to breathe than to speak. On 3 February, the day the tube was removed, her doctors released a guarded statement reporting "satisfaction with her present rate of progress". A week later the medical team issued a much more optimistic bulletin, saying they were "very, very satisfied with her progress". In mid-February Marie Bender announced that Madame Sauvé would soon be leaving hospital.

She went home to Montreal on 3 March in an ambulance. Responding to questions from the press, Marie Bender assured reporters that Madame Sauvé was "feeling very good". This was not entirely accurate, although it was true that she was profoundly grateful for having survived the ordeal. In fact, the illness left her so weak that she couldn't walk, and the breathing-tube had damaged her vocal chords so badly that she couldn't talk. To add to her woes, the respiratory infection had partially collapsed one of her lungs. With the aid of a nurse and a physiotherapist she set about rebuilding her health. Every hour she exercised her legs, and several times each day she exercised her vocal chords to a tape cassette, repeating over and over, "How are you? I am fine. One, two, three. One, two, three." The purpose of the speech exercises was to tighten her vocal chords so that she could modulate her voice, which had been a pleasing contralto before her illness, but now has a permanent rasp. As part of her convalescence she had planned to stay for a few weeks in Florida, but when the time came, she didn't feel up to the journey.

Meanwhile, the date of her Installation had been postponed three times. Ed Schreyer, the outgoing Governor General, was anxious to leave Rideau Hall to take up his appointment as Canada's High Commissioner to Australia. In mid-March, Pierre Trudeau, who had been kept informed of her condition by her doctors, phoned Jeanne to see if she would set a date for the Installation. The Prime Minister caught her at a low point, and she confessed to him that she didn't believe she would ever recover sufficiently to take office. Trudeau said this was nonsense, that her doctors had assured him she would make a complete recovery, and that he would call her again in a month. When he called in April she was still weak, but she was feeling better. Although she knew she should have more time to convalesce, she agreed that the Installation would take place on Monday, 14 May.

On Saturday, 12 May, Jeanne and Maurice Sauvé travelled to Ottawa by train in the viceregal coach. They were welcomed at the Union Station by Prime Minister Trudeau and a half-dozen other dignitaries. Because Madame Sauvé was not yet governor general, instead of going to Government House they went to 7 Rideau Gate, the official residence for visitors of state. That night the Sauvés gave a family dinner party. The following day they went through an arduous rehearsal of the swearing-in ceremony on Parliament Hill. On Sunday evening Serge Senecal and Réal Bastien came to stay at

Rideau Gate. In addition to being guests, these two men had a special role to play.

Serge Senecal and Réal Bastien are partners in the Montreal couturier firm of Serge et Réal. Jeanne Sauvé attended their first fashion show in 1962, and has been their most faithful customer ever since. Looking back, Serge remembers that from the very beginning she had a fashion sense, and she knew how to wear clothes to their best advantage:

"I was amazed, she was an intellectual and I always thought those people weren't interested in clothes, but she had an eye for beauty. She used to love light grey, Wedgwood blues, and mauve, but now she likes stronger colours. She is very feminine and loves soft fabrics for evening. She doesn't like frills — they don't suit her — and she needs to have full skirts because of her hips. The length of the skirts is also a little on the long side to make her look taller and slimmer. She always dresses conservatively during the day, but at night she likes to be a little extravagant."

Jeanne Sauvé keeps her dresses a long time, and wears them over and over. Even so, from the outset her annual account with Serge et Réal has always been at least ten thousand dollars, and she ruefully admits that today it absorbs most of her salary. While Serge and Réal repeat some of their designs in different fabrics for other customers, Madame Sauvé's are one of a kind. Over the years their relationship has evolved into one of close friendship, and she will often spin out a ten-minute fitting at their luxurious Sherbrooke Street salon to more than an hour, happily discussing fashions.

Serge and Réal brought two dresses with them to Rideau Gate, the gown that she would wear for her Installation, and her evening dress for the Gala after the investiture. Dressing her for the ceremony proved to be traumatic for everyone. Her ensemble, designed before she became ill, was an Elizabethan-style coat and gown of grey silk taffeta. Unfortunately the large puffed sleeves of the coat accentuated the puffiness of her face, caused by cortisone treatments. Knowing she would have to walk a considerable distance in her long gown, Serge and Réal pleaded with her to wear low-heeled shoes. But she stubbornly insisted on wearing high heels — a decision she would soon regret.

The morning of the investiture was cool and sunny. As Madame Sauvé's limousine swept through the gates of Parliament Hill she saw the viceregal standard, a royal-blue flag with a gold lion in the centre holding a red maple leaf in its paw, unfurl above the Peace Tower. At this moment she was struck by the realization that after months of uncertainty, the long wait was over — she was about to become governor general of Canada. Smiling happily, she waved to the schoolchildren lining the driveway to the Centre Block. When her car drew abreast of the Peace Tower, a twenty-one-gun salute boomed from nearby Nepean Point, the guard of honour presented arms, and the band played "God Save the Queen". She was greeted on the front steps by Prime Minister Trudeau, who escorted her inside the building. A few minutes later, accompanied by the senior members of the viceregal Household and led by the Gentleman Usher of the Black Rod, she walked in stately procession to the Senate Chamber.

Emerging from the gloom of the corridor she was momentarily dazzled by the brightness of the Chamber. Sunlight pouring through the vaulted windows combined with the television lights to illuminate a sea of faces turned in her direction. The Senate was packed with more than eleven hundred guests, including representatives of the diplomatic corps, lieutenant-governors, a covey of red-robed justices of the Supreme Court, Privy Councillors, Members of Parliament, and friends. Sitting in the front row was her son Jean-François with her three surviving sisters, Berthe, Annette, and Lucille. Her brother Jean sat immediately behind them with other members of the family. Also awaiting her arrival was the Chief Justice of the Supreme Court, who represents the Crown during interim periods, or when the Governor General is incapacitated or out of the country.

Madame Sauvé's entry was heralded by a fanfare of trumpets from the gallery. The mood in the Chamber was both solemn and festive. As she walked slowly up the red-carpeted aisle to the canopied dais, she nodded and smiled to many of her friends and acquaintances. When she was seated on the Senate throne, the Prime Minister made a short speech in which he assured her that she was chosen to be governor general not merely because she was a woman, but because she was the ideal candidate for the position. Esmond Butler then read her commission of appointment from the Queen. After this was completed, Madame Sauvé took her oath of office, and signed the official proclamation. The Bible used to administer her oath was a family Bible that both she and Maurice had used when they were sworn in as cabinet ministers. The investiture concluded with the symbolic presentation of the Great Seal of Canada to Her Excellency by the Secretary of State.

In her twenty-minute address, she stressed the three main themes of her mandate: peace, national unity, and her concern for young people. On the subject of national unity she asked Canadians to be more generous and tolerant towards each other, noting that "This is the price of our happiness, but happiness will never be found in the spirit of 'every man for himself'." Alluding to the violence and unrest in the world, she said, "The effects of this turmoil will be suffered even more tragically by the next generation, living as they will in apocalyptic times. . . . As for myself, I have great faith in the youth of today. My past experience working with youth associations and my daily encounters with young people have revealed to me their spirit and potential. I am certain that, when their time comes, they will take up the challenge and shoulder it with success." She concluded her address with a quote from Ecclesiasticus: "As the governor is, so will be the inhabitants of his city."

The Installation ceremony taxed her strength, but as she left the Chamber her spirits were buoyed by a sense of accomplishment and the majesty of the occasion. On the way out of the building she paused to listen, and to thank the members of a choir who sang a song for her. Before leaving Parliament Hill, Madame Sauvé was given another twenty-one-gun salute, a fly-past of air force jets, and a second royal salute by the guard of honour. The young officer in command then stepped forward and invited her to inspect the guard, comprising one hundred scarlet-coated cadets from the Royal Military College. Seeing the distance she would have to walk, she said to herself, "I'll never make it." Nevertheless, out of a sense of duty she consented to inspect the guard. Holding up her skirt with one hand, she walked along the front rank, bowed to the Colours, and managed to reach the end of the row without incident. But as she turned to walk down the second rank, her heel caught in the pavement and she twisted her ankle. Righting herself, she wobbled grimly along until her heel caught a second time. The pain was so intense that the only way she could prevent herself from falling was to grab the officer's sword arm, which unbalanced him momentarily. Squaring his shoulders, the officer escorted her slowly back to the steps of the Peace Tower. He did this with such aplomb that few people realized anything was amiss, or how close Her Excellency had come to disaster. Maurice, who had watched the whole thing in agony, quickly moved forward to help her up the steps.

Their Excellencies rode back to Rideau Hall in an open landau drawn by four black horses, with an escort of thirty-two Mounties in full dress, the sun glinting from their lances. As the carriage left Parliament Hill the crowd gave a rousing cheer for the new Governor General. At Government House she was greeted by another guard of honour, and then escorted by her Secretary to the ballroom to meet the members of the Household. After lunch Her Excellency received the Prime Minister and the members of his cabinet.

By the end of the afternoon Madame Sauvé's ankle was painfully swollen and she was limping badly. Although she made light of it, Serge Senecal persuaded her to let him bind her ankle with tape, which eased the pain and gave her some support. That evening, dressed in an emerald-green gown, she attended a gala performance in her honour at the National Arts Centre. Sitting with her in the flower-bedecked royal box was her husband, her sister Berthe, and Prime Minister Trudeau. During the playing of the national anthem, all the house lights were turned out except for a single spotlight on the Governor General. As the last chord died away, the audience spontaneously broke into applause for her.

Among the invited guests were people from every period of her life, starting with His Worship Steve Sopotyk, the mayor of her birthplace, Prud'homme. Several childhood friends were present, as was Sister Marguerite Myre, who had taught her at the convent and attended night classes with her at the University of Ottawa. All of her room-mates from the JEC were invited, including Berthe (Deschênes) Bellemare, Françoise (Chamard) Cadieux, Fernande (Martin) Juneau, and Jacqueline (Ratté) Varin. Alex and Gérard Pelletier and Pierre Juneau were also there. The two chaplains from the Centrale, Father Maurice Lafond and Father Germain-Marie Lalande, who were friends as well as spiritual advisers, attended the Gala. (As the night wore on, Father Lalande, who had travelled with her to the West, and also performed her marriage, grumbled that Jeanne was getting tired and everyone should go home.) Françoise Côté and d'Iberville Fortier were among the friends from her days in Europe. Michael Hind-Smith, who had given her her start on TV, was present, as was Fernand Doré, her most important producer from the early years of her broadcasting career. There was also a large political contingent, ranging from constituency workers through to deputy ministers and cabinet colleagues, as well as members of her staff from the Speaker's office. Her most recent friends were the doctors and nurses who had looked after her at Ottawa General Hospital.

Many of these people were among the two hundred guests invited back to Rideau Hall for a dinner-dance after the Gala. For weeks Madame Sauvé had been dreading the Installation and wondering how she could manage it. During the party at Rideau Hall, Pierre Trudeau said to her, "Jeanne, you look much better tonight." Flashing him a smile she replied, "It's because I'm relieved it's nearly over!"

Recalling that memorable day, Serge Senecal observed recently, "Very few people could have gone through the Investiture — when you feel sick and you know you look absolutely awful — that takes courage."

The Regina *Leader-Post* said, "The lady may have kept us waiting but, most Canadians would agree, it was worthwhile." The Halifax *Chronicle-Herald* noted, "There is a sense that this distinguished Canadian and this distinguished constitutional office offer a combination of great promise for the country." Gretta Chambers wrote an editorial on the new Governor General in the Montreal *Gazette* which concluded, "Jeanne Sauvé is just the woman to put her grace and distinction to the determined pursuit of national confidence, generosity and common sense. In the words of her oath of office: May God protect her."

Chapter 10

THE QUEEN'S REPRESENTATIVE

Her Excellency Jeanne Sauvé moved into Rideau Hall the day after the investiture and immediately plunged into her viceregal duties.

Contrary to Mr. Gold's opinion in the *Calgary Herald*, the office of governor general is not a "nest of largely irrelevant ceremonial hokum". Canada is a constitutional monarchy, and the sovereign is the head of state. The Governor General is the Queen's representative; when the sovereign is absent from Canada, the Governor General performs the duties of the head of state. The head of government is the Prime Minister, who is elected, and represents the political majority. The Governor General, who is appointed, must be above politics, and represents the whole country.

As the Queen's representative, Madame Sauvé performs a number of essential duties. Some are ceremonial, some are constitutional, and others are of a social nature. Being the representative of the Crown, Madame Sauvé is at the apex of the Canadian Constitution, and is thus part of both the legislative and the executive branches of the government. In this capacity she opens and prorogues Parliament, as well as swearing in the Prime Minister and members of the cabinet. She gives royal assent to all laws passed by Parliament (until they receive royal assent they aren't legal, and can't be enforced). In addition, she ratifies a host of documents such as Orders-in-Council, Commissions of Appointment, Grants of Pardon, Letters of Credence, and Letters of Recall. As Chancellor of the Order of

Canada, and of the Order of Military Merit, she presides over investitures of these decorations, and also presents national Bravery Awards. As Commander-in-Chief of the Canadian Armed Forces she signs all Officers' Commissions.

Most viceregal duties are performed in accordance with the wishes of the Prime Minister. However, the Governor General has the power to act independently in a constitutional emergency. One of the viceregal responsibilities is to ensure that there is a government, and that the party in power has a leader. If the Prime Minister were to die suddenly (as happened to Sir John Thompson, who suffered a heart attack while lunching with Queen Victoria at Windsor Castle), or be killed in an accident, the Governor General could be called upon to choose an interim leader. Should the House of Commons become locked in a lengthy stalemate and cease to function (as it nearly did during the bell-ringing crisis in 1982) the Governor General has the power to dismiss the Prime Minister, dissolve Parliament, and call an election. If several parties were elected with a similar number of seats, and there was no clear majority, the Governor General could be called upon to intervene. In the words of Professor Norman Ward, "While the Governor General is primarily an impartial head of state, a symbol of the nation, she is not necessarily a figurehead. Her latent powers continue to exist, as a safety-valve to be used in times of crisis and to remain dormant at all other times." Speaking of her latent powers, Madame Sauvé told a CBC interviewer, "The success of a governor general is never to use them."

Another important viceregal role is to advise the Prime Minister. This is embedded in the Constitution as "the right to be consulted, the right to encourage, and the right to warn". The Prime Minister needn't accept the Governor General's advice, but if there is a good rapport between the two, the viceroy can be a valuable confidant. To keep informed on government policy and pending legislation, Madame Sauvé regularly receives confidential cabinet documents. Added to this, the Prime Minister visits her every second Wednesday to discuss matters of state. In turn, Her Excellency writes the Queen on a regular basis to inform her of the situation in

Canada. (Madame Sauvé writes her letters in French and Her Majesty replies in English.) Thus, the Governor General is the link between the Canadian Prime Minister and the Crown.

On the social side, the Governor General is Canada's most important official host, extending hospitality to foreign dignitaries as well as to thousands of Canadians every year. In addition to entertaining at Rideau Hall and at the Citadel, the Governor General travels extensively throughout the land. In recent years, the Queen's representative has also travelled abroad on goodwill tours for Canada.

The viceregal post is the most prestigious in the country, ranking first in the Canadian order of precedence. The Governor General receives the title "The Right Honourable" for life, and is addressed as "His or Her Excellency" while in office. (The viceroy's spouse is also addressed as His or Her Excellency.) Canada pays the Governor General's salary and all the expenses associated with the viceregal office. During the French regime the Governor's salary was set at ten thousand *livres*. When the English took over, this was changed to ten thousand pounds, and it was frozen at that amount for more than a century. In the 1970s it was converted from sterling into 48,666 tax-free dollars. On 1 April 1986, the Governor General's salary was raised to seventy thousand dollars per annum. Although there are many "perks" that go with the job, most governors general have had to dip into their personal savings while in office. Some, like Vincent Massey, have spent considerable amounts of their own money.

As Governor General, Madame Sauvé has two official residences: Rideau Hall in Ottawa and the Governor's Wing at the Citadel in Quebec. Rideau Hall, also known as Government House, is where she spends most of the year. It was built in 1838 by Thomas MacKay, a member of the Legislative Council of Upper Canada and one of the principal contractors on the Rideau Canal. Originally constructed on the lines of a Regency villa, the house is surrounded by eighty-eight acres of woods and parkland. The Canadian government rented Rideau Hall in 1864, and four years later bought the property as a permanent residence for the Governor General. George Brown, one of the Fathers of Confederation and the founder of the Toronto *Globe*, writing to Sir John A. Macdonald in 1864, observed sourly, "The Governor-General's residence is a miserable little house, and the grounds those of an ambitious country squire."

George Brown would be surprised to see the miserable little house today. In the intervening years Rideau Hall has undergone four major expansions and now has 173 rooms. The most dramatic change to the exterior is the massive stone façade with its royal coat of arms, which was added just before the First World War. On the ground floor there is an ornate ballroom decorated with gold leaf, public and private reception rooms, two dining-rooms, administrative offices, and an adjoining greenhouse. The Tent Room is perhaps the most unusual room. Built by Lord Dufferin in 1873 as a wooden addition in which to play court tennis (a game that utilizes the walls and the ceiling to keep the ball in play), from its earliest days the court was disguised with wall hangings so that it could be used for informal entertaining. Court tennis is no longer played in the Tent Room, which for more than a century has been draped in candy-striped cotton, but on muggy days one can still detect a faint athletic aroma.

The second floor consists of bedrooms, sitting-rooms, and a small chapel. The Governor General's personal quarters are on this floor, as are ten bedrooms and suites for guests. The Royal Suite, which the Queen occupies when she is in residence, has an elegant oval bedroom (formerly Thomas MacKay's drawing-room) with a canopied double bed. Her Majesty sat at the writing-desk in this room to deliver the first television broadcast of her reign.

Rideau Hall's spacious grounds, still a mixture of parkland, woods, and formal gardens, are bounded by a heavy iron fence supported at frequent intervals by stone pillars. The main entrance, which has a gatehouse and huge iron gates highlighted in gold leaf, is awkward for tour busses to negotiate because the opening is only the width of a carriage. Within the grounds there are a number of other buildings, among them Rideau Cottage, a rambling brick house that has traditionally been the residence of the Secretary to the Governor General. There are also staff houses, greenhouses, a workshop, and two garages, one of which was formerly the stables.

Recreational facilities on the property hearken back to an earlier era. In the summer cricket is still played on the sweeping lawns to the west of the main residence, and there are two outdoor tennis courts. In the winter there is an outdoor rink for skating and a single sheet of natural ice for curling. Near the rinks, on a hillock, there is also a wooden toboggan slide. Rideau Hall has no swimming-pool.

The nearest thing to a pool is a pond that was dug in the woods behind the skating rink during Edward Schreyer's tenure. Mr. Schreyer stocked this little pond with rainbow trout at his own expense. On summer evenings he used to enjoy strolling down to the pond to feed the trout. As the summer progressed, however, he noticed there were fewer and fewer fish. One evening he discovered two urchins, who had obviously hopped the fence, fishing in his sanctuary. After watching them for a few minutes, he asked, "How are they biting?" Hoisting a freshly caught trout, one of the boys replied, "The fishing's just great, mister. I only got this so far, but my friend has three!"

On another occasion Esmond Butler, the tall and distinguished Secretary to the Governor General, was jogging past the pond early one morning when, to his astonishment, he saw a naked young woman about to plunge in for a swim. The sight stopped him in his tracks. Despite years of viceregal service, he could think of no precedent to deal with the situation. So he simply gave her a nod, bade her "Good morning" in his most formal voice, and continued on his way. For the rest of the summer he jogged faithfully every morning — but he never saw her again.

The Secretary to the Governor General, who is concerned with all matters relating to the Crown of Canada, is the senior member of the Household. While his principal role is to advise and assist the Governor General, he is also responsible for the administration of every aspect of the viceregal office. The job requires talent, diplomacy, and a high degree of dedication. In the Civil Service pecking order the Secretary to the Governor General is equal in rank to a senior deputy minister, which means his salary (before tax) is greater than that of his boss.

Jeanne Sauvé inherited a Secretary with an immense amount of experience and ability in Esmond Butler. A navy veteran, with degrees from the universities of Toronto and Geneva, Butler first came to Rideau Hall in 1955 as assistant press secretary to Vincent Massey. He was later seconded to Buckingham Palace, but returned to Canada in 1959 as Secretary to Governor General Georges Vanier. Roland Michener, Jules Léger, and Edward Schreyer also retained Butler as Secretary for their terms in office. In 1972 Butler was made a Commander of the Royal Victorian Order, an honour awarded for personal service to the sovereign.

Madame Sauvé also has three regular-force officers, one from each service, as aides-de-camp. These young officers are usually chosen from the operational branches: a pilot, a naval deck officer, and an infantry or armoured corps officer. Normally unmarried and of captain's rank (lieutenant in the case of the Navy), they are appointed for a term of approximately two years. An aide-de-camp always accompanies the Governor General, and is easily recognized by the gold-braided cords (aiguillette) hanging from his right shoulder.

The role of an aide-de-camp is to serve Their Excellencies to the best of his ability. To do this effectively he must be sensitive to the personal tastes and preferences of the viceregal couple. When the Governor General agrees to an engagement, it is the responsibility of the ADC to plan the event in detail and to execute it with her. During a tour or an official function, the ADC must ensure that everything goes smoothly. Before the event he briefs the Governor General, and during it he will, if necessary, discreetly remind her of details, such as the name of a local dignitary or where she should stand on the podium.

The image of Rideau Hall is projected more by the ADC's than by anyone else, other than the Governor General. They are in contact with everyone from the Prime Minister down to casual tourists. For this reason, each aide-de-camp is chosen with great care. First, the Department of National Defence selects six possible candidates, all of whom have outstanding records in that particular branch of the service. Government House then weeds out three on the basis of their dossiers, and invites the remaining three to Rideau Hall for interviews. These three are individually screened and graded by senior members of the Household. The qualities they are looking for are a well-developed mind, poise, discretion, decisiveness, and a sense of humour. Her Excellency then personally interviews each of the finalists separately over lunch. After she has seen them all, she makes her choice. Speaking of the candidate's final test, one close observer said, "H.E. is superb — fifteen or twenty minutes in front of the fire and then into lunch. Whether the officer gets the job or not, it's an experience of a lifetime."

An ADC works a twenty-one-day cycle. For seven days he is Aide-de-Camp-in-Waiting, on call round the clock. For the following seven days he is Aide-de-Camp Next-in-Waiting, which means he has a normal working day but is also on call evenings and weekends. For the final seven days he is Aide-de-Camp Out-of-Waiting, during which he works on future programs and is only available for major functions. Being an ADC at Government House carries a certain social cachet, and is often a valuable stepping-stone in one's service career (the most notable example being Harold Macmillan, who went on to become prime minister of Great Britain). It is also a heady but nerve-wracking experience, because one is always in the limelight — and there's no room for error.

For example, a few months after her Installation, Madame Sauvé was giving the Convocation Address at McGill University. The theme of her speech was the challenges youth face upon graduation. She was in top form, and she had the huge audience in the palm of her hand. Suddenly, just as she was reaching the conclusion of her speech, she discovered that the last two pages of her text were missing. Stopping in mid-sentence, she confessed her problem to the audience. After frantic scrambling, her aide-de-camp (who should have checked this detail) eventually produced the missing pages. He will remember the incident to his grave.

In June, Madame Sauvé went to England to see the Queen, a visit that would normally have taken place before she assumed office, but had been postponed because of her illness. On the morning of 12 June, at Kensington Palace in London, His Royal Highness the Duke of Gloucester, a younger cousin of the Queen, invested Madame Sauvé as a Dame of Justice in the Venerable Order of the Hospital of St. John of Jerusalem. (As governor general, she is Prior of the Canadian branch of the Order.) At the same investiture her husband Maurice was made a Knight of Grace in the Order of St. John. Following the ceremony, she went to Buckingham Palace — her first visit there since 1948 — to have lunch with the Queen. Madame Sauvé was delighted with the warm welcome she received, and was put at ease by the Queen's vivacity and sense of humour. She was also impressed by Her Majesty's knowledge of Canada, and her obvious affection for the country.

While she was chatting happily with the Queen over lunch, back in Canada an Ottawa television station was reporting that Madame Sauvé had cancer. Television station CJOH said in its six o'clock news that according to "informed sources" she was receiving treatments for Hodgkin's disease. This form of cancer, which is treated by radiation and chemotherapy, is curable in about seventy per cent of cases. Symptoms of the disease include painless enlargement of the lymph glands, fever, weight loss, and anaemia.

Both Government House and the Prime Minister's Office refused to comment on the report. The following day at a press conference in London, Madame Sauvé also declined to discuss the allegation, telling reporters, "What I owe the public is the assurance that I am capable of fulfilling my duties. They will have to take my word for it."

Speaking privately, she explained, "The reason I don't want to talk about it is I don't want sensational stories in the press — I'm not a sick person and I don't want the country to have that kind of image. When I was ill I was a private citizen; now I would owe it to the country if I became ill to tell them what's wrong with me."

This was Madame Sauvé's first skirmish with the press as governor general. In the briefing she received from Esmond Butler before taking office, she was warned that dealing with the press can be like walking through a minefield. The notes on this subject read in part: "The media is traditionally sophist in philosophy . . . Good news is no news. Bad news is good for them. Thus, it's a constant game for the media to try and embarrass the government, no matter the political stripe. And what better way to do it than through the Governor General who is in a constitutional strait-jacket with severe limitations as to what she can or cannot say. Hypothetical questions as to what would happen 'if' have to be turned down like the bubonic plague."

The Governor General's Press Secretary is responsible for providing, and screening, information to the media. This office also replies to hundreds of letters from the public, many of them from children seeking information on the Governor General for school projects. Because the Press Secretary must have direct access to the Governor General at all times, the relationship is a close one. To fill this sensitive position Her Excellency brought in Marie Bender, her former Press Officer in the Speaker's office. Ms. Bender, who is fluently bilingual and highly competent, maintains a friendly rapport with the media of both languages. At the same time she is fiercely protective of her boss — as a vigilant Press Secretary should be.

A significant amount of Madame Sauvé's time is spent travelling around the country. The purpose of these trips is to bring the vice-regal office to the people, and to foster national unity, an ongoing viceregal theme. By meeting and speaking to people from all regions, she can, in a sense, take the nation's pulse. However, protocol decrees that before attending the first event in a province, the Governor General must be officially received by that province. For this reason, one of Madame Sauvé's priorities after taking office was to formally visit all the provinces, as well as the Yukon and the

Northwest Territories. Two days after she returned from England she flew to Quebec City for her first provincial visit. On hand to greet her at l'Ancienne Lorette airport was the Lieutenant-Governor (the provincial representative of the Crown), the mayor of Quebec City, a senior Quebec cabinet minister, and a guard of honour provided by the Royal 22e Régiment. After a warm welcome, Her Excellency proceeded to her residence in the Citadel.

The Citadel is an ancient fortress located on a promontory overlooking the broad St. Lawrence. From its ramparts the view of the river and the surrounding countryside is truly spectacular. Built to withstand attacks from land and sea, the Citadel is laid out in the shape of a star. Founded during the French regime, it was enlarged and rebuilt by the British in the 1820s. All the buildings within the fort are of stone, as are its massive earth-covered ramparts. Since its earliest days it has been an army garrison — for the past sixty years the Home Station of the famous Royal 22e Régiment, familiarly known in English Canada as the "Van Doos".

Because of its historic nature, the Citadel is a prime tourist attraction, especially during the summer, when the Royal 22e Régiment puts on a daily Changing of the Guard ceremony. This is a colourful event because the dress uniform of the regiment is scarlet and bearskin, similar to that worn by the Guards on Parliament Hill. The regimental mascot, a goat, also takes part in the parade.

The Governor General's residence is in the Governor's Wing, a two-storey building with a breathtaking view of the St. Lawrence. Much of it was destroyed by fire in 1976, but fortunately most of the old furniture and paintings were saved. At heavy cost the gutted part was rebuilt, and the smoke-damaged section was also completely refurbished. Aside from one stridently modern fireplace, with jagged stonework that resembles the mouth of a lamprey eel, the overall effect of the restoration is magnificent. As the Governor's Wing is much smaller than Rideau Hall, it will accommodate relatively few members of the viceregal Household, which helps to create a family atmosphere. While the Governor General is in residence, the Royal 22e Régiment mounts a special guard to salute her arrivals and departures, and also posts sentries in full dress at the viceregal entrance to the building. Madame Sauvé loves Quebec, and she treasures her time at the Citadel.

Following a three-day round of receptions in Quebec, Their Excellencies returned to Ottawa. One of Madame Sauvé's first and most noteworthy duties at Rideau Hall was to bid farewell to the outgoing Prime Minister, Pierre Trudeau. It was a sad occasion for both of them, and one that she found "very moving". Later that day in her constitutional role she received another old friend, the newly elected Liberal leader and Prime Minister-designate, John Turner. The conversation at this meeting, in which she formally asked him to take over the reins of government, was spiced with reminiscences of the days when they sat across from each other at the cabinet table.

A week later she was back in Quebec City to participate in the festivities marking the 450th anniversary of Jacques Cartier's voyage to Canada. The arrival of the Tall Ships was one of the most impressive events of this celebration. Among the receptions she gave at the Citadel was one for the captains of these legendary sailing vessels. In the midst of her schedule she had to fly back to Ottawa to swear in the new Prime Minister and his cabinet at Government House. Because she had several events to attend in Quebec that same day, and she was also giving a reception, she reluctantly agreed to take a helicopter from Rideau Hall. Fortunately her son Jean-François was with her and she was able to clutch his arm as they clattered aloft. It wasn't until the helicopter reached cruising altitude that she opened her eyes. Stealing a glance out the window, she found her fear replaced by delight at the sight of the autumn panorama unfolding beneath her. It was so entrancing that when they reached Quebec she told the pilot to swoop low over the St. Lawrence so they could have a bird's eye view of the Tall Ships.

On the first of July Their Excellencies were in Ottawa to attend the Canada Day celebrations on Parliament Hill. Earlier, while they were in Quebec, Maurice Sauvé had presided at an unveiling ceremony in the ballroom of the Citadel of twelve stamps commemorating Canada Day, his first solo function. When Madame Sauvé was asked by Barbara Frum on CBC television whether her husband was prepared to be the viceregal spouse, she replied with a laugh, "He says he's going to have a ball entertaining the ladies at luncheons. I'm sure he's going to be a great support."

On the morning of 9 July, Prime Minister Turner went to Rideau Hall to obtain permission from the Governor General to dissolve Parliament and call a general election. Her Excellency granted him permission to do so without comment.

That afternoon she was hostess at the annual Garden Party. This used to be a very formal affair, by invitation only, but is now open to the public, and the dress code has been relaxed so that guests may wear whatever they wish. Refreshments consist of sandwiches, cakes, tea, and fruit punch. Hoping to catch a glimpse of the new Governor General, more than five thousand people flooded the lawns of Rideau Hall for her inaugural party. During her walkabout she shook hands with hundreds of people, and one eight-year-old girl gave her a stuffed doll she had made. Another youngster, a little boy, dodged through the crowd in search of his mother yelling excitedly, "I've seen her. I've seen the Queen!"

In fact, the Queen had been scheduled to come to Canada the following week, but her trip was postponed by the election. Traditionally, royal visits don't take place during an election campaign because the head of state could conceivably influence the vote. For this reason, Madame Sauvé, as the Queen's representative in Canada, postponed several provincial visits and deliberately kept a low profile.

The interlude gave Madame Sauvé a much-needed rest. Still weak from her illness, she had been working twelve hours a day and travelling constantly. Added to this, she was still receiving regular treatments at the Ottawa General Hospital. Sheer will-power had carried her through her first few months in office. "I was really dying with weakness in my chair," she later admitted. For the balance of the summer, while the politicians criss-crossed the country, she enjoyed an unexpected holiday. It did her a world of good.

The visit to Canada in 1984 of His Holiness Pope John Paul II, whose directness and warmth have endeared him to people around the world, was an historic event that had been anticipated for more than a year. His Holiness arrived in Quebec City on Sunday morning, 9 September. The excitement was intense at l'Ancienne Lorette airport on that sparkling autumn day. As head of the Vatican, a sovereign state, he was met by the Governor General. When the Pope stepped off his plane he was given a twenty-one-gun salute. Unfortunately, however, the first salvo was fired just as he knelt to kiss the ground, which momentarily startled everyone. Aside from this small incident, the ceremony went off like clockwork. In her welcoming address to the Pontiff, Madame Sauvé concluded with these words:

> *What reassures us and has power to move the young is the boldness, the selflessness and the tranquil assurance of your message which ... reveals your love for us. ...*
>
> *When the tumult surrounding this unprecedented visit has died away, we will be able to delve further into the mystery of an encounter that, we will come to realize, was not like any other. It will leave in our very soul a permanent mark. ...*
>
> *Your Holiness, Canada salutes you and thanks you. ...*

The Governor General's speech, one of the best of her career, set the tone for the Pope's visit. That afternoon, Their Excellencies attended the Celebration of the Eucharist at Laval University celebrated by His Holiness. The next day the Pontiff embarked on his week-long tour of the country.

Meanwhile, the federal election had taken place on 4 September. The Conservatives swept the board with 211 seats, the Liberals were reduced to 40, and the NDP took 30 seats. John Turner, who had been prime minister for less than three months, presented his resignation to the Governor General at the Citadel. Her Excellency then summoned Brian Mulroney to Quebec and asked him to form a government. Although the Papal Visit was in progress, it was agreed that the new Prime Minister and his cabinet would be sworn in at

Rideau Hall the following week. While the Pope was in western Canada, the Governor General returned to Ottawa for the swearing-in of the new Prime Minister and his cabinet on 17 September.

The following Sunday Madame Sauvé gave a large reception for the Pope at Government House. Before meeting the assembled guests, who had been anxiously awaiting his arrival for more than an hour, His Holiness spent fifteen minutes with Their Excellencies and Jean-François in Madame Sauvé's study. Ignoring the pomp and ceremony that was going on outside, the Pope spoke to the Sauvés with the kindness and simplicity of a parish priest. After the family audience, the Pontiff met privately with the Governor General for a quarter of an hour, and then spent another fifteen minutes with Madame Sauvé and Prime Minister Brian Mulroney. In their public appearances it was obvious that Madame Sauvé and the Pope got along very well together, so much so that a French television announcer covering the farewell ceremony was moved to comment, "They make a lovely couple!"

The day after the Pope left Canada, the Governor General made her first official visit to New Brunswick. On the following Monday she and her husband returned to Moncton to greet Her Majesty the Queen and the Duke of Edinburgh, who had flown from England to celebrate New Brunswick's bicentenary. Their Excellencies dined privately with the Queen and Prince Philip that evening and flew back to Ottawa the same night.

The next day, at a ceremony in the ballroom of Rideau Hall, Madame Sauvé presented the 1983 Governor General's Literary Awards, the most prestigious prizes in Canadian literature. (Although the awards are given in the Governor General's name, selection of the winners is made by an independent jury under the supervision of the Canada Council.) Because of her interest in literature and her personal experience as a journalist, it was a special pleasure for her to present these awards.

The Queen and Prince Philip arrived in Ottawa the following day, where they were welcomed at a ceremony on Parliament Hill. Afterwards they returned to Rideau Hall to meet Prime Minister

Mulroney and his cabinet. During this event the Queen had an opportunity to test her well-known expertise as a judge of good horseflesh. The Mounties had given Her Majesty a black mare, "Burmese", that she had ridden in the Queen's Birthday parade since 1969. As Burmese was now getting old, the Force wanted to give the Queen another horse. They had three for her to choose from, but because of her tight schedule she didn't have time to view them at Rockcliffe barracks. To get around this problem, it was arranged that when she rode from Parliament Hill to Government House in the state landau, the three "gift" horses, ridden by outriders, would be in the procession. This way the Queen would have ample time to look them over.

While Her Majesty was receiving the cabinet in the Long Gallery at Rideau Hall, the outriders quietly took the three horses around to the back of the building, and stood with them on the Upper Terrace. They didn't have long to wait. Thirty seconds after the Queen caught sight of the horses, she was out on the terrace to tell the Mounties of her choice.

Madame Sauvé had a full schedule for the remainder of the autumn. On Sunday, 7 October, she was in Winnipeg to bid farewell to the Queen and the Duke of Edinburgh at the conclusion of their Canadian visit. At the end of October she travelled west again for her state visit to Saskatchewan.

Among her Ottawa engagements, she attended morning service at St. Bartholomew's Anglican Church, where she read the Epistle. This Gothic chapel, built in 1868 on land donated by Thomas MacKay, faces Rideau Hall. From the outset it has been the parish church of Government House, and it is now also the chapel of the Governor General's Foot Guards. The interior of St. Bartholomew's contains many reminders of these connections, including memorials and heraldic shields of past governors general as well as the regimental colours of the Guards. By tradition the first two pews are reserved for the Governor General and members of the Household.

There is also a chapel at Rideau Hall that was established by General Vanier, and was converted to ecumenical use by Mr. Michener. For some years Government House has had two honorary chaplains, the rector of St. Bartholomew's and a Roman Catholic priest from the Archdiocese of Ottawa. On most Sundays when she is in Ottawa, Madame Sauvé goes to the Notre Dame Basilica, but as Governor General she also attends churches of other denominations.

Paying ceremonial visits to religious institutions is a custom that dates back to the governors of New France. Among the institutions in Quebec City that have participated in this ritual for more than two hundred years are the Ursuline Monastery, l'Hôpital Général and l'Hôtel-Dieu. It is the Governor General's prerogative on these visits to grant *congé royal*, a viceregal holiday. The Governor General may also pay formal calls on cloistered orders. When Madame Sauvé was given a tour of the Carmelite Monastery, and was taken into the cloistered section, she was struck by the beatific expressions of the nuns at prayer. "They looked as though they were in heaven."

On a less beatific note, the Opening of Parliament is another important viceregal duty. The heart of this ceremony is the Speech from the Throne by the Governor General, which outlines the legislative plans of the government. The speech is read to the Senate, while the members of the Commons stand respectfully at the entrance to the Chamber. (In practice, there's so little space for them behind the "bar" that most MP's listen outside in the hall.) After opening the new session, the Governor General gives a ball for parliamentarians at Rideau Hall.

At the beginning of November Her Excellency opened the first session of the Thirty-third Parliament. Her arrival on the Hill in the state landau was accompanied by all the traditional pomp and pageantry. Although she was in a mink coat and a long gown, this time she took the precaution of wearing low heels, and the inspection of the guard of honour went off without incident. Not only was she sure-footed, but her voice was much stronger than when she had read her Installation address. Although the Governor General has little room for creativity in the Throne Speech, which is written by the Prime Minister, Madame Sauvé was able to voice her own hopes in the preamble:

"This is the inauguration of a new Parliament. Let it be also a new era of national reconciliation, economic renewal and social justice. In this spirit, my ministers will honour the mandate entrusted to them by the people of Canada."

That night, more than seven hundred formally dressed MP's, senators, and their spouses attended the ball at Government House. After being greeted by Her Excellency, they passed through to the ballroom, where two bars were doing a land-office business. The guests were in a jovial mood as many of them had just come from receptions given by the Speaker of the House of Commons or the Speaker of the Senate — sometimes both. When a good number of parliamentarians had been received, Madame Sauvé left her post and went into the ballroom to start the dancing. Having launched the party, she returned to the Ambassadors' Room to greet the last stragglers. For the rest of the night she danced almost continuously. Only once did she find herself trapped with a partner (a tall Tory MP) who had partaken too generously of the grape. Spotting her predicament, Jean-François smoothly cut in and rescued his mother. At eleven o'clock, a sumptuous buffet supper was served. Tables in the Tent Room accommodated some of the guests, but there were so many people that the rest had to perch wherever they could find a space — on the stairs, in the drawing-room, the Petit Salon, even the Greenhouse. The party broke up at one o'clock with the playing of "God Save the Queen" and the national anthem. Everyone agreed that with Jeanne Sauvé as chatelaine, the glitter had returned to Government House.

Her Excellency was in Montreal the following day to give the Convocation Address at McGill University. Then she returned to Ottawa to receive Laurent Fabius, the Prime Minister of France. The next day she presided over an investiture of Bravery Awards, received the legendary skier Herman (Jackrabbit) Johannsen on the occasion of his 110th birthday, and attended an eightieth-birthday dinner in honour of physicist Dr. Gerhard Herzberg, winner of the 1971 Nobel Prize for chemistry. On Saturday evening at Rideau Hall she presented the Michener Award, which is given for "meritorious and disinterested public service in journalism". The presentation of this coveted prize is made in the ballroom. Usually it is a sedate, even solemn, ceremony. On this occasion, however, Madame Sauvé's sense of humour got the better of her. In the midst of her speech, a paean of praise to the nobility and unselfishness of the press, she suddenly stopped, looked around the room, and said, "My God! Who wrote this?" After a stunned silence, the audience broke into roars of laughter.

Madame Sauvé made her first official visit to Ontario in mid-November. During her five-day stay in Toronto she was formally received at Queen's Park and at City Hall. She was also guest of honour at a dinner given by the Vice-President of the Royal Winter Fair at the Toronto Club, and attended the Royal Horse Show at the Coliseum — the latter being one of the few events in Canada where white tie and decorations are still the order of dress. On the last night of her visit she was guest of honour at the annual Mess dinner of the Governor General's Horse Guards at the Denison Armoury.

Her Excellency is Honorary Colonel of the Governor General's Horse Guards, a former cavalry regiment (now armoured) that still provides mounted escorts on ceremonial occasions. In addition, she is Honorary Colonel of two infantry regiments, the Governor General's Foot Guards in Ottawa, and the Canadian Grenadier Guards of Montreal. Aside from their ceremonial roles, all three units have distinguished war records.

At the end of December, Madame Sauvé hosted the annual Christmas Party at Rideau Hall for children of the Ottawa Boys and Girls Club and its French counterpart, the Patro d'Ottawa. It was one of her favourite events of the year. The party began at noon with lunch in the gaily decorated Tent Room. Her Excellency, wearing a party hat, and assisted by two of her smallest guests, carved the first piece of turkey. Following tradition, she and her staff then served the children their meal. The Christmas dinner had all the trimmings, but the chef had taken care to eliminate most of the seasoning, and milk was served rather than soft drinks (previous experience having shown that over-excitement and pop are a lethal combination). After lunch everyone trooped into the ballroom for the entertainment. The room had been transformed: cushions on the floor, the walls covered with Christmas decorations, and a mass of balloons suspended from the ceiling. Snuggling close to Madame Sauvé, the youngsters, most of whom came from underprivileged homes, watched spellbound as a magician displayed his sleight-of-hand. The climax of the party, which brought shrieks of delight, was the entrance of Santa Claus and the Christmas Fairy (played by the senior aide-de-camp and his fiancée). Their arrival signalled that the moment had come to give out the presents. Each child sat on Santa's lap, was handed a present by the Christmas Fairy, and then was given a big hug by the Governor General. The party ended in a shower of popping balloons.

Her Excellency also gave a Christmas dinner for her family at Rideau Hall. The day after Christmas, she and her husband left for a three-week holiday in Palm Beach as guests of Paul and Jacqueline Desmarais.

It had been a tempestuous year. Having nearly died in the early part of the year, during her first six months in office she had had three prime ministers, accepted the resignation of two of them, sworn in two of them, experienced a general election, received both the sovereign and the leader of the Roman Catholic Church, and opened a new Parliament.

By the end of her stay in Florida, her friends were remarking how well she looked. "When I came back to Ottawa in January I felt much stronger, and I knew I was better."

Madame Sauvé's first engagement on her return was the New Year's Levée. This centuries-old ritual used to take place in the Parliament Buildings, but is now held at Rideau Hall. In essence, guests pay a courtesy call on the Governor General. At noon, senior government, church, and military officials are received in order of precedence (starting with the Prime Minister, followed by the Chief Justice, and so on down the line). Each person brings a calling-card, which is handed to the ADC Next-in-Waiting, who gives it to the ADC-in-Waiting, who in turn announces the guest's name. After shaking hands with the Governor General, guests go into the ballroom for non-alcoholic refreshments. In the afternoon, members of the general public are received. Nearly three thousand people showed up for Madame Sauvé's first Levée.

Security is a growing concern since the assassination of a Turkish diplomat in Ottawa and the assault on the Turkish ambassador's residence. The RCMP is responsible for the Governor General's personal security, and that of her residences. The Governor General is not a high-risk target, but a few crackpots inevitably turn up at public viceregal functions. For this reason, plainclothes Mounties mingle with the guests at the Levée and the Garden Party. (When a potentially dangerous person is spotted, he is firmly but courteously escorted off the premises.) There is also an RCMP detachment who patrol the grounds of Rideau Hall around the clock. The policy is to make Government House as accessible as possible to the public while at the same time maintaining adequate security. Thus, the grounds and public rooms are open for guided tours, but general access is restricted. As an added security precaution, all incoming mail is screened by a fluoroscope machine located in the Gatehouse.

Whenever the Governor General attends an outside event, Mounties check the site and are waiting for her when she arrives. Indeed, Madame Sauvé is required to have a bodyguard wherever she goes — even to the dentist. Many politicians treat the RCMP security people as a necessary evil—part of the furniture—and ignore them. Madame Sauvé has a different, more personal rapport with the plainclothes officers, and makes a point of talking to them when she meets them around the country. The Montreal detachment of the RCMP, responsible for the surveillance of her house in Outremont, and her safety when she travels in Quebec, affectionately refer to her (among themselves) as "tante Jeanne". If Her Excellency goes outside the country she must be accompanied by an RCMP inspector, designated as her "travel officer", who in fact is her bodyguard. Before leaving Canada for Florida, Madame Sauvé had asked Gabrielle Léger (widow of Jules Léger) what she should do with her bodyguard while she was shopping. Madame Léger answered, "Get him to carry your parcels." When she went to Palm Beach that Christmas, her travel officer was Inspector Claude Thériault. As is the custom, while he was outside the country Inspector Thériault wore civilian clothes.

One morning, as Madame Sauvé came out of a Palm Beach shop, she was seen by two Canadian matrons, who rushed over to shake her hand. While they were chatting, Her Excellency casually turned to a tall, grey-haired man who had joined them, and with a smile gave him her parcels. The two ladies, who knew the handsome stranger wasn't Maurice Sauvé, stared in shocked disbelief and hurriedly excused themselves.

The RCMP also serve the Governor General by escorting foreign ambassadors to Rideau Hall when they present their Letters of Credence. The ambassador is driven to Government House in an enclosed landau drawn by four horses, with two Mounties riding postillion and two riding behind the carriage. The only time the landau isn't used is during the winter. Then, rather than having the ambassador shiver in the unheated carriage, he is whisked to Government House in a warm limousine.

When an ambassador presents his Letters of Credence, he is formally recognized as the representative of his country. This dignified ceremony takes place in the ballroom, usually in the morning. While the ambassador is coming up the drive, Her Excellency takes her place seated at the far end of the room. Outside, a procession forms up in three ranks. On one side are the embassy staff and the Secretary to the Governor General, in the centre, by himself, the ambassador, and on the other side the members of the Household and the Chief of Protocol from External Affairs. They march solemnly into the ballroom like two opposing teams. The ambassador, led by the Chief of Protocol, stops five paces from the Governor General and is presented. He then makes a short and flowery speech, hands his Letters of Credence to Madame Sauvé, and returns to his place. She makes a brief speech of welcome, and they shake hands. At the conclusion of the ceremony Her Excellency retires with the ambassador to her study for a ten-minute chat. To prepare herself for this conversation she has studied a two-page briefing on the ambassador's career and his country. This briefing is essential because some mornings as many as three ambassadors present their credentials. In this connection, Madame Sauvé's staff marvel at how quickly she absorbs information, and at her ability to turn it into sparkling conversation.

On a typical day Madame Sauvé rises at seven o'clock. Over breakfast she reads at least four newspapers: *The Globe and Mail*, *Le Devoir*, *The Gazette*, and the Ottawa *Citizen*. Shortly after nine she goes downstairs to her office, a spacious round room panelled in walnut, with a fireplace and a fine view of the grounds. At nine-thirty she is briefed by her personal secretary, Renée Langevin, who was also her secretary when she was Speaker. A tall, attractive woman with a charming smile, Langevin combines diplomacy with efficiency in dealing with her formidable work-load. Her briefing covers the day's events as well as future activities, and usually takes about half an hour. During this meeting Her Excellency may give Mlle Langevin instructions to be passed on to the chef, to the head gardener, or to other members of the support staff. The rest of Madame Sauvé's morning, if no events are scheduled, is devoted to her voluminous correspondence. On most days there are guests for lunch.

When the House is sitting, Madame Sauvé always watches Question Period on TV, which lasts from two until three o'clock. Although she does this to keep informed, it is no hardship — politics continue to fascinate her. With the passage of time, her own political views have shifted from the left to the centre of the spectrum. A few years ago Madame Sauvé told *Chatelaine*, "When I was younger, I was considered to be left wing, but I discovered that among the left wingers are a lot of people who believe they can decide things for everybody else. Now I believe in such supposedly right wing things as more freedom for the individual to plan her or his life; more freedom for enterprise — and the basic ideas of freedom often denied in government planning.''

From three until six o'clock she receives visitors, reads confidential cabinet documents, or works with senior members of the Household. If she wants to discuss family matters, she can visit her husband in his adjoining office. However, as he is still active with his corporate directorships, he is often out of town. When he's away, he phones her every day, and she also speaks with her son daily. At least once a month Jean-François comes to Rideau Hall for the weekend. Despite her change in status, she has maintained a close relationship with old friends, among them Sylvia and Bernard Ostry, Françoise Côté, Bluma Appel, Lisa Philips, Jacqueline and Paul Desmarais, and Anna Abromeit. Another friend she keeps in touch with is Gaetana Enders, the wife of the former U.S. ambassador to Canada, who is now in Spain.

At the end of January and the beginning of February, Madame Sauvé held Winter Parties at Rideau Hall for the diplomatic corps, the Parliamentary Press Gallery, and senior public servants. These parties are a tradition that has been observed for more than a hundred years. Although they are informal, guests are invited by engraved invitation, with their names written in calligraphic lettering (by a Government House employee nicknamed "Madame Gothique"). Because of the sub-zero temperatures and the fact that most of the entertainment takes place outside, the dress is warm clothing. The parties begin at seven-thirty in the evening at the rink, where there is skating to music, round-robin curling matches, sleigh rides, and tobogganing on the nearby lighted hill. In 1985 there were also dog-sled rides through the lower woods provided by a driver and his team of dogs from Baffin Island. Their Excellencies, wearing racoon coats, always invite a few guests (two at a time) for a ride with them in their high-backed cutter. For a few fortunate guests snuggly wrapped in buffalo robes a moonlit sleigh ride over the snow-covered lawns of Rideau Hall is an unforgettable experience. For those who don't care to exert themselves, there is a huge log fire behind the rink where they can simply relax, or toast marshmallows on long pointed sticks.

Around nine o'clock everyone goes inside to be received by Her Excellency, and then they pass through to the ballroom for mulled wine. A half-hour later, a buffet supper is served featuring hearty fare like baked beans and boeuf bourguignon, as well as other dishes that make the cuisine of Rideau Hall famous. Supper is eaten in the Tent Room, at round tables for eight covered with checked table-cloths. Their Excellencies sit at separate tables so they can meet as many of their guests as possible. After the meal, there is dancing to recorded music, an eclectic selection that ranges from "golden oldies" to current pop tunes. In keeping with the informal atmosphere, little protocol is observed except for the normal courtesy of wait-ing for Her Excellency to finish each course, and to start the danc-ing. Because Winter Parties are normally given on a weekday, they end quite early, often before midnight.

Early in 1985 Madame Sauvé was faced with a challenge to her office which she met with grace and firmness. In February, Esmond Butler was informed by the Prime Minister's Office that Mr. Mulroney had invited President Reagan to Quebec City in March. Although the U.S. President is head of state as well as head of gov-ernment, Madame Sauvé was told it was to be a low-profile work-ing visit, rather than a formal state visit, so she need not be present. However, the Prime Minister wished to stay with the President in the Citadel — and indeed have adjoining rooms so that they could enjoy breakfast and late-night chats together. Butler went to Her Excellency and warned her that in all likelihood this would be a very public event, designed to enhance the Prime Minister's image. Madame Sauvé's reaction was, "The Citadel is my residence, and nobody is going to entertain there unless I'm the host." Her senti-ments, couched in slightly more diplomatic terms, were relayed to the Prime Minister's Office.

During the ensuing weeks Butler was badgered by Gordon Osbaldeston (Secretary to the Cabinet and Clerk of the Privy Council) to persuade Madame Sauvé to change her mind about the Citadel. In doing this, Osbaldeston placed himself in an invidious position, because as Secretary to the Cabinet he was, in effect, deputy minister to the Prime Minister, while as Clerk of the Privy Council he had a duty to protect the role of the Crown. Butler refused to intercede, but pointed out that the Prime Minister could ask the Governor General himself when he next came to Rideau Hall. Osbaldeston said this wasn't feasible, because "the PM hates confrontation." Negotiations dragged on. Finally, after being assured by the Prime Minister's office that it really was a private working visit, Madame Sauvé agreed to remain in Ottawa, and to let the Citadel be used as the site for the signing of the Accord. Although she wouldn't be in Quebec herself, she would, however, send her Secretary to the Citadel as her representative.

When President Reagan landed in Quebec City on St. Patrick's Day (a date carefully chosen by Mulroney's public relations people), he was greeted by the Prime Minister, 101 scarlet-coated Mounties, a full military guard of honour, a thirty-five-piece band, and a twenty-one-gun salute. All the trappings of a state welcome — except for the Governor General.

That night Mulroney and Reagan appeared on national television at a special St. Patrick's Day gala. The highlight of the performance was when they went on stage and warbled "When Irish Eyes Are Smiling". From a public relations standpoint it was a smashing success. Indeed, even before the President arrived, the press had picked up the significance of two Irishmen meeting on St. Patrick's Day and had dubbed their get-together "The Shamrock Summit". The next morning, Reagan and Mulroney went to the Citadel, where more pictures were taken of them signing the Accord, and then the President flew back to Washington.

The French-language press were the first to realize what had happened: that the Prime Minister had shunted the Governor General aside so that he could play head of state and have the limelight to himself. Then the English media jumped on the story, noting that although the Shamrock Summit was billed as a working visit, only two hours were spent in discussion — less time than was spent at the St. Patrick's Day gala. Madame Sauvé, who knew she'd been misled, was not amused, but she could say nothing.

A month later, at the Parliamentary Press Gallery Dinner, she got a measure of revenge. This black-tie function, traditionally attended by the Governor General and political leaders, is unique in that the most scurrilous things can be said about the guests of honour, and all the proceedings are supposedly off the record. At first Madame Sauvé wasn't sure whether she would go, because if she did she would be expected to speak. To say the Gallery is a tough audience is a gross understatement. Two years earlier, when she was Speaker, she had sat beside Mr. Schreyer when he was pelted with buns for giving a tedious speech, and she had even caught a few. At the last minute, although she was "scared stiff", she decided to attend the dinner, which was to be held in the Parliamentary Restaurant.

A long cocktail hour precedes the dinner and there is an endless supply of wine with the meal. Thus, when the time comes for the speeches, most of the guests are in an uninhibited mood. Madame Sauvé, being Governor General, was the first to speak. Her opening remark, "I'd like to thank the Prime Minister for allowing me an opportunity to appear on the same platform," brought hoots of laughter and whistles of approval. Then she launched into a parody of a letter to the Queen, telling the monarch in verse of recent happenings in Canada. One of the verses was:

> *The Irish were at it, the shamrocks were golden,*
> *Mulroney and Reagan don't seem beholden*
> *For the use of the Fort, and the loan of the key;*
> *They were workin', they said, there was no use for me.*

She had to pause after this verse because most of the guests were on their feet chanting "Jeanne! Jeanne! Jeanne!". When she finished her poem, she got another standing ovation, the loudest of the night. In clear, albeit humorous, terms, she had served notice to the Prime Minister that she wouldn't tolerate any further poaching on her territory. Mr. Mulroney, who is sensitive to the media, was also left in no doubt as to what the press thought of the Shamrock Summit. In contrast to Her Excellency's speech, his speech received muted applause. A few days later, columnist Allan Fotheringham (who had escorted Mila Mulroney to the dinner) wrote a column titled "Lady from Rideau Hall floored 'em". Breaking the Gallery's rule of secrecy, Fotheringham said:

> ... *it was with some surprise on the weekend that the ink-stained wretches found that the new boffo queen of the oneliners is none other than Governor General Jeanne Sauvé.*
>
> *She brought down the house — while bringing down Brian Mulroney — with her getting-even shafts for being excluded from the Shamrock Summit in Quebec City.*
>
> *The chaps forgot she was once a journalist herself, so she knew the tradition and she slayed them, even bringing her own equerry from Government House who brandished signs* — Applause, Groan — *at the appropriate moments.*

Notwithstanding the controversy over the Reagan visit, the Governor General and the Prime Minister get along well together. Indeed, they knew each other socially in Montreal long before Mr. Mulroney entered politics. Any lingering ill will from the Shamrock Summit was erased a few months after the event when the Prime Minister threw a private party for Her Excellency at 24 Sussex Drive and invited many of her close friends. Mulroney also meets with Madame Sauvé at Rideau Hall twice a month to discuss confidential matters of state.

At a State Dinner there is no danger from flying buns or shafts of barbed wit; decorum is everything. A few days before the Press Gallery bash, Madame Sauvé gave a State Dinner for the President of the Socialist Republic of Romania and Mrs. Ceausescu. At seven-thirty that evening the guests assembled for drinks in the Long Gallery. At the same time, the Prime Minister and Mrs. Mulroney joined Their Excellencies in Madame Sauvé's study. The Governor General's Secretary then went upstairs to escort the President of

Romania and his wife down to the study. At five to eight the vice-regal party proceeded to the Reception Room, where the President and the Governor General, with their spouses, lined up to receive the guests: first Her Excellency, then the President, the President's wife, and His Excellency. While the guests were going through the receiving line in strict order of precedence, the Prime Minister and his wife stood on the other side of the room with the Secretary (because only a head of state can receive at a State Dinner).

Normally there are 120 guests at a State Dinner. The usual format is a head table, seating sixteen along one side, at the far end of the ballroom, under the portraits, with the rest of the guests at separate tables that accommodate nine or ten people. Seating is also by precedence, and the golden rule is, the closer to the centre of the head table, the better (which invariably produces complaints from people who feel they have been slighted in the seating arrangement). After the main course, Her Excellency rises and proposes a toast to the head of state, who responds in turn with a toast to "The Queen of Canada — La Reine du Canada". The meal continues until liqueurs and cigars are served, and then Madame Sauvé makes a speech to the guest of honour, who may or may not respond. Sometimes there is also fifteen or twenty minutes of entertainment by a noted pianist or a cellist at the conclusion of the meal. After dinner, led by the Governor General and the head of state, the guests return to the Long Gallery. Everyone stands while couples are brought up to meet the head of state. Around ten-thirty, the head of state and his wife nod their way out of the room and are escorted by Their Excellencies to the foot of the stairs. After they have gone up to bed, Their Excellencies continue down the hall and retire to their own quarters.

Because the proceedings are so rigidly governed by protocol, state dinners usually go off without a hitch. One exception was a State Dinner given at Rideau Hall in 1967 for Haile Selassie, Lion of Judah and Emperor of Ethiopia. During this dinner the Emperor's little dog, a Mexican hairless named "Lulu", who was roaming about under the head table, created a diplomatic precedent by urinating on the foot of one of the most distinguished guests.

Some people believe that state dinners and formal receptions are a waste of time, but Madame Sauvé views them in a different light: "As far as dinners and receptions go — I've never thought of them as useless — you can do a lot of work at them."

She also enjoys planning the menus for important dinners with her chef, Michel Pourbaix, who has been at Rideau Hall for many years (as have the under-chef and the pastry chef). Madame Sauvé is a gourmet to whom a meal is not simply eating, but an artistic adventure. When she returns from a trip she will often suggest a new dish to the chef, giving a detailed description of the particular treat she has enjoyed. Chef Pourbaix is delighted with her enthusiasm, and affectionately refers to her as "une femme gastronomique".

Not only magnificent flowers, but spices and tropical fruits are grown in the three greenhouses at Government House. Rideau Hall also has its own sugar bush behind the rink. These trees are tapped every spring, and the sap is boiled on the premises. Although most of the syrup is used by the kitchen (maple *mousse* is a house specialty), some of it is put up in small bottles for gifts.

Madame Sauvé loves food, but she watches her weight and eats sparingly. Breakfast consists of dry toast and coffee, and lunch, if she is alone, is usually fruit salad, a meal that she had virtually every day when she was Speaker. At tea in the afternoon, Her Excellency will accept a cookie or a piece of cake from the footman, but this is merely to put her guest at ease. It is left untouched on her plate. Dinner is the only meal where she allows herself any leeway. Sometimes, when there's been a lot of entertaining, to get a break from fancy food she'll have the chef produce something simple, like spaghetti. At other times, she'll dine on nothing more than a green salad.

Travelling plays havoc with her diet, and 1985 was a particular busy year for travel. In addition to many brief excursions, she paid official visits to British Columbia, Nova Scotia, Manitoba, Alberta, Prince Edward Island, Newfoundland, and the Yukon.

While she was in Victoria she was guest of honour at the re-commissioning of a Canadian destroyer, HMCS *Yukon*, which had just come out of drydock. The climax of a re-commissioning ceremony is the breaking out of the ship's flags, which are simultaneously run up to the masthead in two lines from the forepeak and the stern. On this occasion, when the order to break out the flags was given, the row of flags from the stern got tangled in the line. On board, the Signal Officer could be seen frantically trying to correct the problem. Meanwhile, on the dock, the ship's company stood rigidly at attention, and the officers were frozen in the saluting position. After several long minutes a seaman shinnied up the mast and untangled the flags. Later, in the wardroom, Her Excellency asked the captain what would happen to the officer responsible for the flags. The captain replied that he would be Officer-of-the-Day for thirty days. Madame Sauvé then asked her aide-de-camp, a naval lieutenant, what this meant. Her ADC explained that the officer would be confined to the ship, on duty round the clock, for a solid month. Turning back to the captain, Her Excellency said, "We can't have that! Please remit the punishment." Because the Governor General is Commander-in-Chief of the Armed Forces, the captain had no alternative but to accede to her request.

During her first official visit to Nova Scotia, Madame Sauvé was given a reception at City Hall in Halifax. In the middle of her speech she noticed a little girl, three-year-old Christine Dewell, across the room. Christine had a bouquet of flowers, and was obviously anxious to present them — in fact, she was being restrained by her father. When Her Excellency finished her address she beamed at Christine and said, "Okay, you can come now!" The little girl, as though released by a spring, shot across the room and flew into Madame Sauvé's arms, nearly bowling her over. In her thank-you letter to the Mayor, Madame Sauvé mentioned Christine, noting with tongue in cheek, "we could say that she carried out her duties with unusual singlemindedness and dispatch."

While in Nova Scotia, Her Excellency also visited the historic fortress of Louisbourg in Cape Breton. Driving from Sydney that morning, she stopped to meet the children of Albert Bridge School, who were waiting for her on the highway. Accompanied by her ADC, she started down the line shaking hands and patting heads. But the number of children in front of her never diminished. When she recognized a child she'd spoken to a few moments before, it dawned on her that after shaking hands the children were running down to the end of the line for a second greeting. Had she not called a good-natured halt to the proceedings, it could have gone on all day.

After lunch at the Fortress, she was given a ride in a sedan chair carried by four men in period costumes. Bouncing around in the little box, supported by four poles, was an amusing experience for her until one of the bearers got a cramp in his hand and let go of the pole. The sedan chair crashed to the ground with such force that Madame Sauvé was nearly pitched out of the window. Seeing how mortified the man was who'd dropped the pole, she quipped, "It was all my fault — I had too much for lunch."

One of the highlights of her first official visit to Manitoba was a dance for young people at the Manitoba Legislature. At the beginning of the party the youngsters, who ranged in age from fourteen to eighteen, were so awed by their surroundings and the presence of the Governor General that they wouldn't dance. Madame Sauvé, who is a very good dancer, got things rolling by going up to boys and asking them to dance with her. After several young men had been dragooned onto the floor, everyone joined in the fun.

On her first official visit to Alberta, Madame Sauvé participated in Lethbridge's one-hundredth-anniversary celebrations. The city of Lethbridge gave her a tremendous welcome, which included many signs and banners in French. All the schools turned out to greet her. When she passed one of the schools, she noticed a series of one-word signs at intervals that read "Madame — Sauvé — We — Want — to — Give — You — a — Present". Unfortunately, by the time her car passed the last word, it was too late to stop the motorcade. Her Excellency, not wanting to disappoint the students, arranged for a bus to bring them out to the airport just before she left so that she could speak to them and they could make their presentation.

She also received a surprise present at the closing ceremonies of the 1985 Summer Games in Saint John, New Brunswick. It was a joyous, high-spirited occasion for the young athletes. As each provincial contingent marched around the stadium they threw souvenirs — pins, hats, and other small items — into the stands. The team from Alberta tossed Frisbees, one of which landed at Madame Sauvé's feet. Picking it up, she saw that the owner had taped his name and phone number to the underside. When she returned to Ottawa, she had the address traced and wrote the young man a letter.

As well as touring Canada in 1985, Her Excellency visited the Canadian forces in Lahr and Baden, West Germany. During her inspection of the Canadian NATO squadron, she was asked if she would like to take a ride in the new CF-18 fighter. To no one's surprise, she declined this invitation, but she did sit in the cockpit of the plane for a minute or two. That night, at a Mess Dinner given by the squadron, she began her speech by saying, "I was told by the former Minister of Defence, Gilles Lamontagne, that flying in the CF-18 was better than sex. I've only sat in the cockpit of the plane, but I find this very hard to believe!"

In addition to being Commander-in-Chief of the Armed Forces, Her Excellency is Chancellor of the Order of Military Merit. In this capacity, she presides over investitures of the Order at Government House. Twice a year she also presents Bravery Awards at Rideau Hall. Unlike the Order of Military Merit, which is restricted to members of the armed forces, most of the recipients of the Bravery Awards are civilians. The Bravery Awards ceremony, like most other presentations, takes place in the ballroom. The person to be decorated stands before the Governor General while the citation is read, and then steps forward for the presentation. Because of the extraordinary feats of courage that are revealed, it is a very moving ceremony. The youngest person ever to be decorated was seven-year-old Jonathan Carter of Souris, Prince Edward Island. Jonathan received the Medal of Bravery for saving the life of an eight-year-old girl who had fallen through the ice. When Madame Sauvé presented Jonathan with his medal, she couldn't help thinking, "If I was your mother, I would have told you not to do that!"

Because she is patron to more than one hundred and fifty charitable, benevolent, and military organizations, Her Excellency participates in many other ceremonies. One of her more unusual presentations was to a goat, the mascot of the Royal 22e Régiment. At a full-dress parade at the Citadel in September 1985, Madame Sauvé presented the goat, Baptisse V, with a new brass headband. Trained to kneel when the National Anthem is played, Baptisse knelt to the Governor General after receiving this decoration. As the original mascot, Baptisse I, was presented to the Regiment by Governor General Massey, the ceremony was part of an ongoing viceregal tradition. That night, Madame Sauvé was guest of honour at a Mess Dinner given by the officers of the Royal 22e Régiment at the Citadel.

The Order of Canada investiture is one of the most prestigious Government House events. Held in the ballroom twice each year, the investiture is similar in format to that of the Bravery Awards. The Secretary to the Governor General, standing to the right of Their Excellencies, who are seated, reads the citation. An aide-de-camp then hands Madame Sauvé the appropriate decoration (there are three levels: Companion, Officer, and Member), and the person steps forward to be invested. After shaking hands with Her Excellency the recipient steps back, bows, and walks to the right side of the room to sign the Register. Following the ceremony, Madame Sauvé receives the guests in the Reception Room. While this is taking place, the chairs are removed from the ballroom, where the reception continues with before-dinner refreshments. People who haven't been been to Government House before often don't realize they're in the same room. Following the reception, a buffet dinner is served in the Tent Room.

In October 1985, four outstanding Canadians were made Companions of the Order, one of whom was Pierre Trudeau. As Trudeau bowed to receive his neck decoration, Madame Sauvé thought to herself, "How strange life is. Here I am, one of his junior ministers, giving him the Order of Canada."

This investiture was also the last official duty for Esmond Butler as Secretary. Unquestionably the most knowledgeable person in Canada on the viceregal role, he had served five governors general. He was a popular man, and his departure raised eyebrows across the country. On hearing the news that he was being replaced, one feisty woman senator offered to circulate a petition on Parliament Hill to have him reinstated. Butler declined her offer with thanks, saying he felt it was time to step down: "I can understand Her Excellency wanting her own team." Leopold Amyot, Canada's ambassador to Morocco, was appointed the new Secretary to the Governor General. Butler and Amyot, in fact, simply exchanged jobs. When Amyot came to Rideau Hall, Butler replaced him as ambassador to Morocco. Before he left Canada, Madame Sauvé gave a black-tie dinner for Esmond Butler at Government House. In her speech that night she spoke of the extraordinary contribution he had made during his twenty-six years at Rideau Hall, and noted that in his new posting he too would have the well-deserved title of "Your Excellency".

The appointment of a new Secretary was the last, and most important, in a series of personnel changes made by Madame Sauvé. The changes began on the day of her Installation, when she brought with her to Rideau Hall eleven of her former staff from the Speaker's office. Shortly after her appointment she arranged for a firm of management consultants, Price Waterhouse, to make a comprehensive study of the administrative set-up at Government House. Their report, which recommended restructuring and strengthening middle management, was considered by a committee chaired by Madame Sauvé. The changes that were adopted were done gradually, over a period of many months.

A high percentage of the Household are francophone, all of whom are bilingual. One of the few people who isn't fluent in French is Madame Sauvé's niece, Liane Benoit, her Attaché and English-speech writer. A vivacious woman in her late twenties, Ms. Benoit is well qualified for the job, holding three university degrees. After the success of Her Excellency's speech at the Press Gallery dinner, Liane Benoit received an overture to work for the Prime Minister's Office — at a considerably higher salary. She declined to follow it up because, like the rest of her aunt's team, she is loyal to her boss.

Since Madame Sauvé took office there have also been some physical changes to the residence. Most have been prompted by necessity. Except for recent additions, the main residence is more than one hundred years old, and the quality of construction varies from fair to poor. In the public rooms there is a danger that the floors might collapse, and fire is another serious hazard. Her Excellency's personal quarters, a large master bedroom with a bathroom and dressing-room ensuite, and a drawing-room across the hall, were badly in need of repair when she moved into Rideau Hall. Madame Sauvé wanted to have a private firm of interior decorators undertake the renovations, but the Department of Public Works (which at that time was responsible for the maintenance of the buildings) insisted it was perfectly competent to do the job. Willing to give DPW a chance, Her Excellency said, "All right, do one room and we'll see what it looks like." The upshot of this test was that the viceregal quarters were done by the private firm.

During 1985 more than $700,000 was spent renovating the kitchens at Government House. This was sensationalized by the press as a fearful extravagance. In fact, the fifty-year-old kitchens — which serve more than 100,000 meals to guests each year — had been condemned as a serious health hazard. To make matters worse, when construction started it was found that portions of the building were rotten, which caused the cost to skyrocket. In the near future two of the greenhouses — which provide flowers not only to Rideau Hall but to all the official residences, including the Prime Minister's — will also have to undergo expensive repairs. They too have been classified as structurally unsafe by the Department of Public Works.

Of equal importance, the interior of Rideau Hall has been spruced up, and so has the quality of service. A stickler for doing things properly, soon after she arrived Madame Sauvé told the footmen, "Put on your white gloves, fellas." She also made a thorough inspection of the basement, an area rarely visited by viceregal occupants. Explaining this sortie to a *Globe and Mail* reporter, she said, "I am a compulsive housekeeper. Everything is going to be in order down there. I can't stand disorder. I can't stand that good things are not looked after, if the silverware is not placed in felt bags. I went down and said this is the way I want things done."

She demands excellence of herself, and sets equally high standards for the senior members of her Household. Esmond Butler says of her style at staff meetings, "She's very businesslike, she has a clear mind, and states her case with clarity — even severity, if things aren't going the way she wants." Her efforts have definitely improved the image of Government House. In the words of *The Gazette*:

> *Not since Vincent Massey was appointed in 1952 have we seen a governor general with such an innate sense of flair and elegance. This is more than just an asset on Ottawa's social scene. It can be a useful means — one of the few available to governors general — to remind Canadians that in our political system, prime ministers come and go but the head of state remains above politics, symbolizing the country itself, and its best values.*

Speaking of the way she conducts award ceremonies (one of the most important functions at Rideau Hall), her former Secretary said recently, "She does it very nicely — she's not as verbose as some of her predecessors — she does it with warmth and grace." On the same subject, but in a broader context, Charles Lynch observed, "Without being snobby or elitist, Jeanne entertains beautifully at Government House; she does it with great aplomb and obviously enjoys it."

She also takes a great interest in the political aspects of her role, and is arguably one of the best-informed people in Canada. This is due in part to having access to cabinet documents, but also to her own political sensitivity. Of her discussions with the Prime Minister she says, "I have knowingly traded power for influence."

During her first eighteen months in office she made more than two hundred speeches, and, to the amazement of one close observer, "She hasn't resorted to governor-generalities — she almost always says something relevant." She has also travelled extensively, making forty-seven trips out of Ottawa during this period. Judging from the welcome she has received across the country, she is achieving her goal to foster national unity. Nowhere is this truer than in Quebec.

One Sunday in September 1985, while she was in residence at the Citadel, Her Excellency attended Mass at Notre Dame des Victoires. This ancient church is located in La Place Royale, a restored section of Lower Town Quebec. The previous Thursday, her aide-de-camp had phoned the priest to say that she would be attending Sunday Mass, but wished to make it an unofficial visit. When she arrived, the priest greeted her on the steps of the church and then escorted her to the *banc du Gouverneur* (the front right-hand pew). In his sermon, which was on Madame Sauvé's humanity, he quoted extensively from her welcoming address to the Pope. At the end of the Mass, she was astounded when the congregation rose and sang "O Canada". The priest then came down from the altar and shook hands with her. As he did so, the congregation broke into loud clapping. When Her Excellency emerged from the church, the square was so densely packed with people, who had been waiting for her, that her limousine couldn't get through the crowd. There had been no publicity prior to her appearance; the word had spread entirely by mouth.

Madame Sauvé was very moved by this spontaneous display. Another memory she treasures was a conversation she had with a five-year-old boy in Edmonton.

As she does with many little children, she asked him, half teasing, "Do you know who I am?"

"Yes, you're the Governor General."

"What does the Governor General do?"

"You work for the people of Canada."

ACKNOWLEDGMENTS

The first person I must thank is Her Excellency Jeanne Sauvé, whose generosity and kindness made this book possible. Although I was often a nuisance, continually asking questions and popping up at viceregal functions, Madame Sauvé was unfailingly courteous to me. His Excellency Maurice Sauvé was also immensely helpful.

The core of my research consisted of a series of interviews with Madame Sauvé. I am especially grateful to Renée Langevin, who listened to my requests for interviews with sympathy, and somehow always managed to shoehorn me into Her Excellency's crowded schedule.

Madame Berthe Belisle, Jean Benoit, Mrs. Annette Peters, Liane Benoit, and Jean-François Sauvé all granted interviews that shed valuable light on the family history.

Esmond Butler, the senior member of the Household staff, smoothed my path in many ways, and provided perceptive insights into the viceregal office. I am also indebted to Major Colin Sangster, who, at some inconvenience, arranged for me to accompany Madame Sauvé on two provincial tours.

The three aides-de-camp, Captain Pierre Richard, Captain André Lévesque, and Lieutenant (N) Paul Maddison, were also consistently helpful.

Marie Bender, Madame Sauvé's Press Secretary, and her assistant, Manon Caris, spent an inordinate amount of time ferreting out information on my behalf. Looking back, I marvel at their patience and good humour.

Robert Hubbard, the author of two excellent books on Rideau Hall, provided both encouragement and sound historical advice.

Among others who granted interviews, or contributed in some special way, I should like to thank:

Dominique Balas, Robert Blain, Don Boudria, Les Brown, The Hon. Jean Chrétien, Major-General Maurice Cloutier, Susan Cornell, Françoise Côté, Ramsay Derry, James Ferrabee, Douglas Fisher, d'Iberville Fortier, Guy Fortier, Douglas Fullerton, Edgar Gallant, Harold "Sonny" Gordon, Charles Greenwell, Richard Gwyn, Fernande Juneau, Pierre Juneau, Floralove Katz, Deputy Commissioner William Kelley, Beverley Koester, Pierre Lafleur, Father Maurice Lafond, Marie Tessier-Lavigne, Father Georges-Henri Lévesque, Charles Lynch, Bernard Ostry, John deB. Payne, Alex Pelletier, The Hon. Gérard Pelletier, Simon Reisman, Denise Robichaud, Blair Seaborn, Serge Senecal, The Rt. Hon. John Turner, Jacqueline Varin, Patrick Watson, and Peter White.

My research was made easier by Erik Spicer, who kindly permitted me to use the facilities of the Library of Parliament. To him, and to his dedicated staff, I extend my sincere appreciation. The staff in the Reference Section of the Ottawa Public Library also deserve my thanks, as they provided me with instant answers to all sorts of esoteric questions.

Many of the photographs come from the Sauvé family albums, for which I am most grateful. Government House, the Public Archives, the Department of the Secretary of State, and the Canadian Government Film and Video Centre were other valuable sources of photos. I am indebted to the Protocol Office of Saskatchewan who provided two fine pictures of Her Excellency's visit to Prud'homme. I also thank the Ottawa *Citizen*, the source of many excellent photographs. Yousuf Karsh graciously granted permission to use his portrait of Madame Sauvé on the front cover of the book.

All of the Sauvé family photographs were painstakingly reproduced by Michael S. Heney, who took a good number of the original photos, including the ones on the back jacket and the inside flap. This is the third book that we've worked on together; with each I've had doubts about the text, but I've never had to worry about the illustrations.

Finally, I must thank my wife, Sandrea. For many things, including her tolerance of my obsessive behaviour during the past two years. Sandrea had the unenviable task of reading every word I wrote — sometimes three or four drafts of the same passage — and commenting upon it. The very least I could do, as a token of my gratitude, was to dedicate this book to her.

INDEX